Bunny Yeager's

Beautiful Backsides

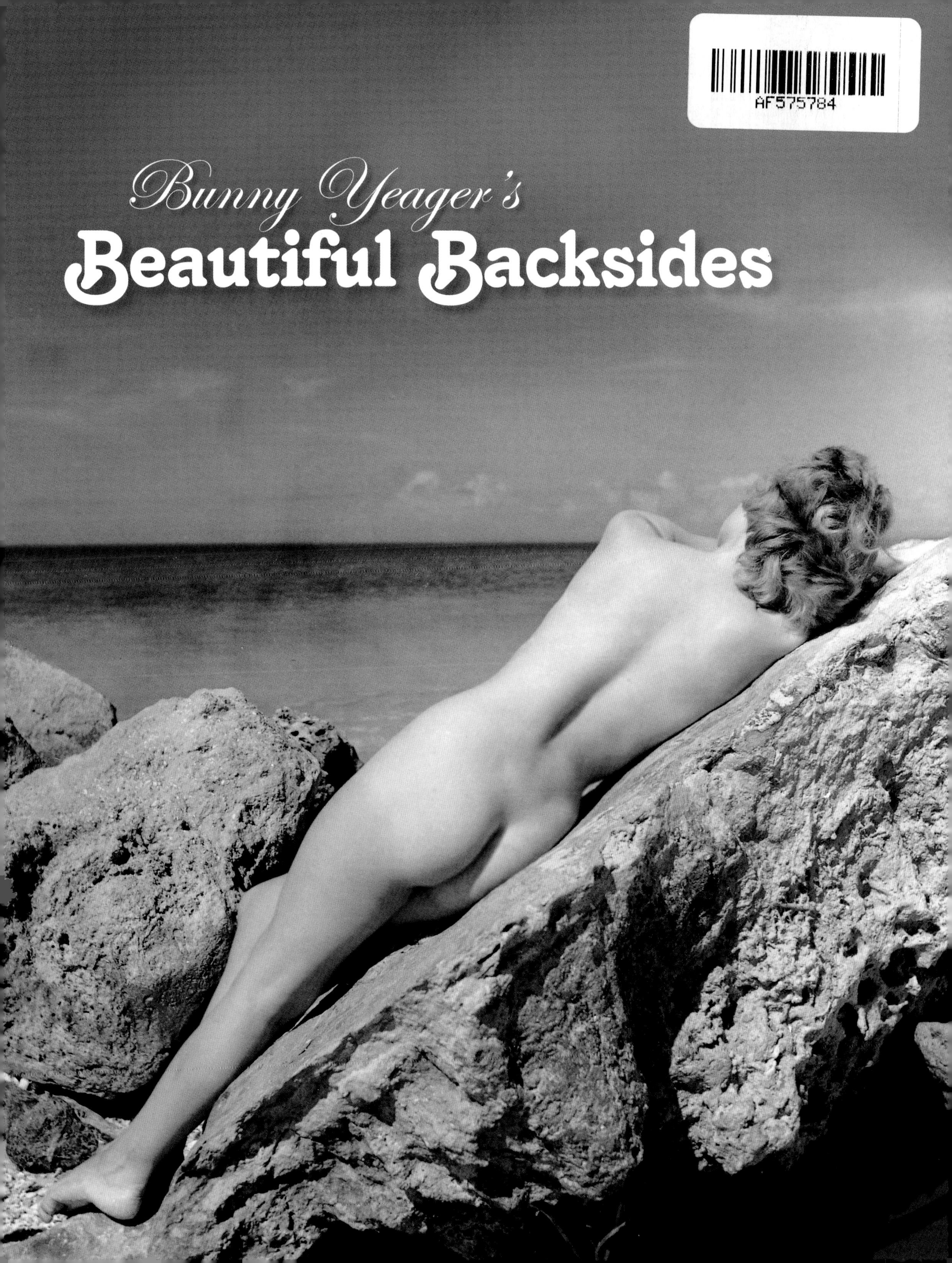

Other Schiffer Books By The Author:

Bunny Yeager's Bouffant Beauties, 978-0-7643-3225-8, $ 24.99

Bikini Girls of the 1960s, 978-0-7643-1735-0, $24.95

Bunny Yeager's Pin-Up Girls of the 1960s, 978-0-7643-2334-2, $29.95

Bunny Yeager's Bikini Girls of the 1950s, 978-0-7643-2002-5, $19.95

Bunny Yeager's Pin-Up Girls of the 1950s, 978-0-7643-1473-4, $24.95

Flirts of the Fifties, 978-0-7643-2637-0, $19.95

Femmes Fatales of the 1950s, 978-0-7643-3030-8, $19.99

Library of Congress Control Number: 2011942209

Cover and book designed by: Bruce Waters
Type set in Gill Sans Lt./Tango

ISBN: 978-0-7643-3963-9
Printed in China

Schiffer Books are available at special discounts for bulk purchases for sales promotions or premiums. Special editions, including personalized covers, corporate imprints, and excerpts can be created in large quantities for special needs. For more information contact the publisher:

Published by Schiffer Publishing Ltd.
4880 Lower Valley Road
Atglen, PA 19310
Phone: (610) 593-1777; Fax: (610) 593-2002
E-mail: Info@schifferbooks.com

For the largest selection of fine reference books on this and related subjects, please visit our website at **www.schifferbooks.com**
We are always looking for people to write books on new and related subjects. If you have an idea for a book, please contact us at proposals@schifferbooks.com

This book may be purchased from the publisher.
Include $5.00 for shipping.
Please try your bookstore first.
You may write for a free catalog.

In Europe, Schiffer books are distributed by
Bushwood Books
6 Marksbury Ave.
Kew Gardens
Surrey TW9 4JF England
Phone: 44 (0) 20 8392 8585; Fax: 44 (0) 20 8392 9876
E-mail: info@bushwoodbooks.co.uk
Website: www.bushwoodbooks.co.uk

Introduction

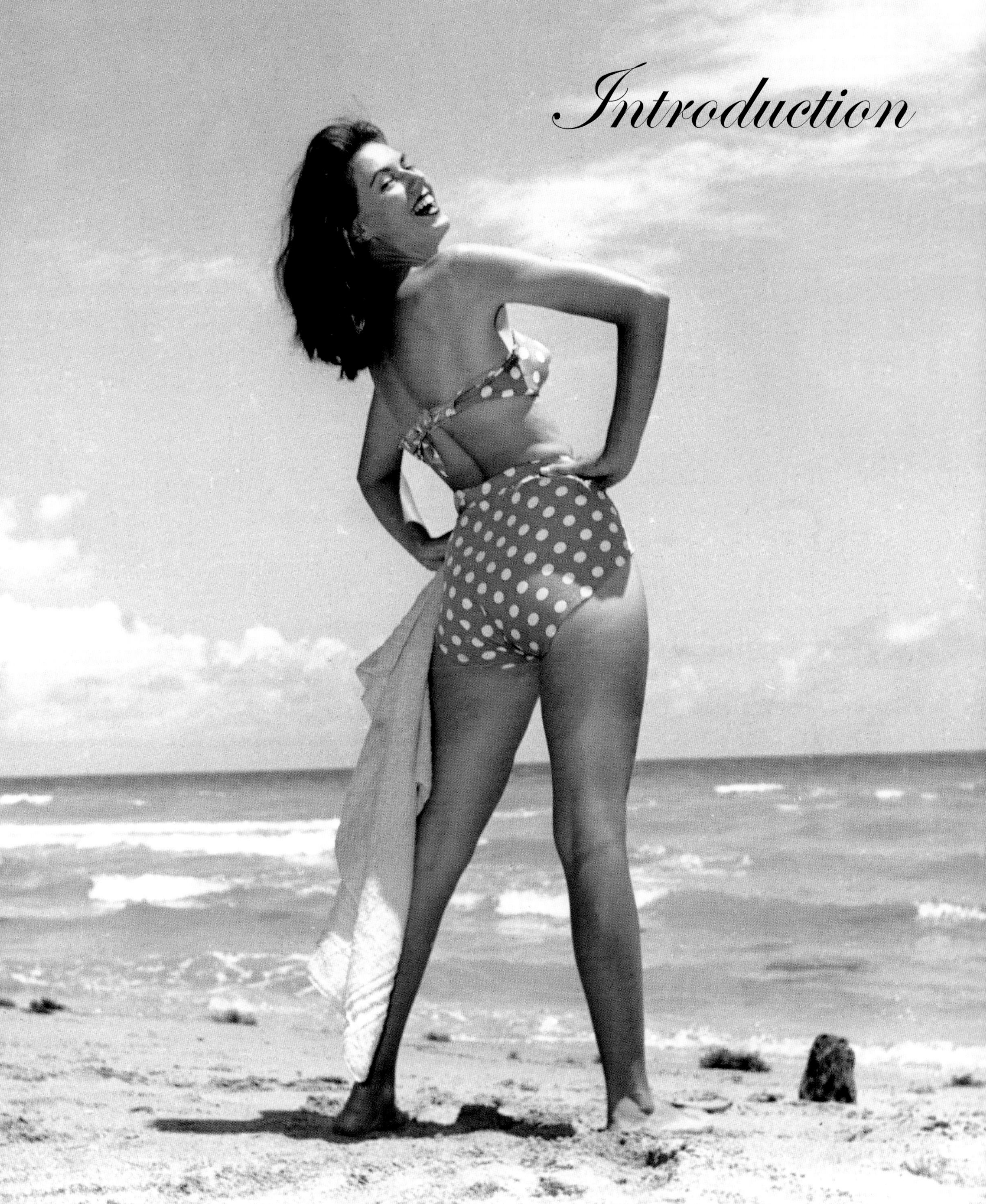

Bunny Yeager, self-portrait

Bunny Yeager, camera in hand, was ready and waiting on the frontlines as society's moral boundaries started to shift in the 1950s. In fact, as she transitioned from a model posing for others to a model posing for her own photos to a photographer capturing images of beautiful young women in luxurious locations, one could argue that she had a direct role in redefining these so-called moral boundaries.

She has done it all, really. She made the move to behind the lens where she first photographed herself and experimented with lighting, posing, costuming, props, backgrounds, and setting to develop her skills and style. This gave her confidence and creativity as she began capturing images of models other than herself.

But constructing a complete vision for her work wasn't just limited to her photography skills. Spending a good deal of time shooting on the beach or in other warm locales in the early fifties, Bunny realized that there was a significant lack of options for women's swimwear. New one-piece styles would be released and every woman would have that one style. How was Bunny to make creative images of beautiful models if they were wearing the same suit? So until the bikini suit was popularized and manufactured in numbers for the American market in the 1960s, Bunny designed and sewed suits for her models to wear. She created her own swimwear aesthetic and introduced a large variety of swimwear for her models. This set her images apart from other photographers and caught the eye of editors looking for something fresh.

Bunny knew what men's magazines were looking for; she shot on speculation rather than assignment. Perhaps the best instance of this was when after a shoot with Bettie Page, Bunny planned on using the images to create a calendar photo, but instead sent the transparencies to *Playboy* magazine. Hugh Hefner called her soon after and asked to use one of the images for their 1955 holiday issue. She went on to shoot eight centerfolds for *Playboy*.

But Bunny wasn't chasing fame. When she sold her first cover photo in 1954, the thrill of getting paid for what she loved to do fueled her drive to continue taking photos of beautiful young women. And this is how we have such a fabulous photographic archive to pull from for new collections like this. Bunny's natural, fun approach to her work is also why her images are so full of character and how she is able to elicit such playful, artful, and smoldering looks and poses from her models.

It was this very talent that interested Johnny Carson and landed her as a guest on "The Tonight Show" in 1964. In conjunction with promoting her book *How I Photograph Myself* (Carson rarely featured guests promoting books), Bunny's appearance on the show featured a 23-minute spot teaching the host how to photograph a beautiful woman. In this case, guest comedienne Edie Adams served as the model.

You will find many beautiful women, and more specifically, their beautiful posterior assets, in this book, which makes this a special group of Bunny Yeager images. Images of the backside were not in high demand from men's magazines at the time these photos were taken. In fact, Bunny always concentrated on shooting bosoms because that's what was selling. Bunny did not go out of her way to capture these gorgeous backsides, but her approach to her craft is so thorough that whenever Bunny starts working with a new model, she sees how the woman looks in all possible poses. Sometimes the good stuff only reveals itself organically after multiple poses. While the Bunny models featured in this book surely look good from all angles, this is a best of the best of their backsides.

Not unlike Bunny's other collections, many of the photos were shot on the beach, a location Bunny credits for being the first place society's moral boundaries started to shift. But unlike her other Schiffer collections which feature one era and theme, *Bunny's Beautiful Backsides* includes images from the 1950s to the 1970s. They reflect a range of moods and explore just how far those moral boundaries moved in that time period. Describing this transition, Bunny says that in "the 1950s things were very calm in terms of nudity. Images were mostly artistic study pieces. Things changed in the 1960s when the real nudity started. And then by the 70s everything was nude." Frame by frame these differing aesthetics and eras are clear.

Stylistically these images are just as diverse, including statuesque nudes shot with artistic studio lighting, flirtatious and fun bikini-clad models playing in the surf, and slightly less modest lusty ladies in bedroom scenes with come-hither eyes and poses. From bikinis to cover ups to completely nude, these gorgeous ladies display their equally divine derrieres for Bunny Yeager's lens in these teasingly tasteful portraits.

All in all this collection encapsulates three pivotal decades in Bunny Yeager's career. Without the pioneering creativity, enterprise, and natural talent that defines Bunny's career we would not have the bounty of beautiful backsides you find in this rare vintage look at the female derriere.

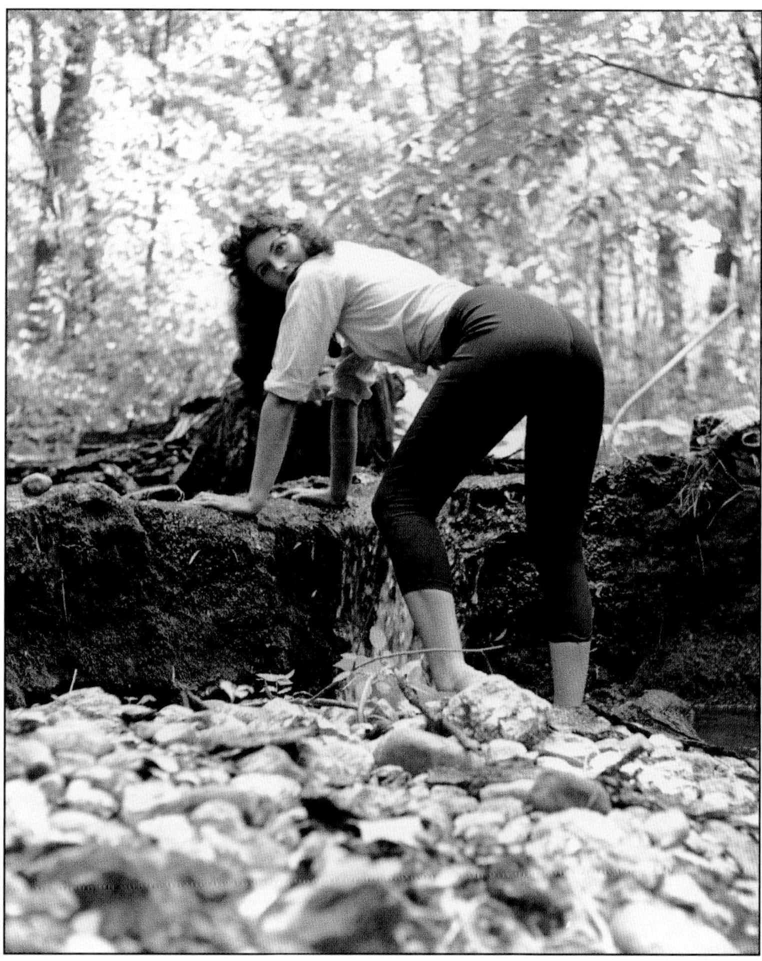

Bunny Yeager, photo by Ben Correa

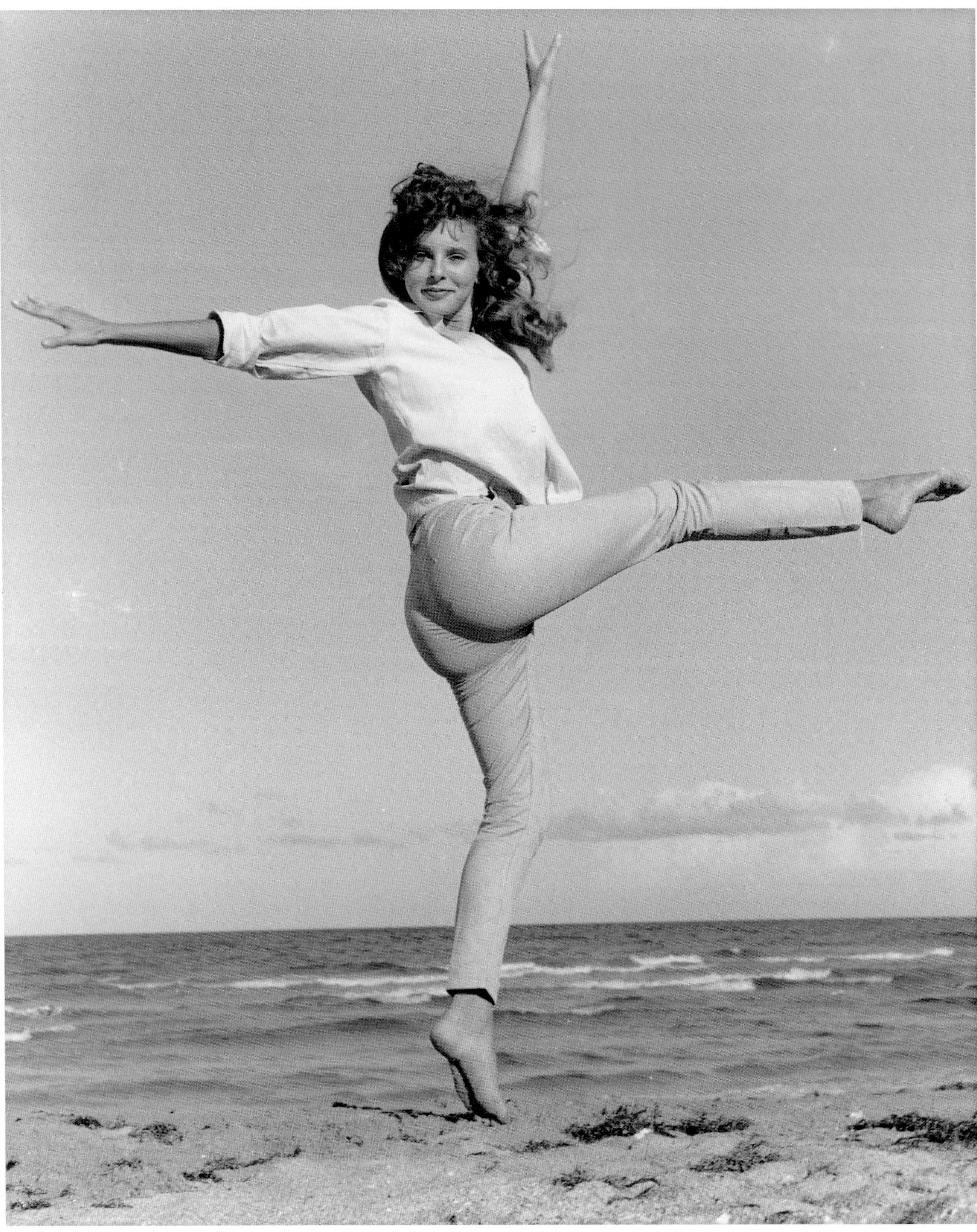

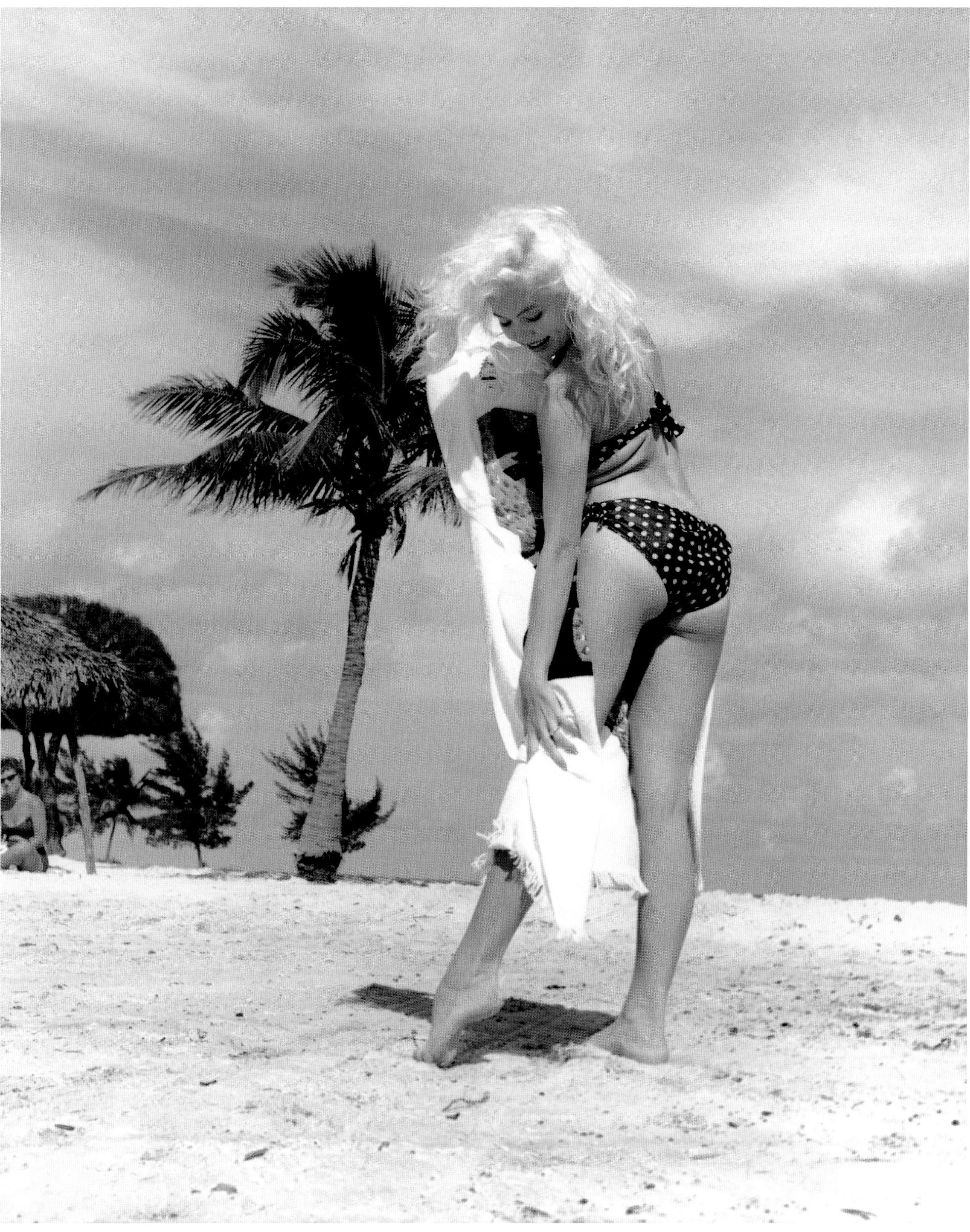

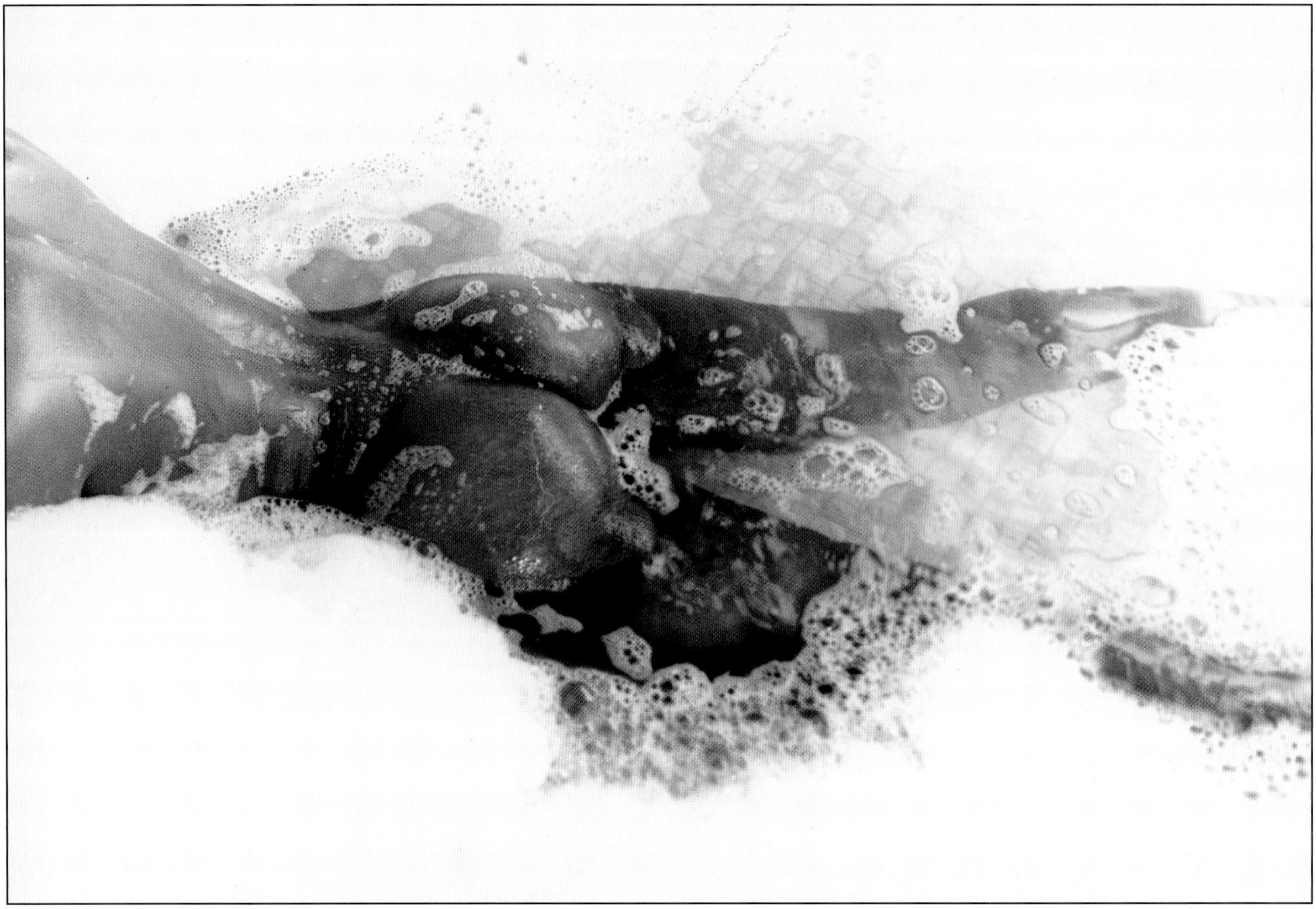

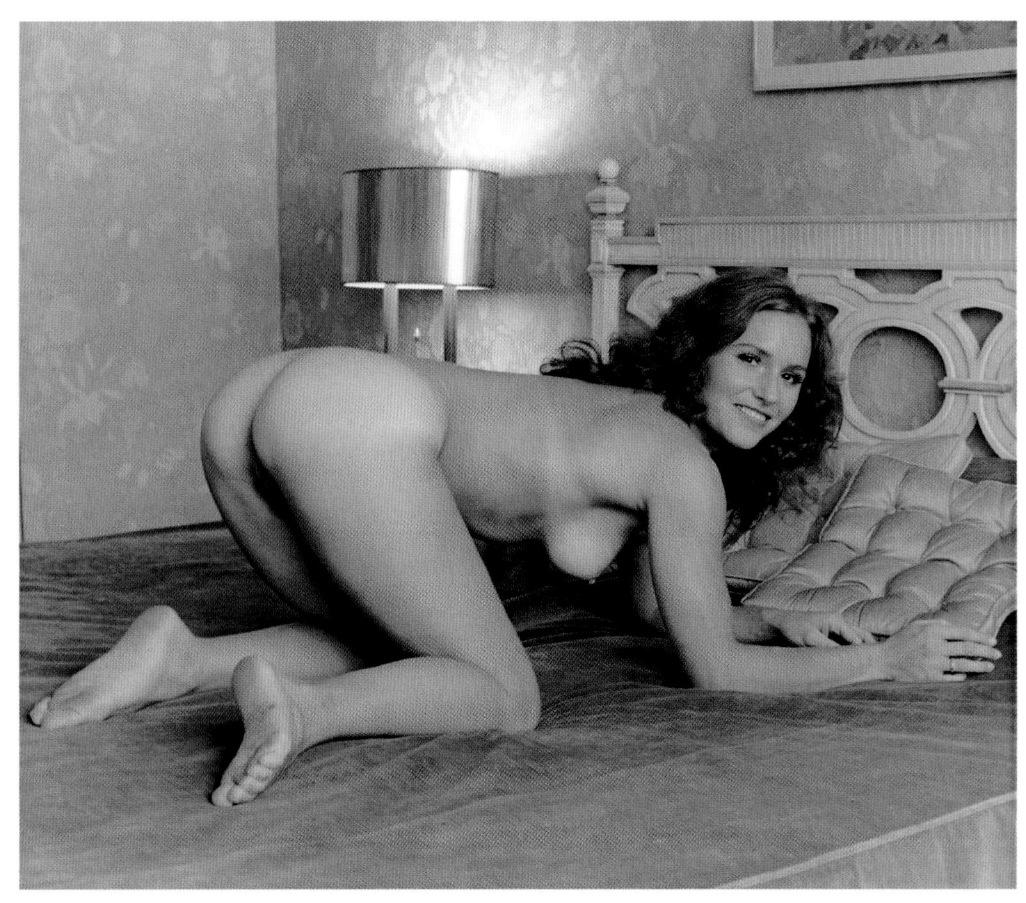

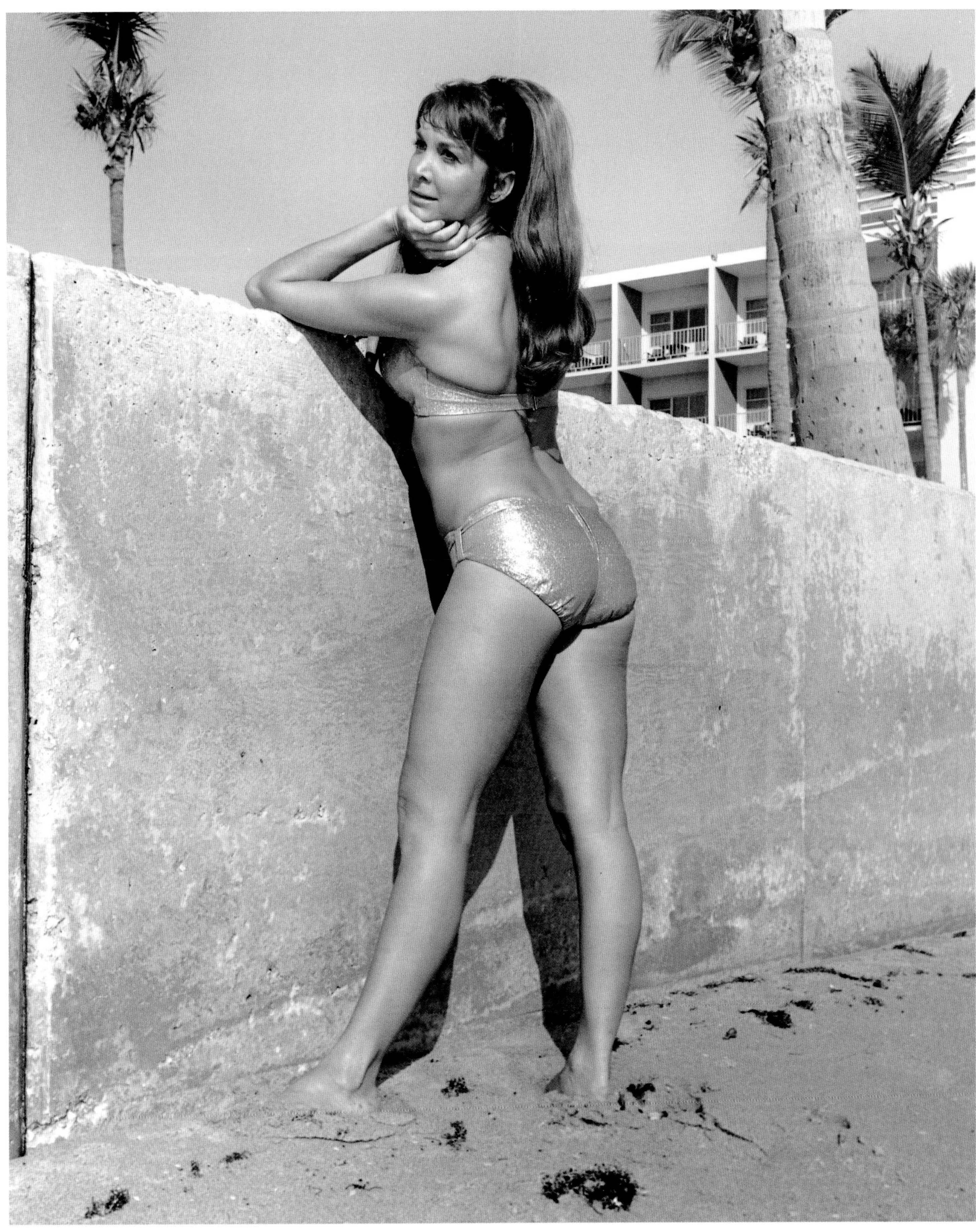

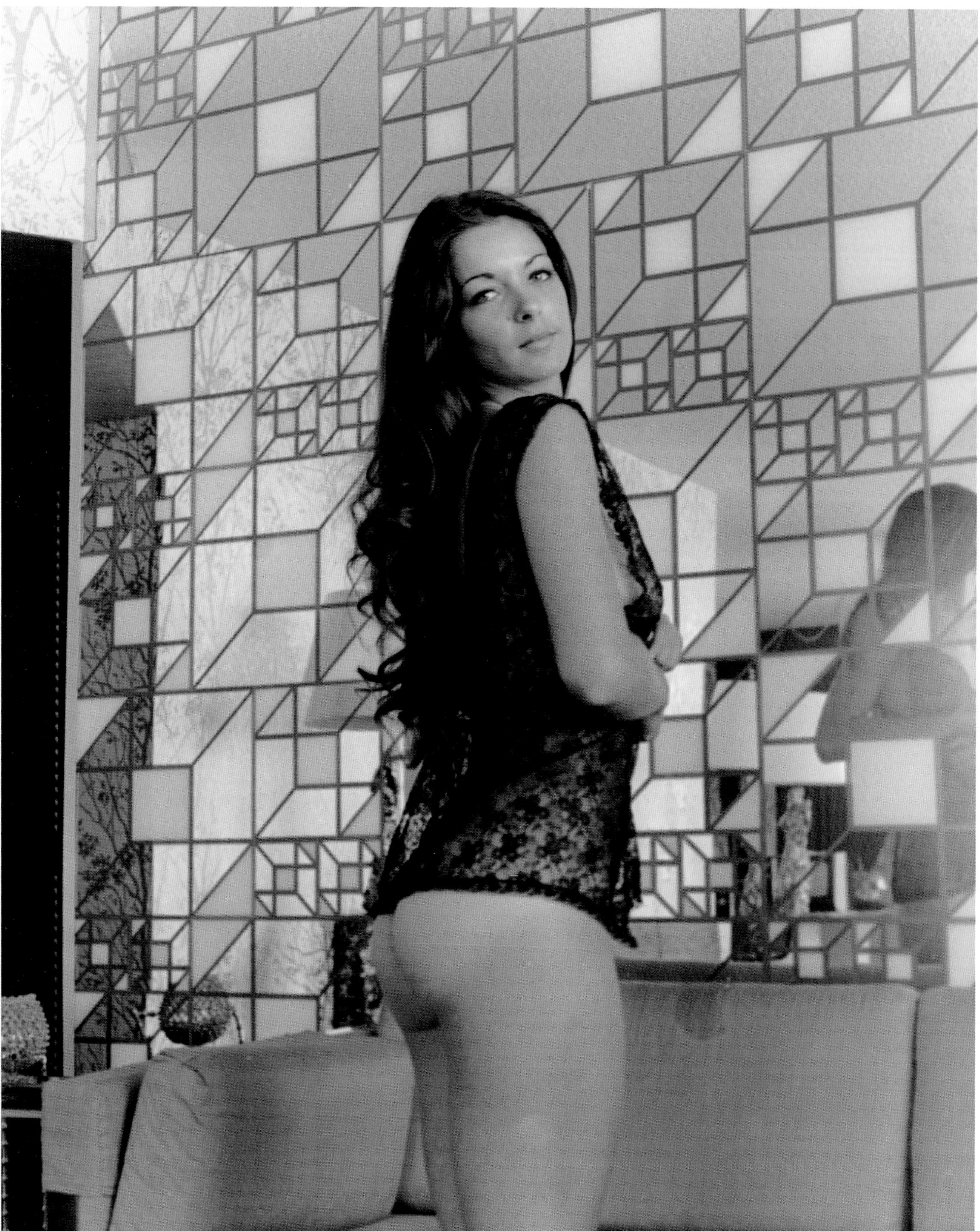

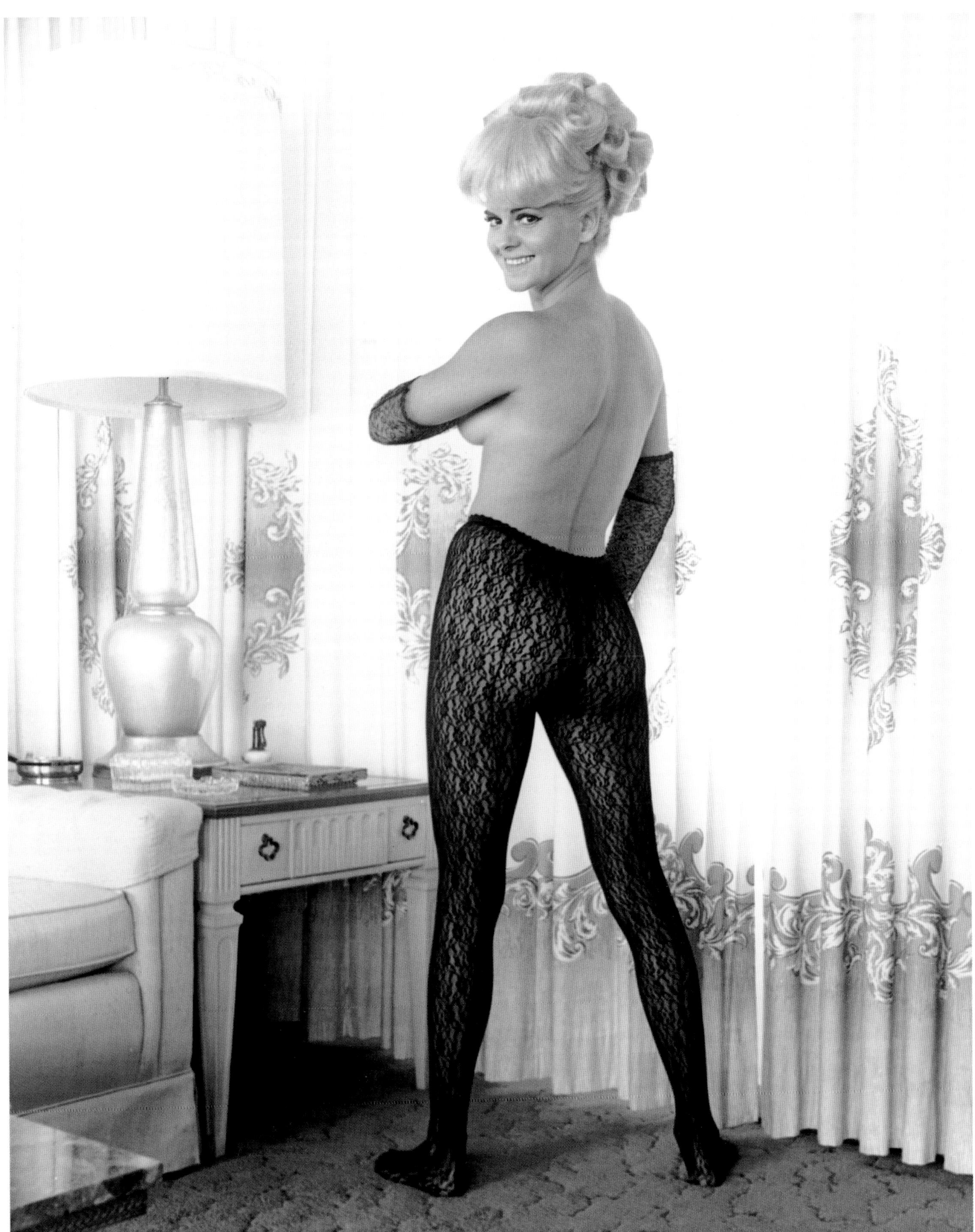

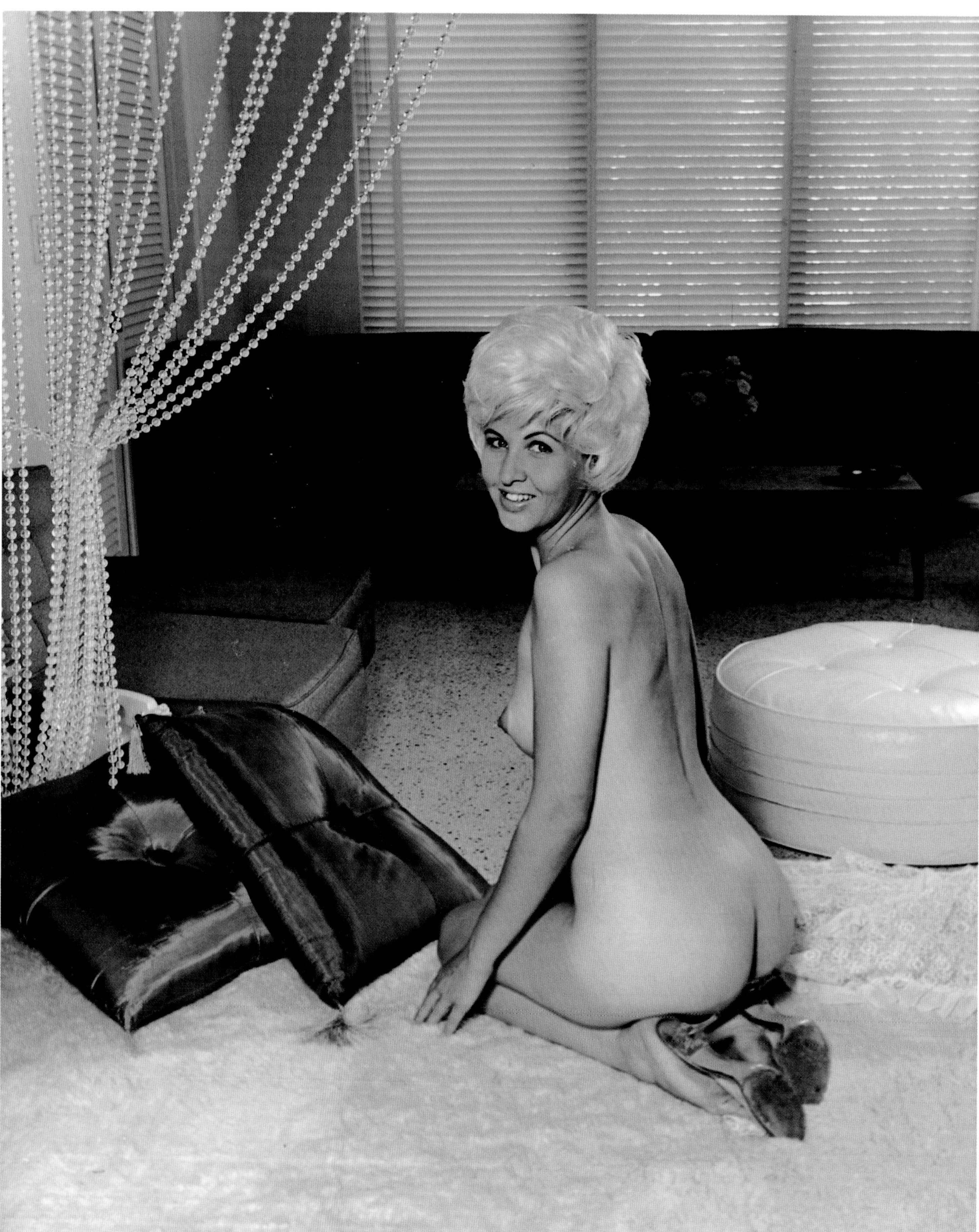

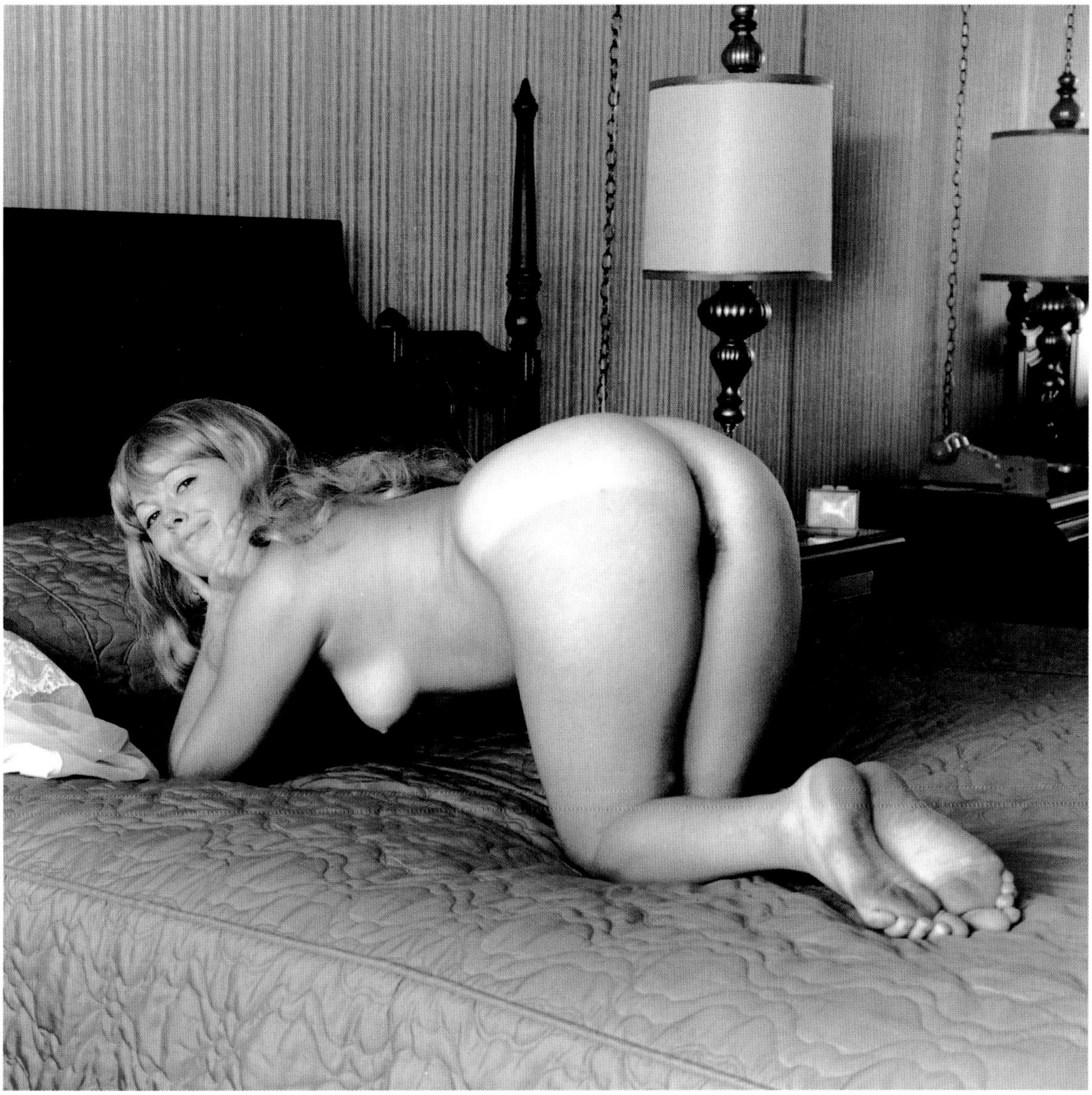

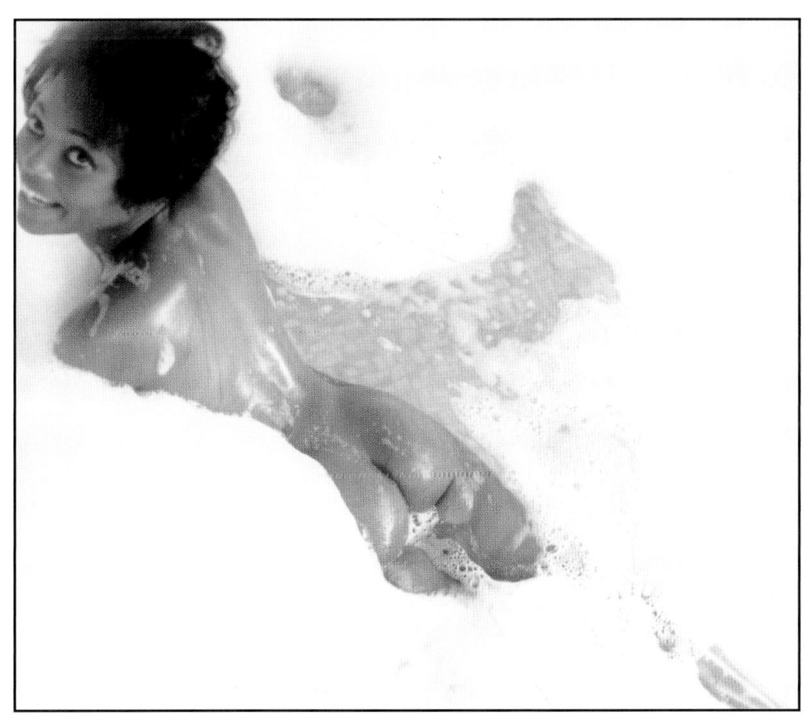

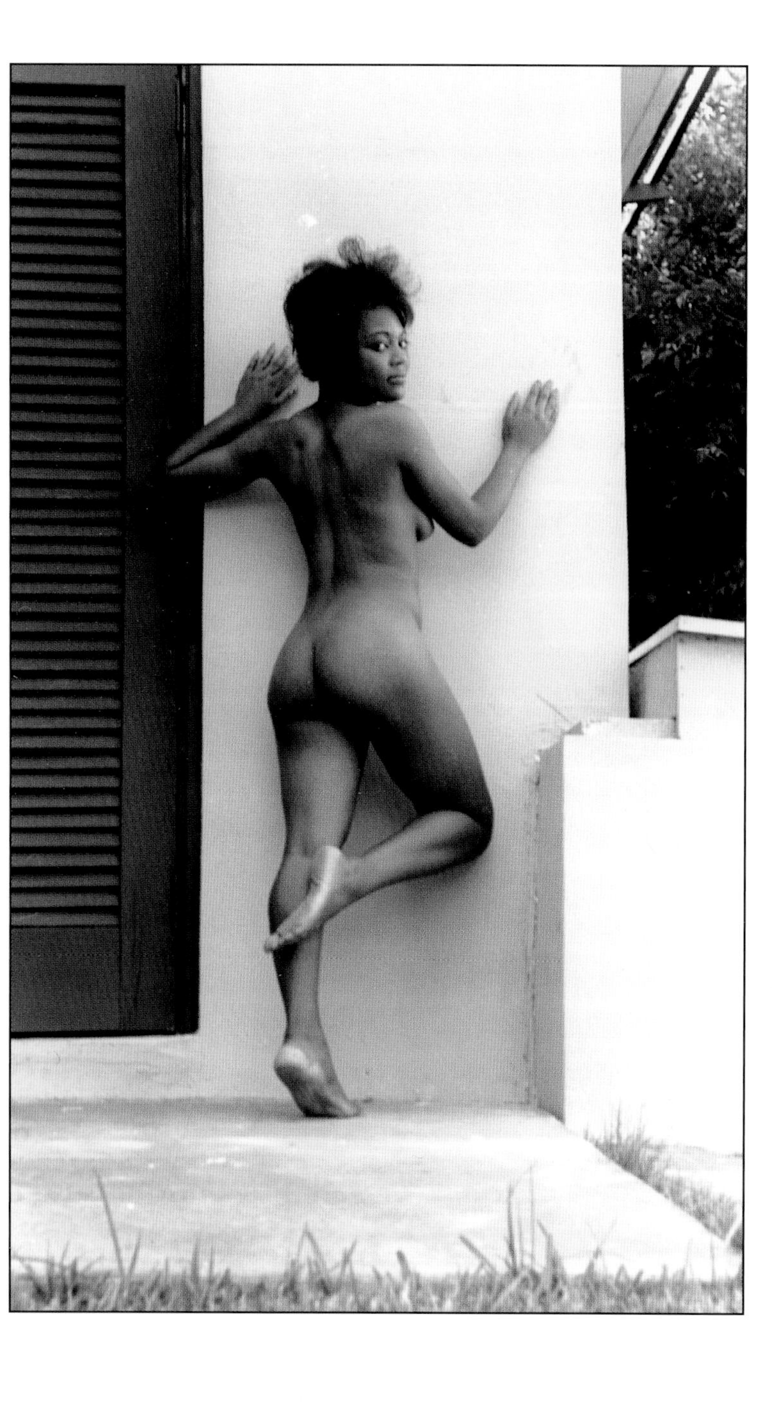

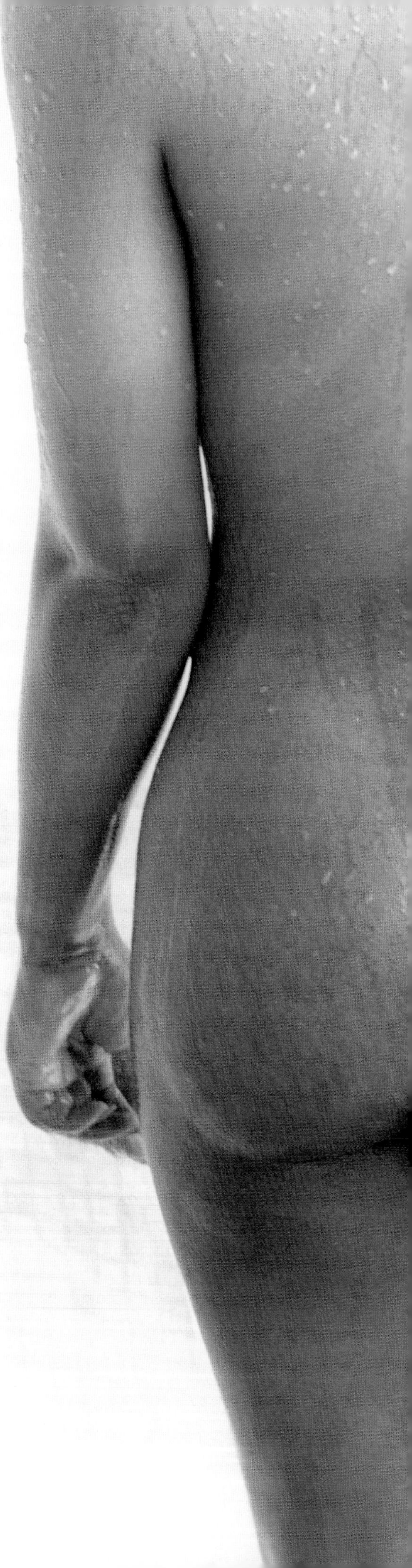

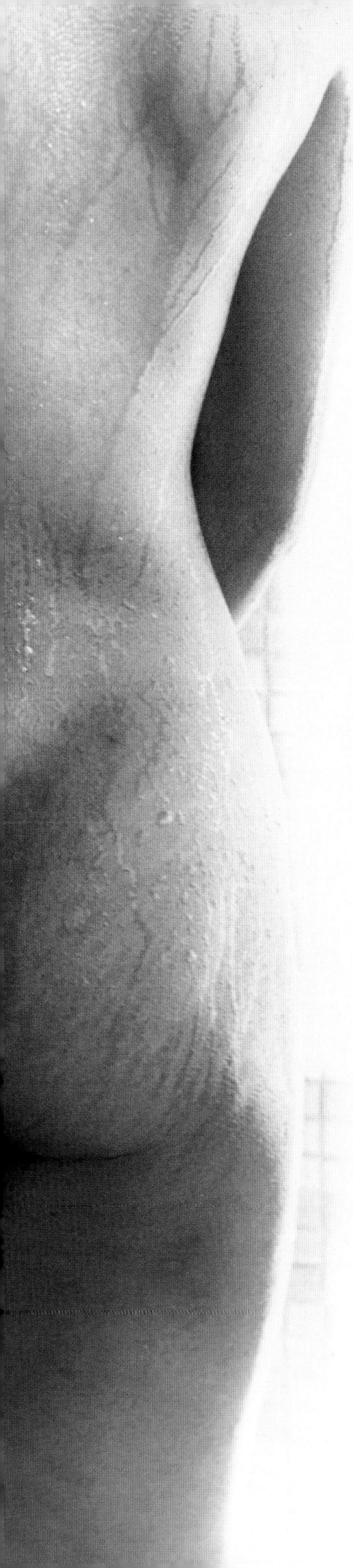

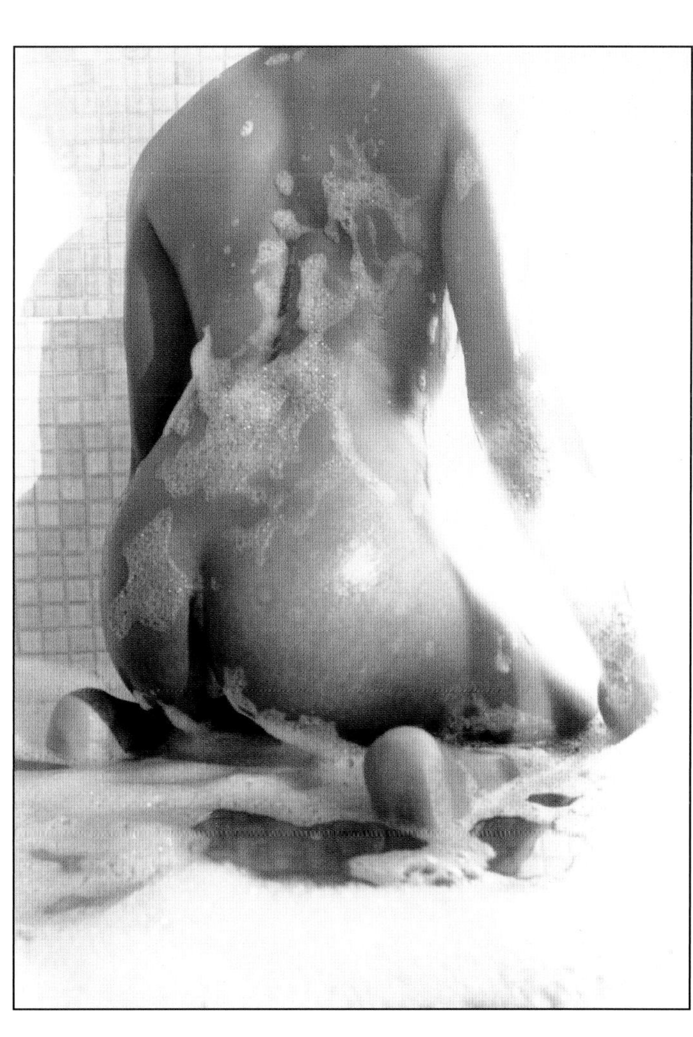

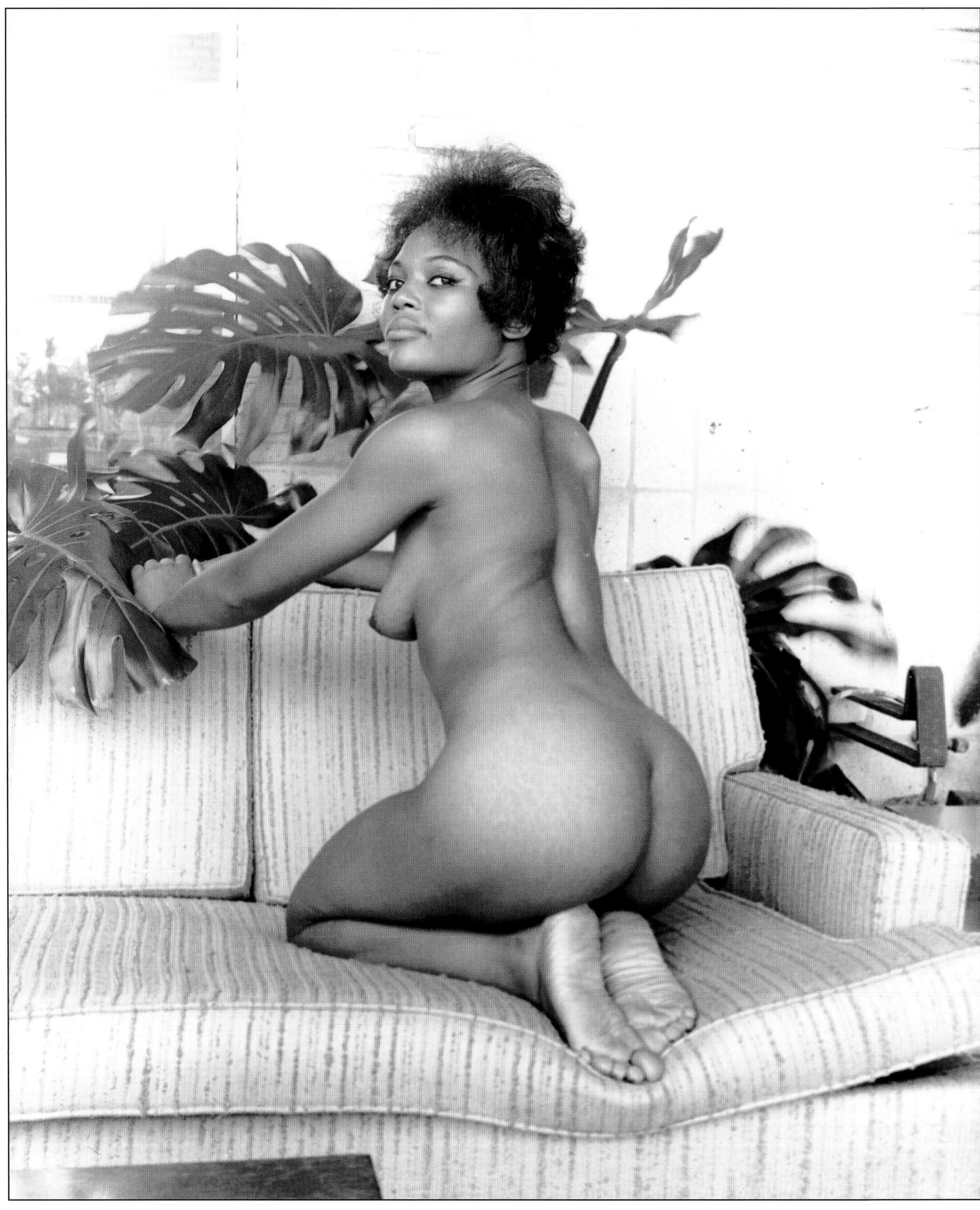

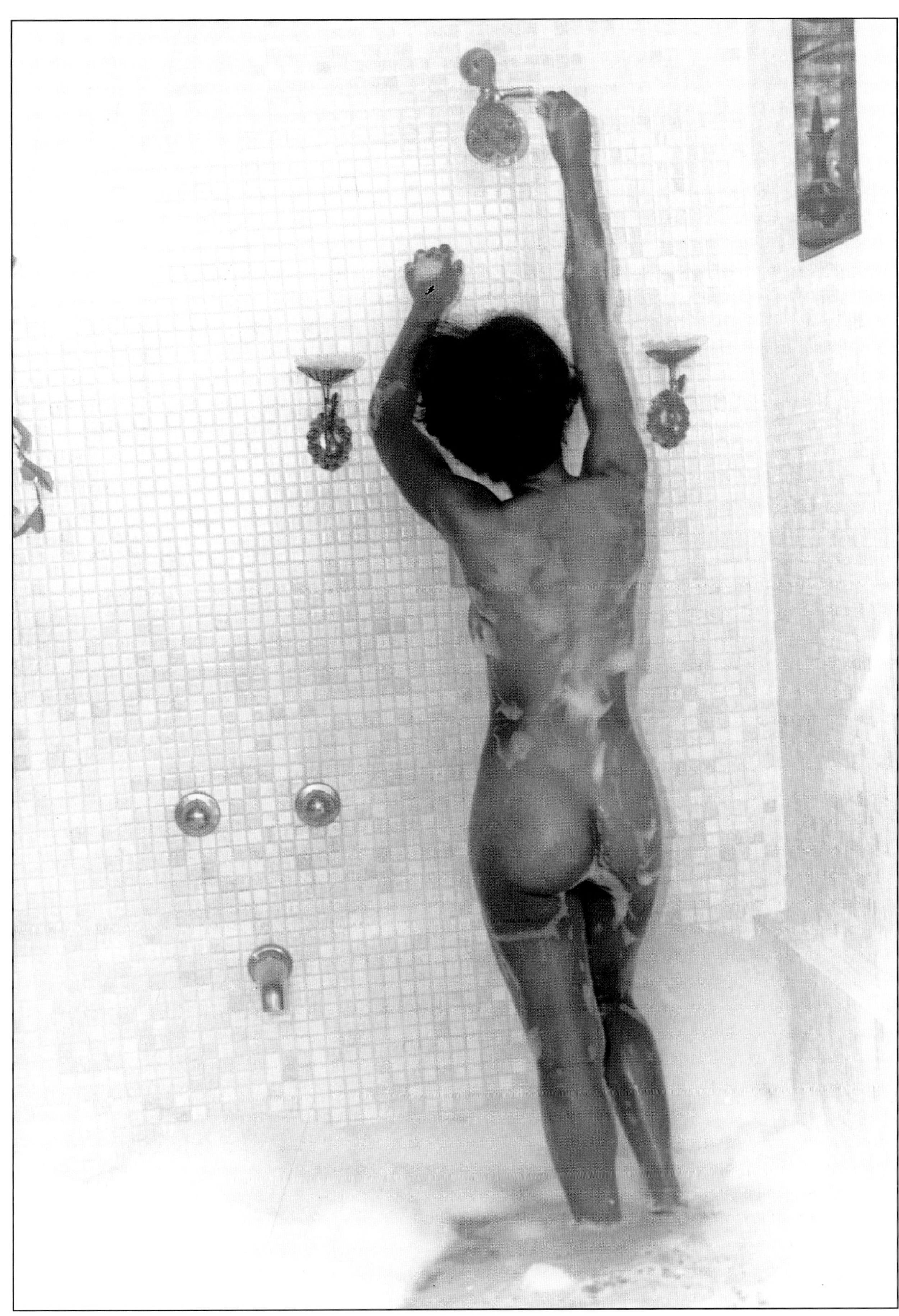

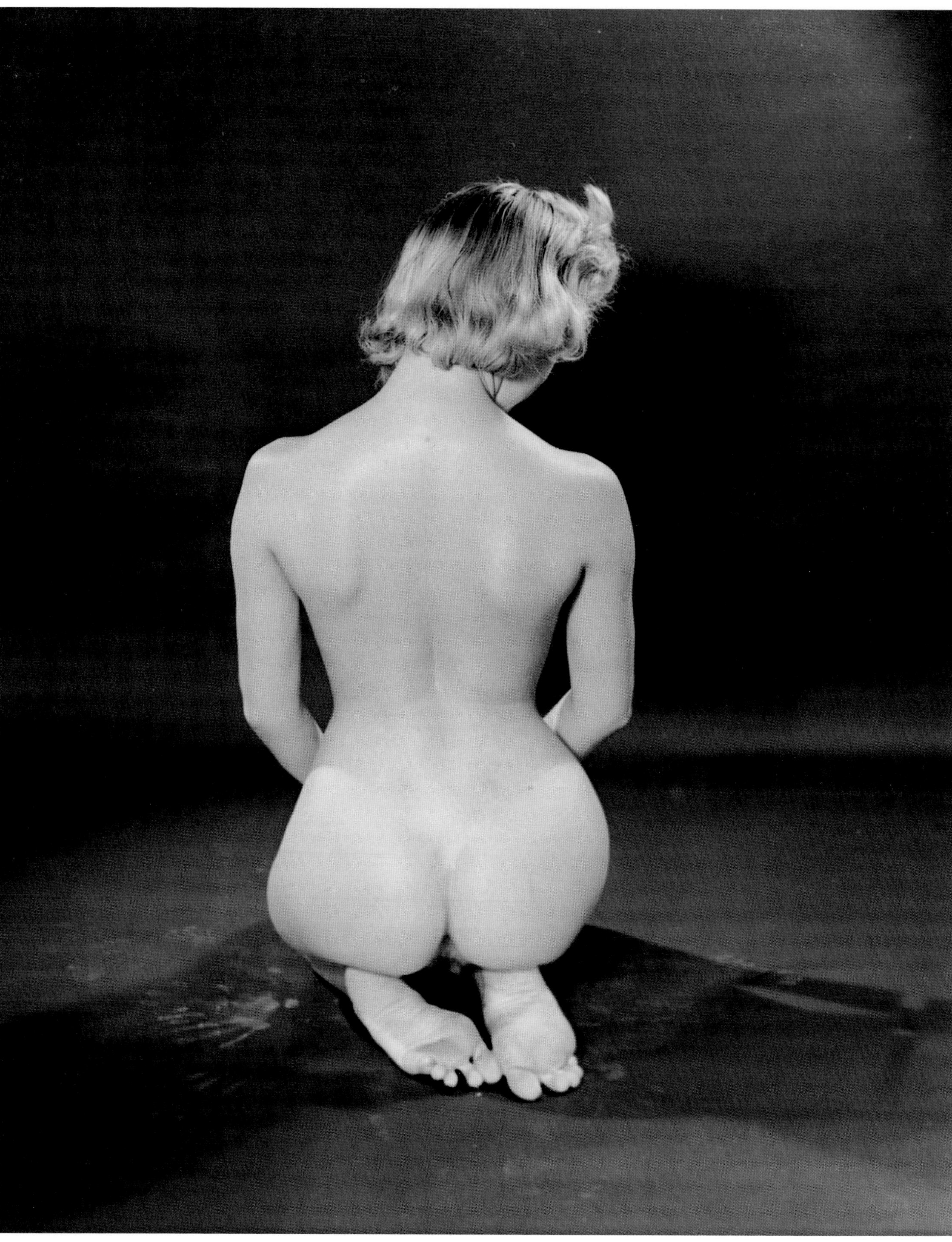

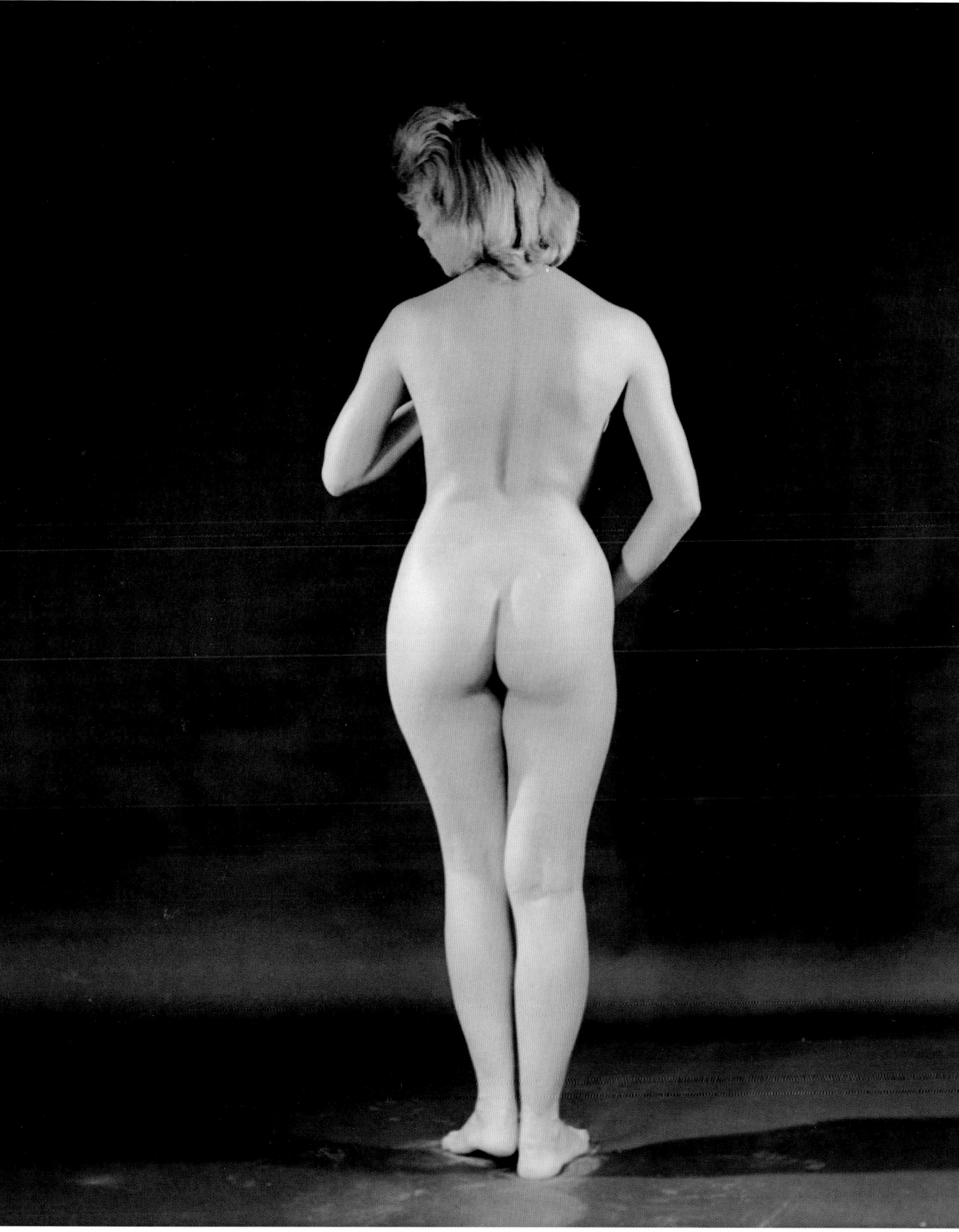

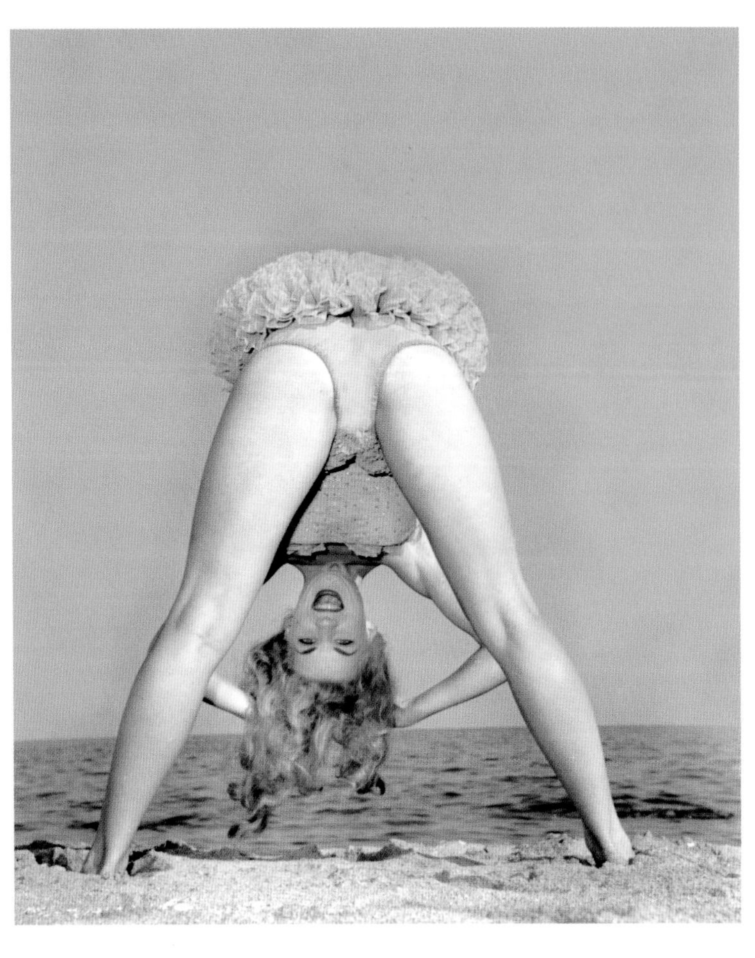

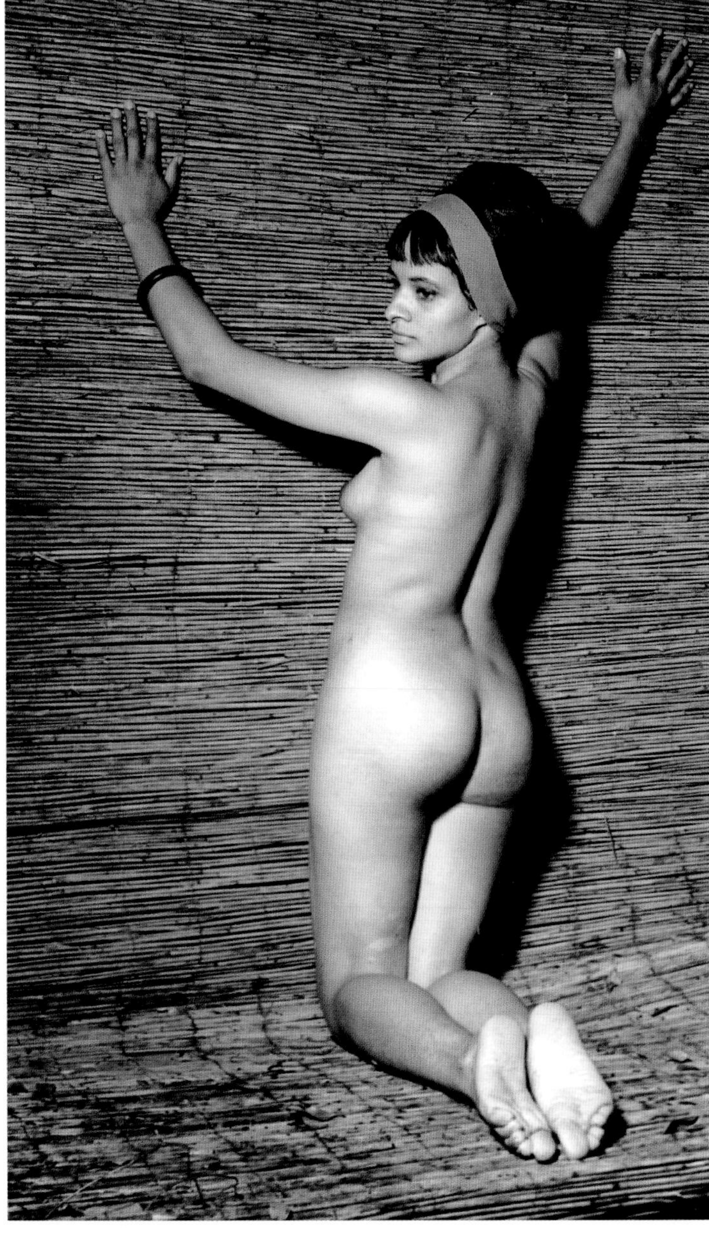

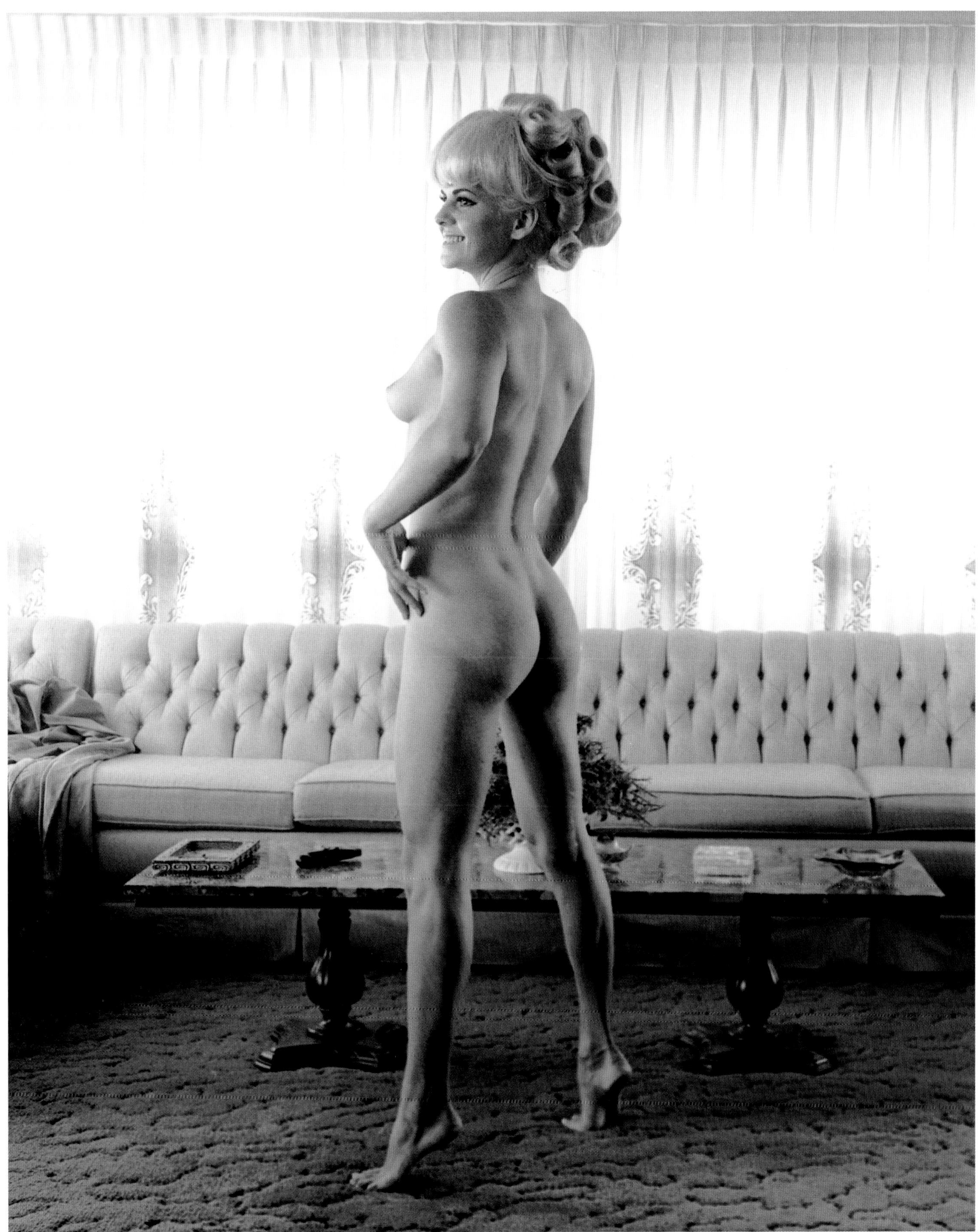

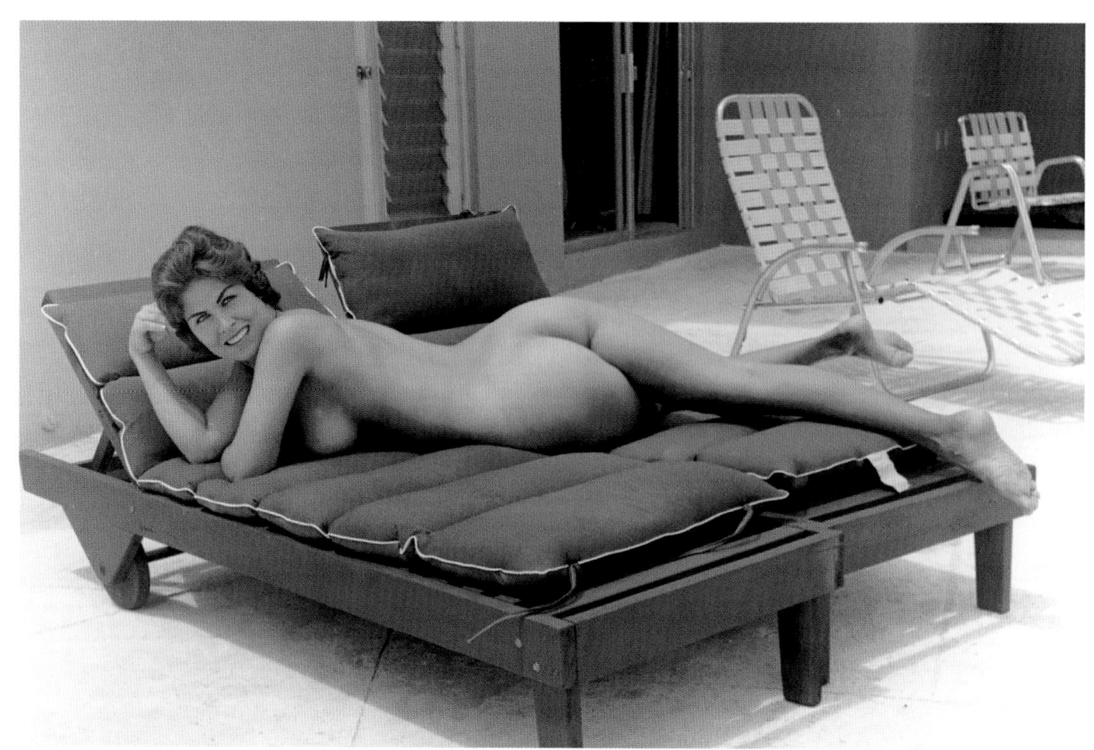

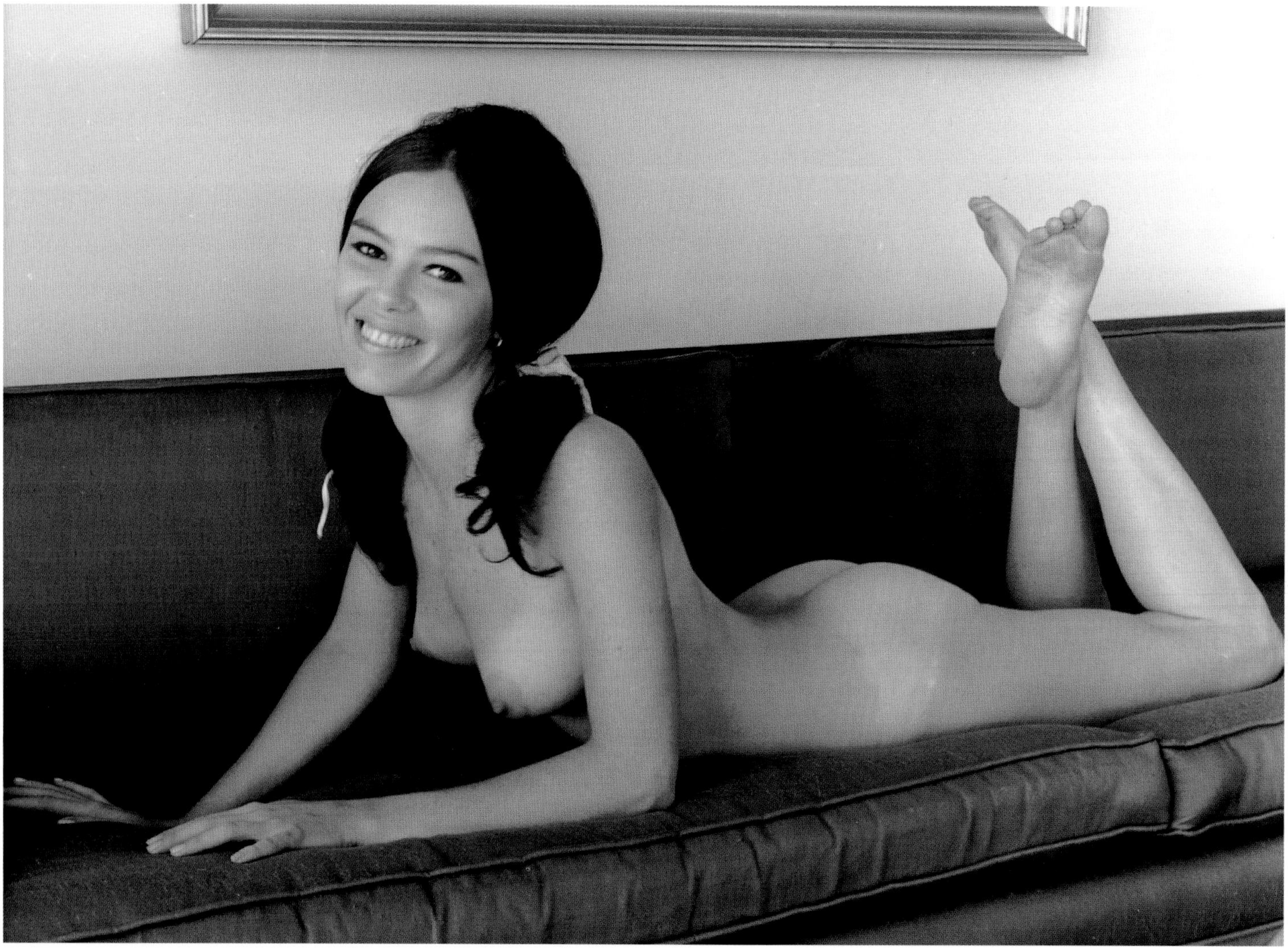

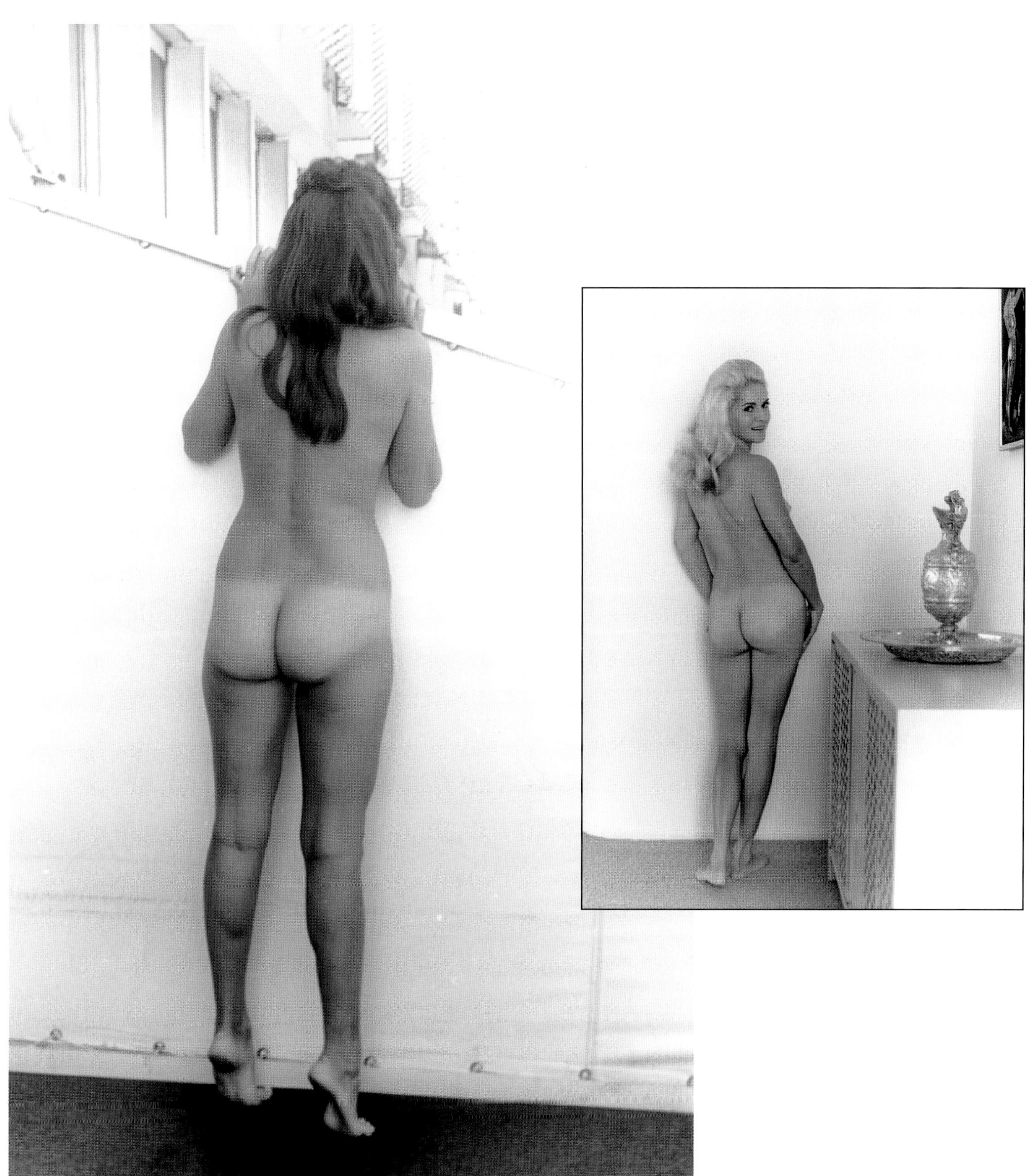

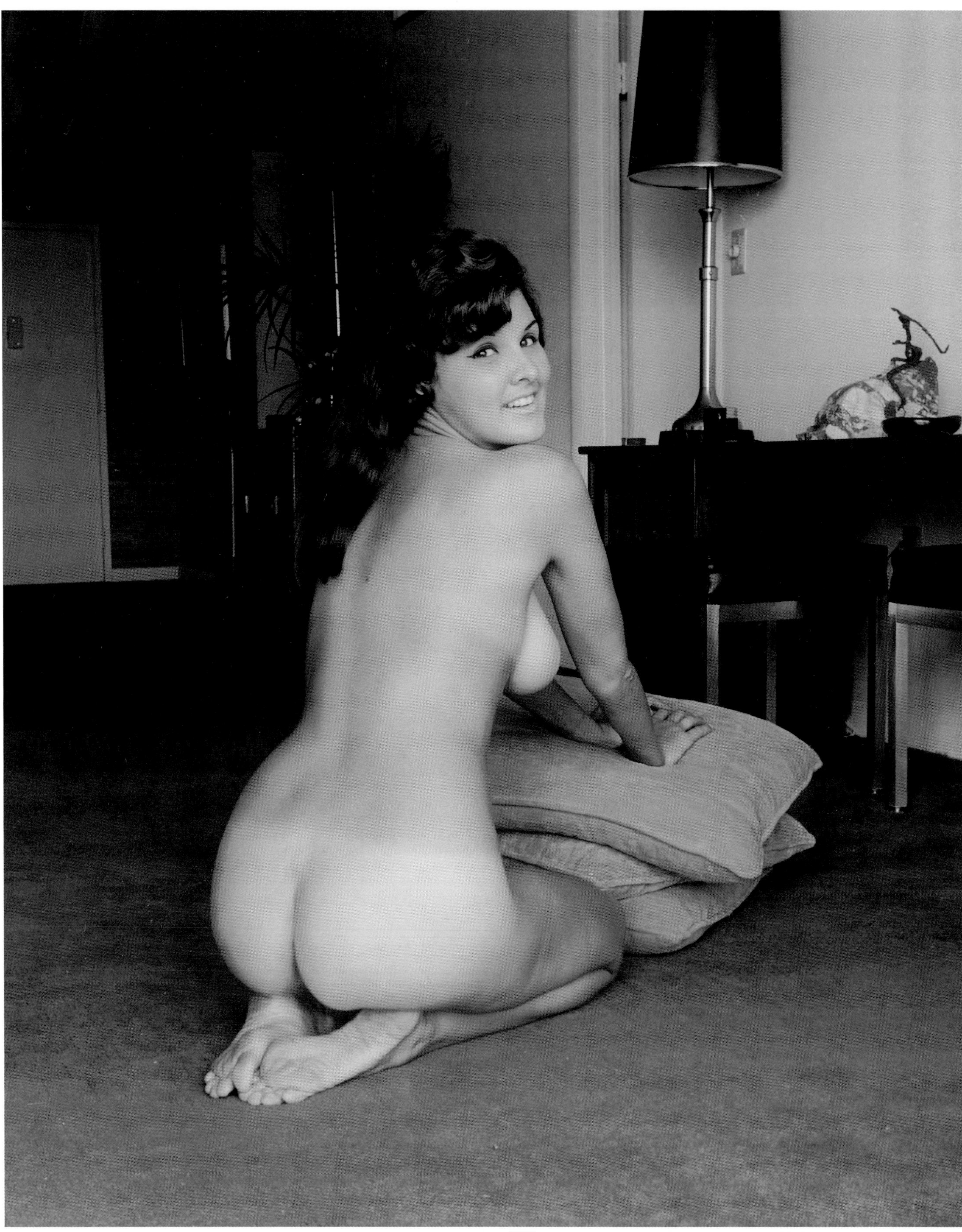

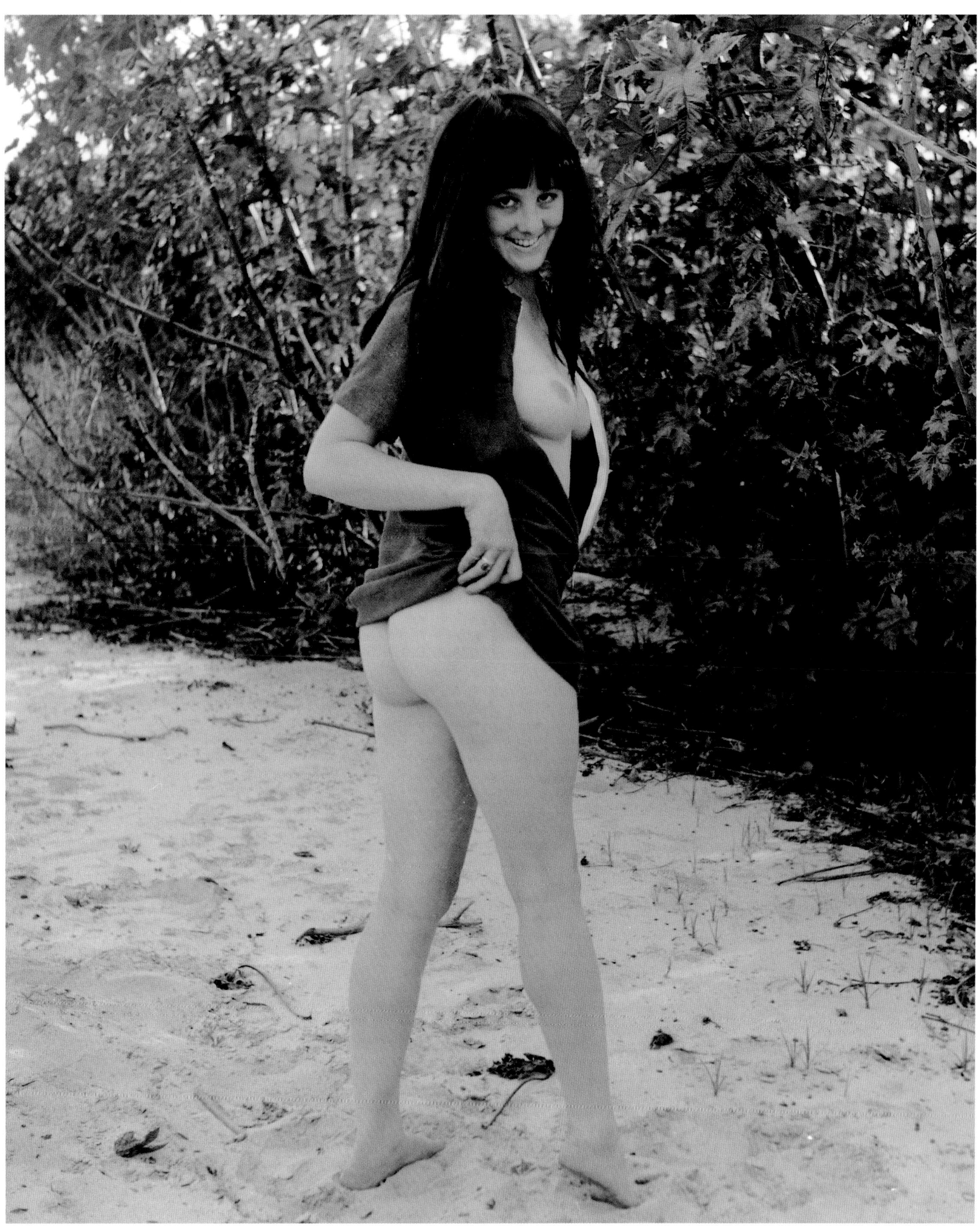

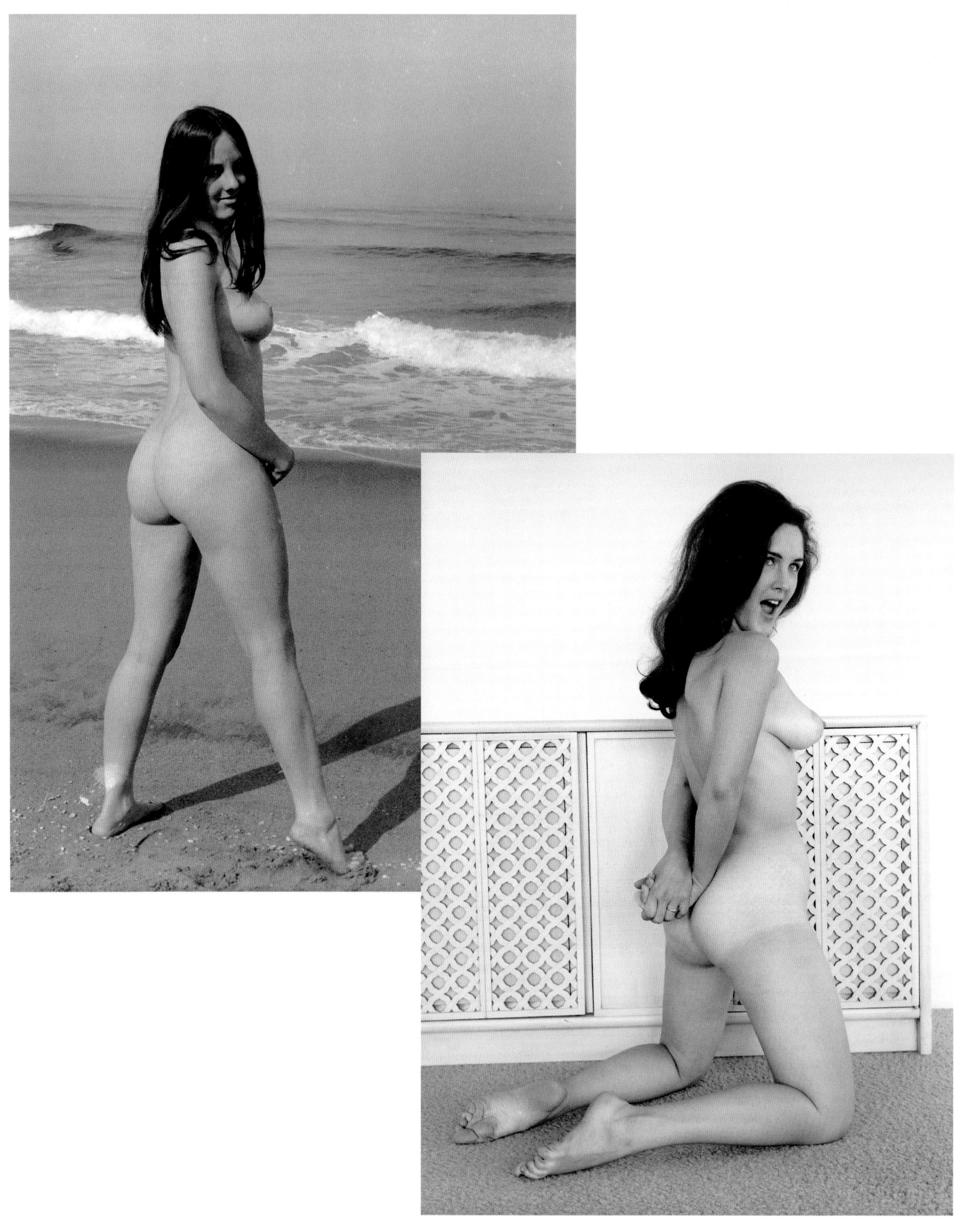

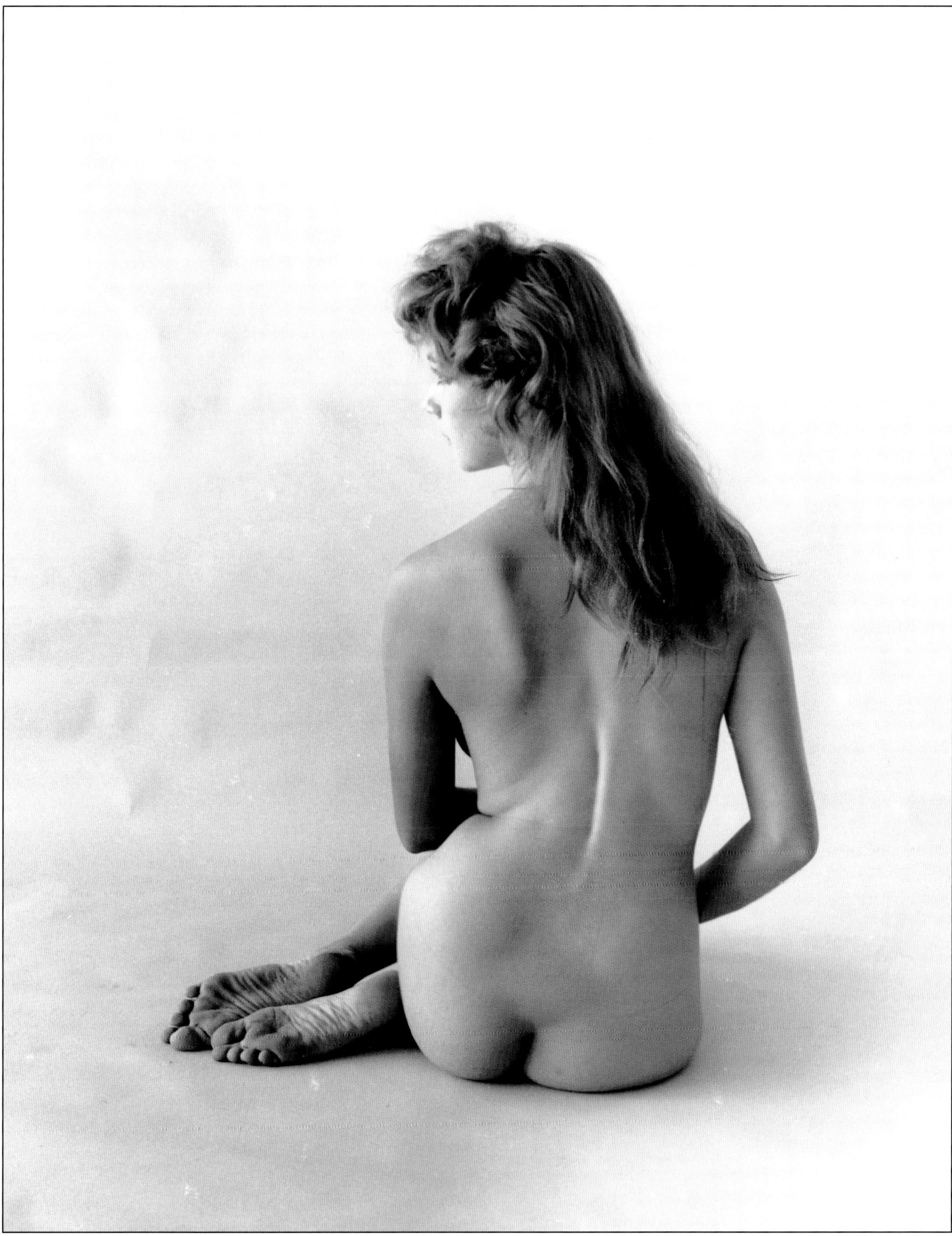

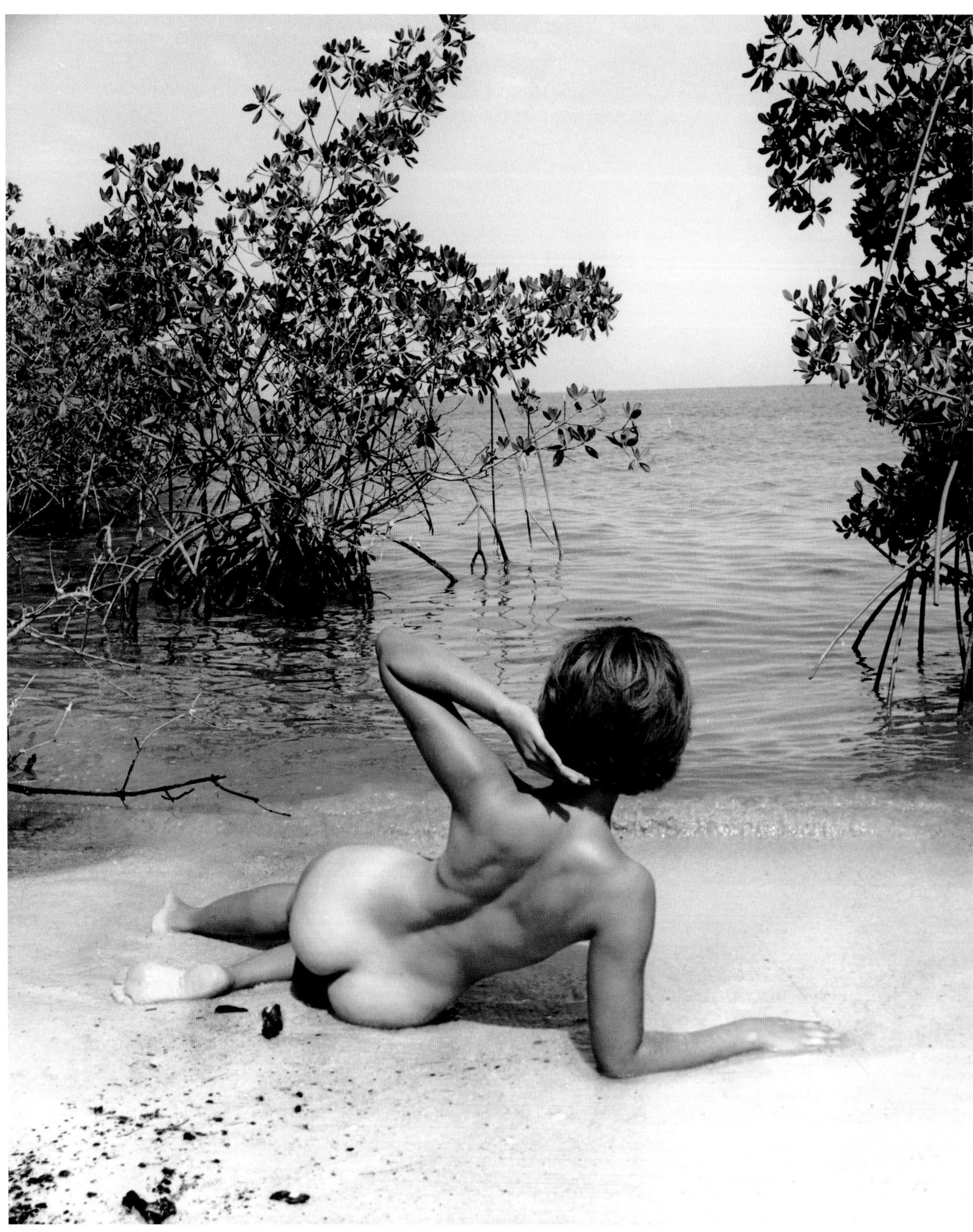

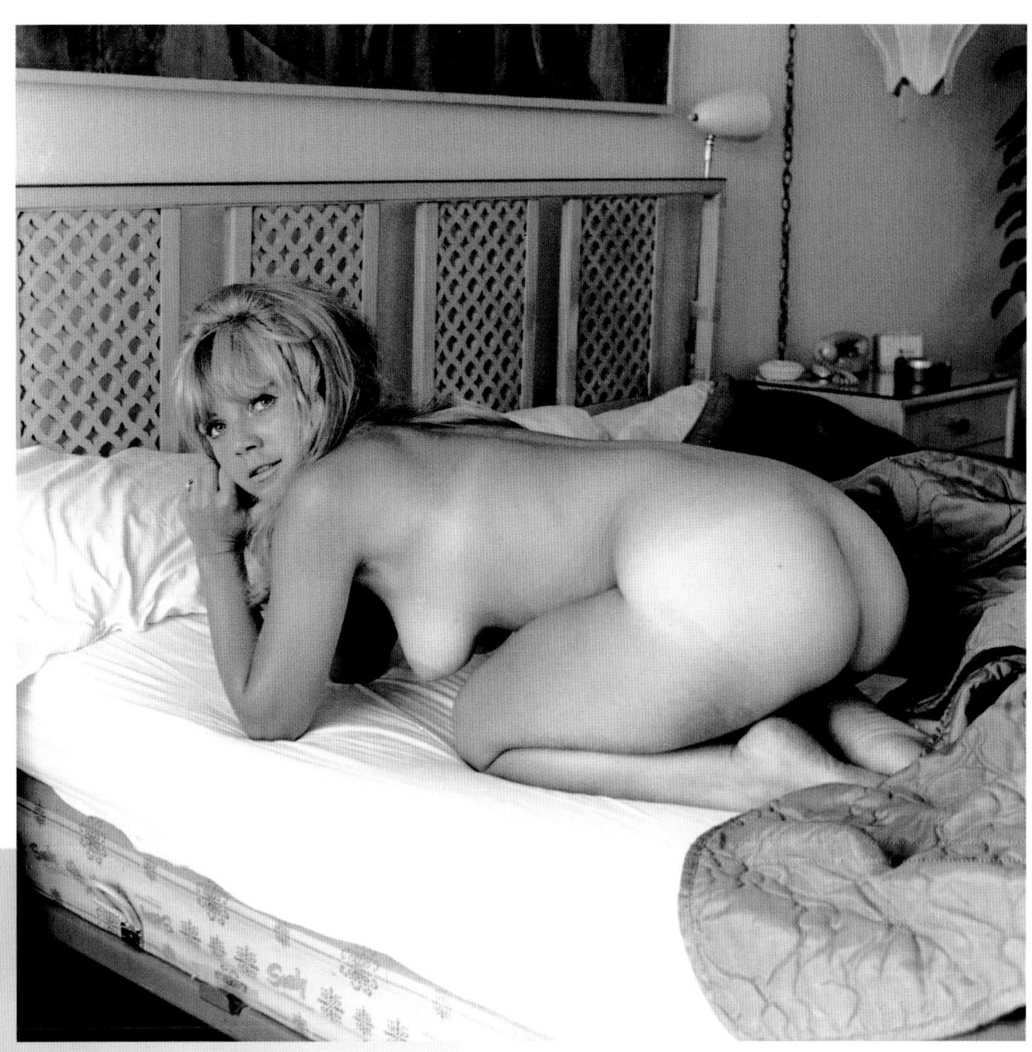

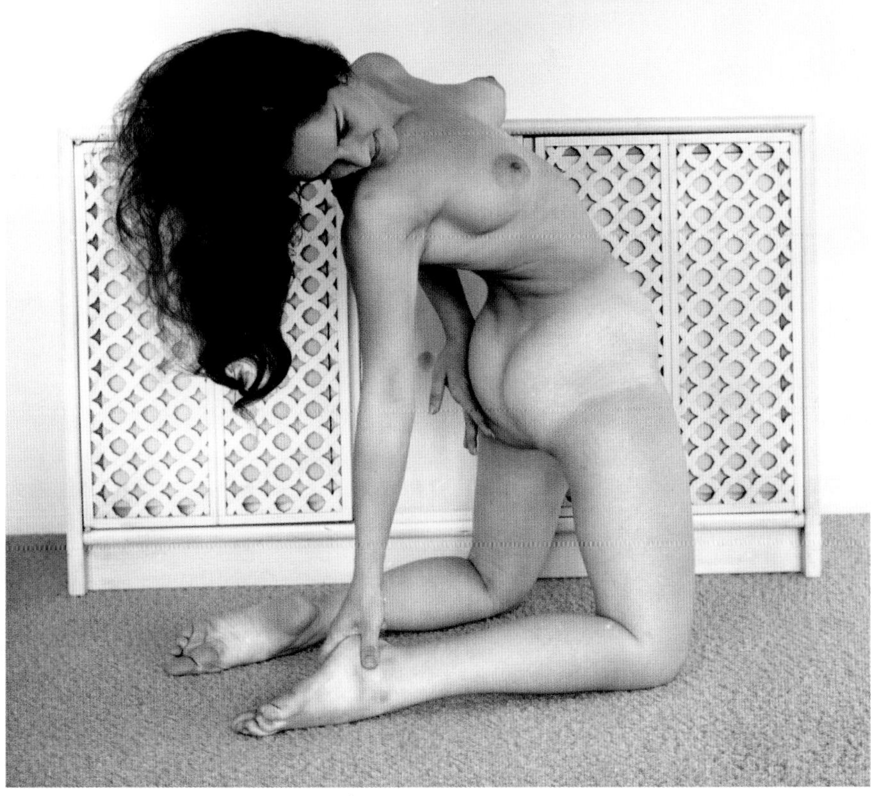

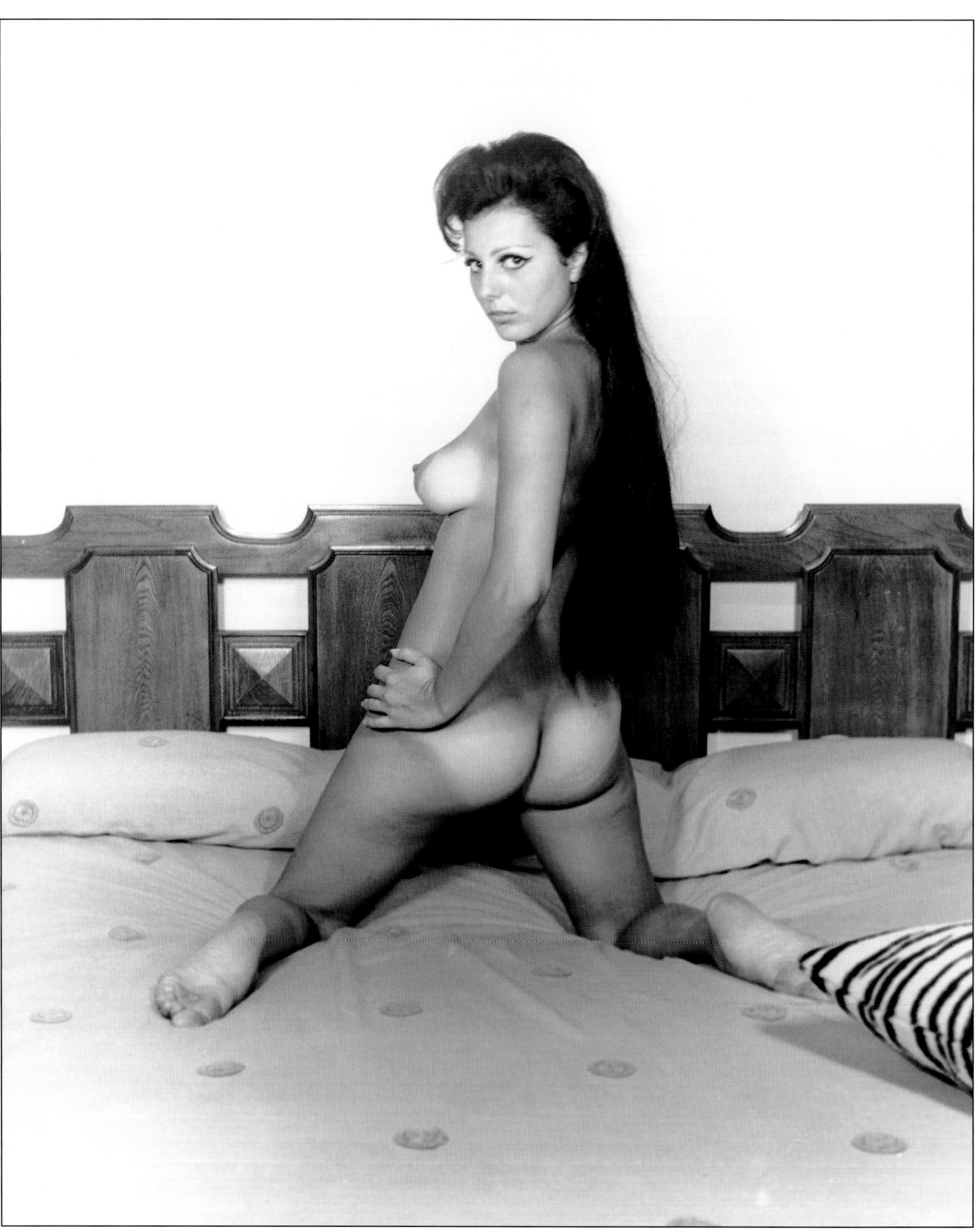

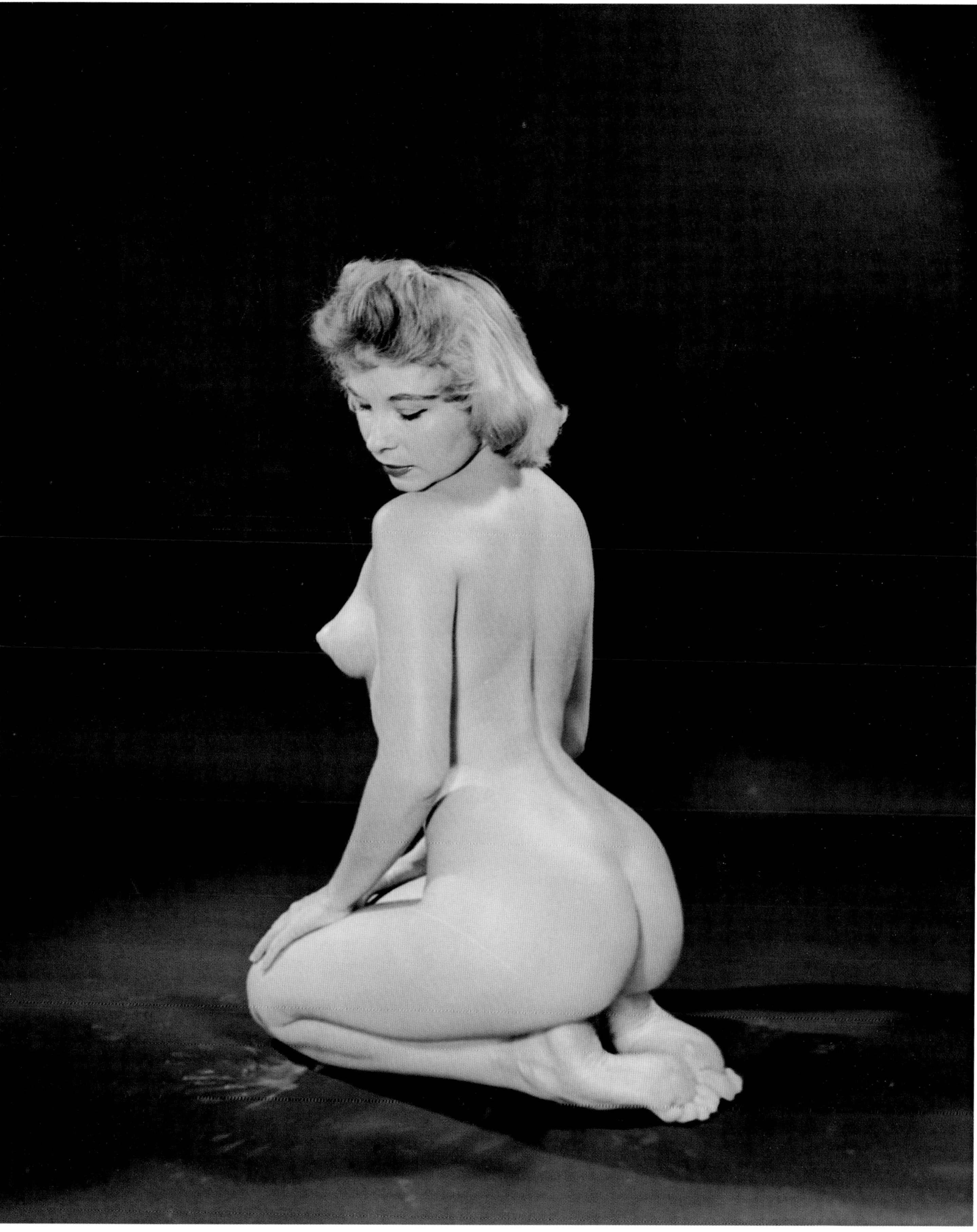

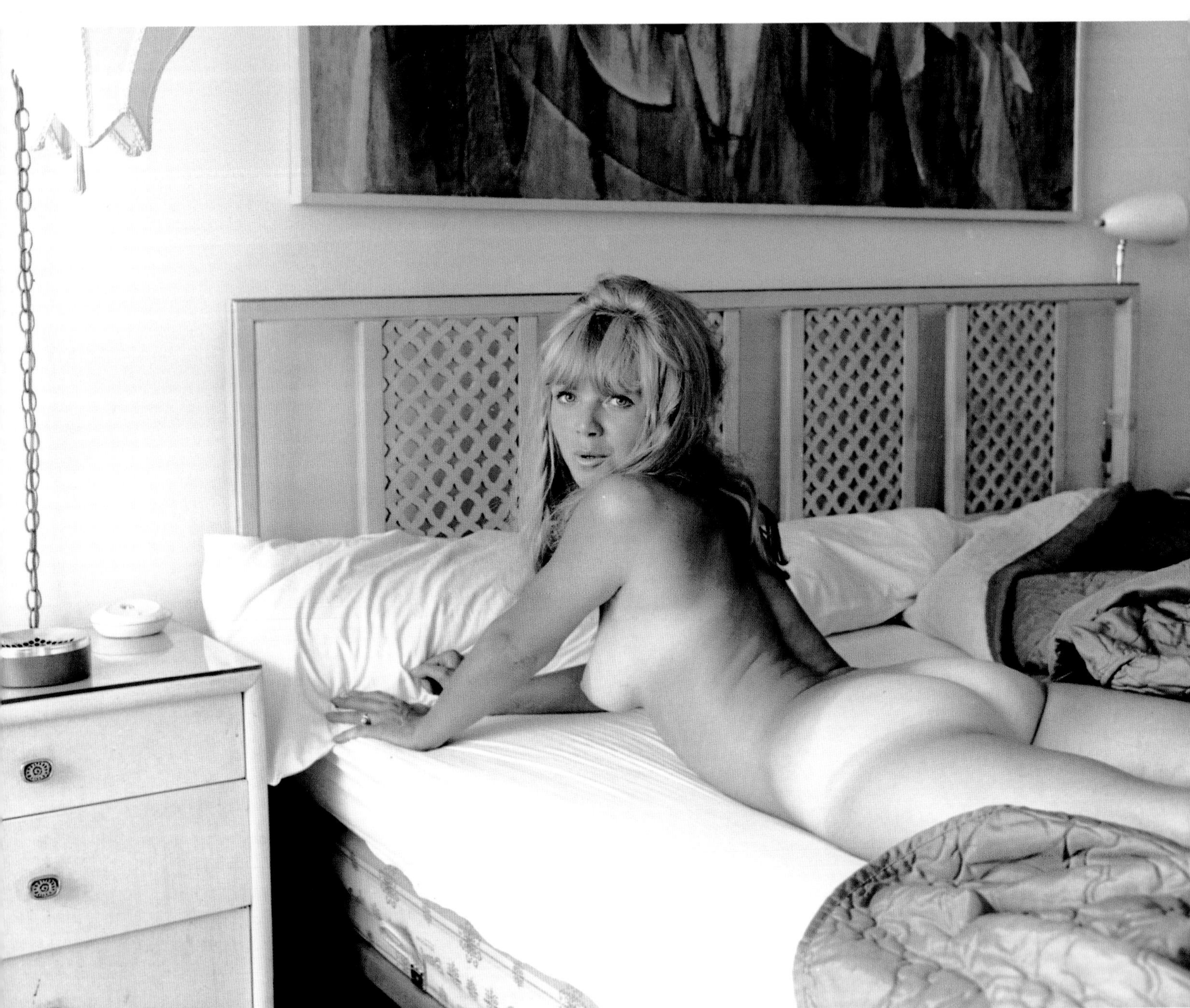

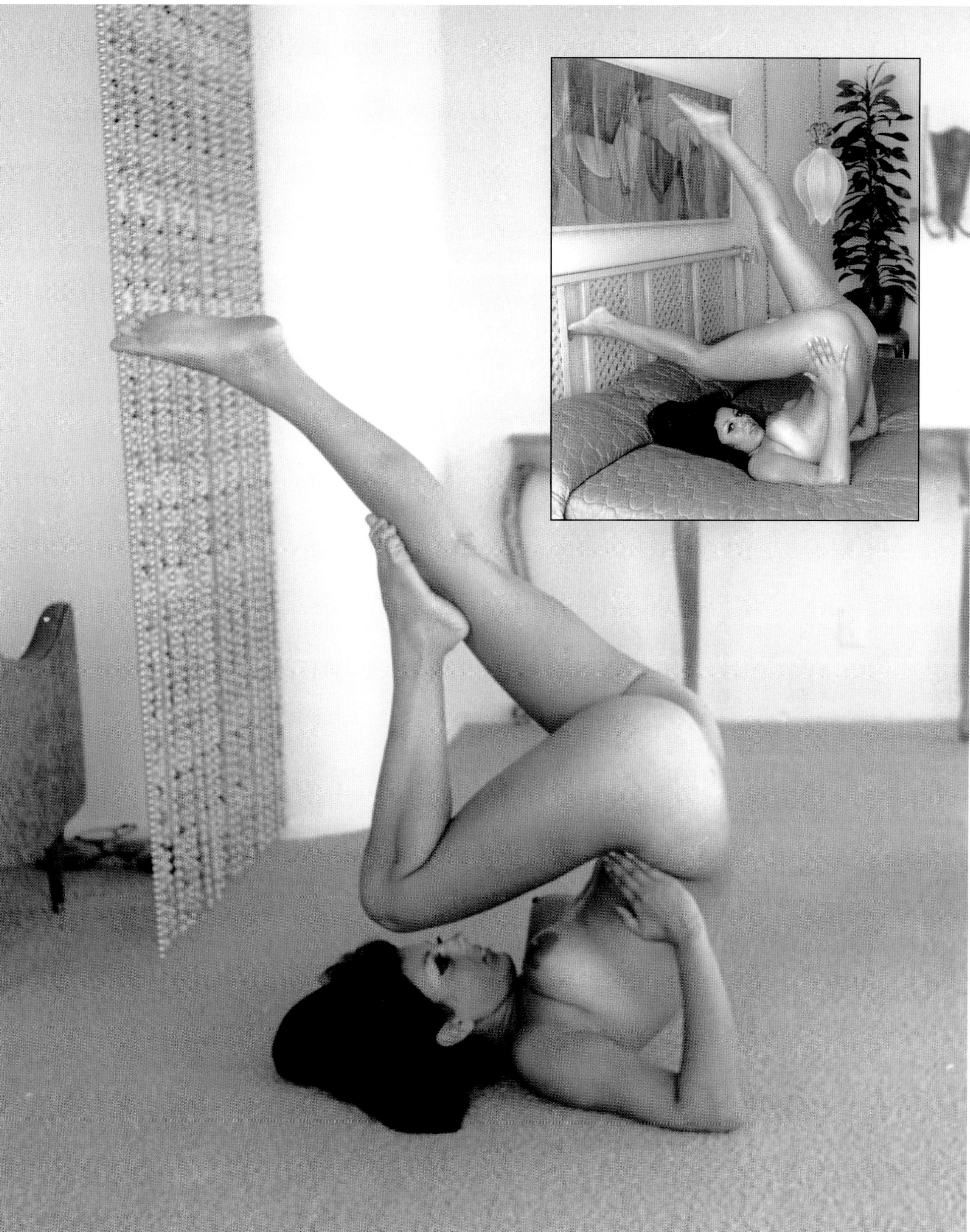

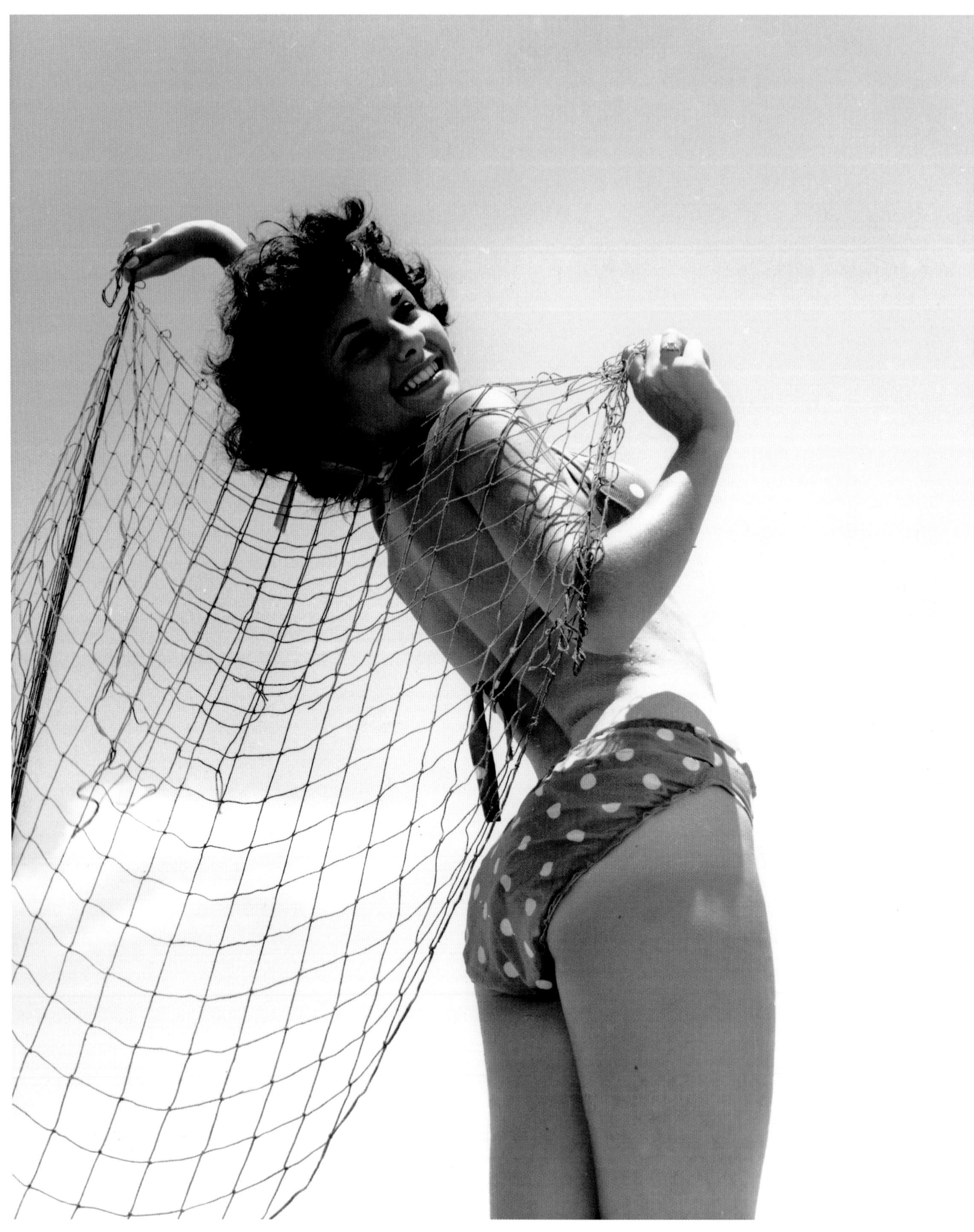

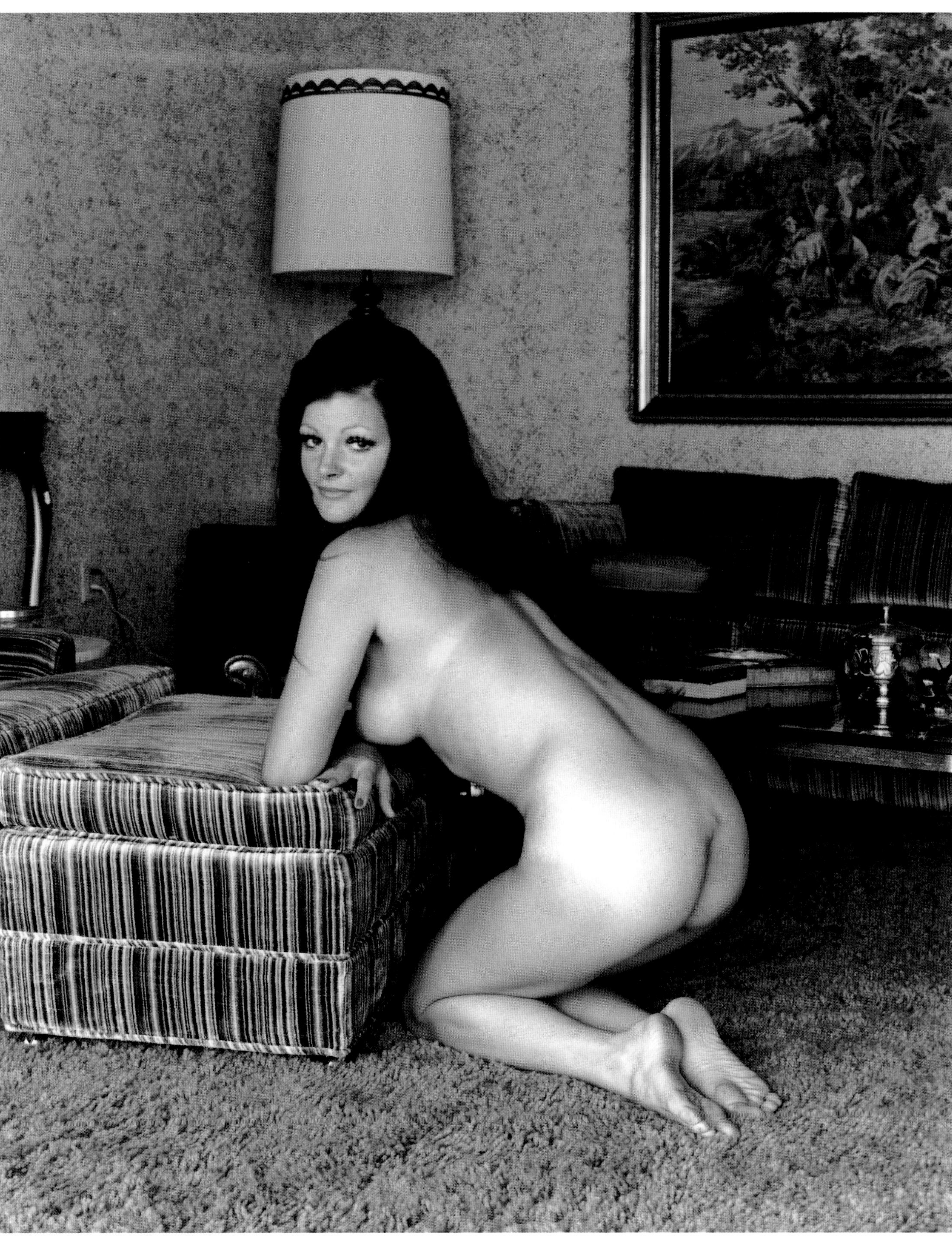

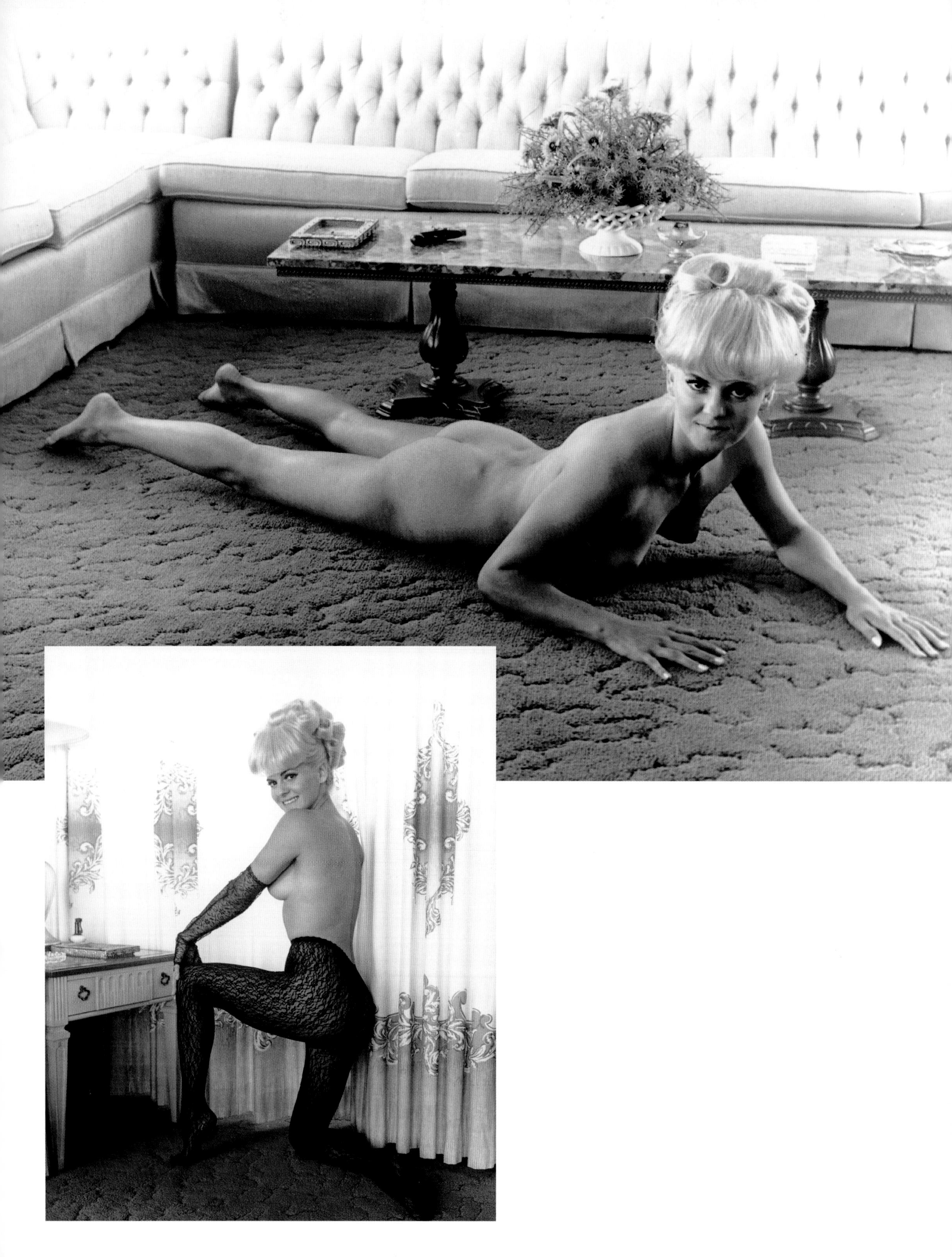

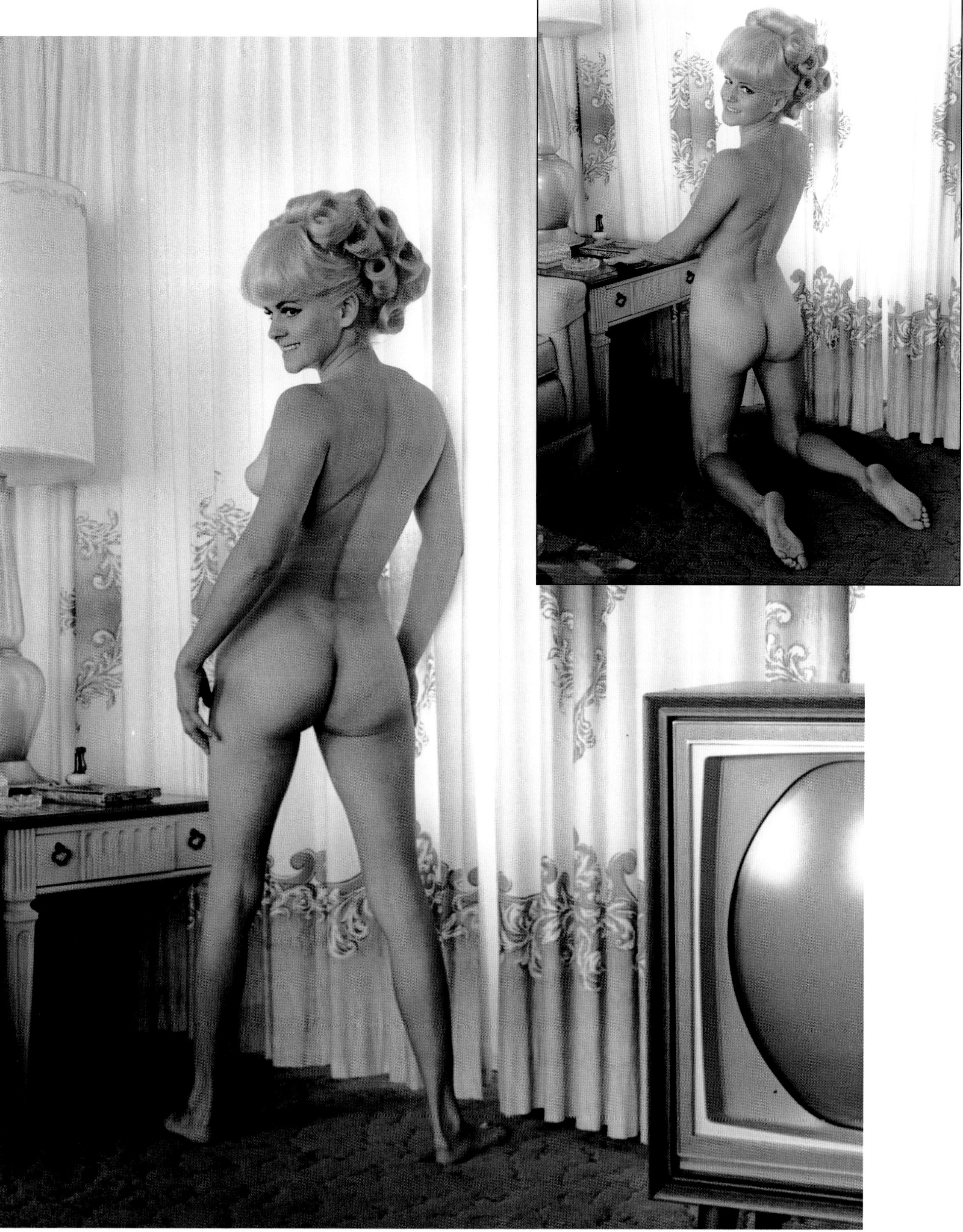

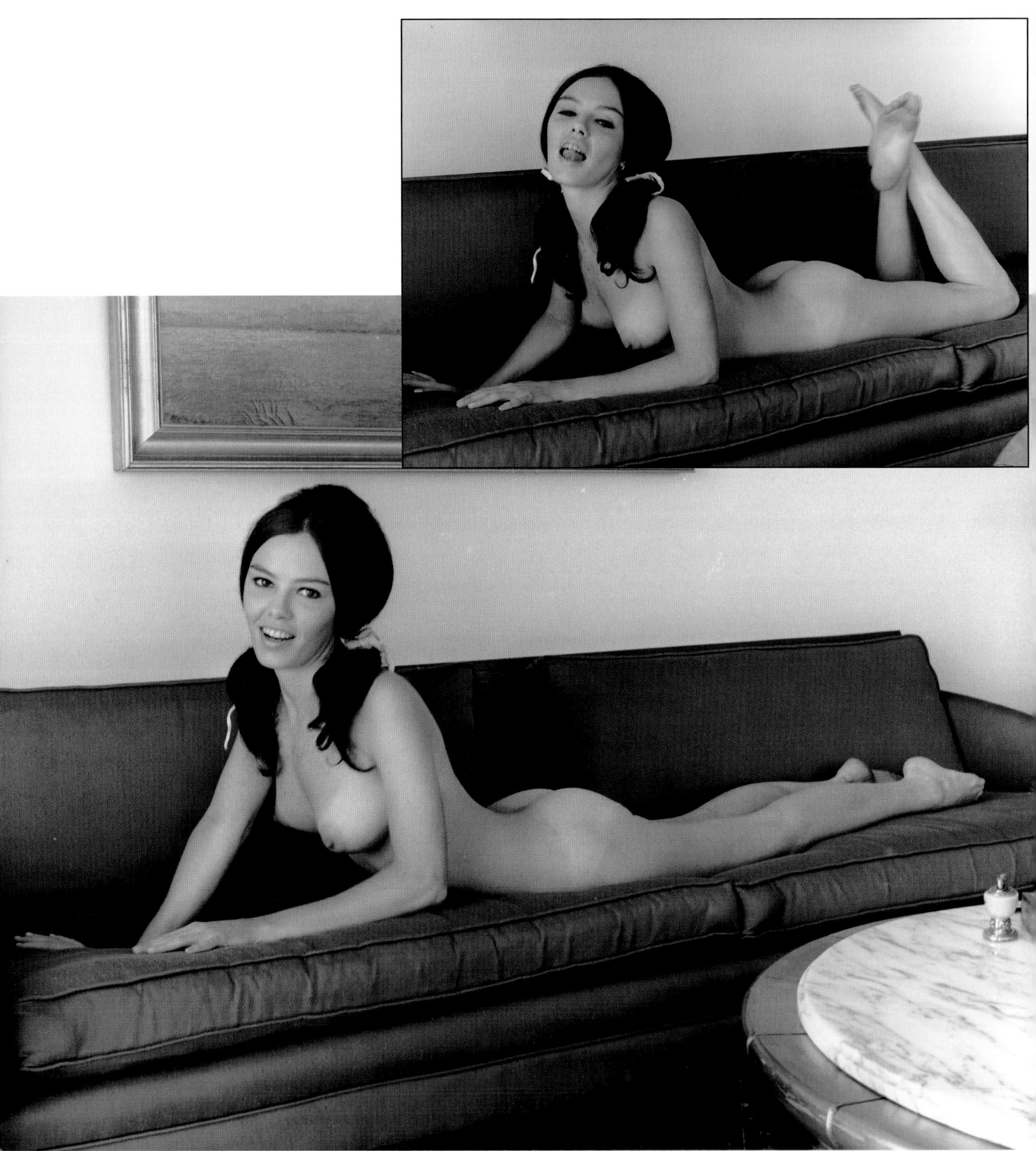

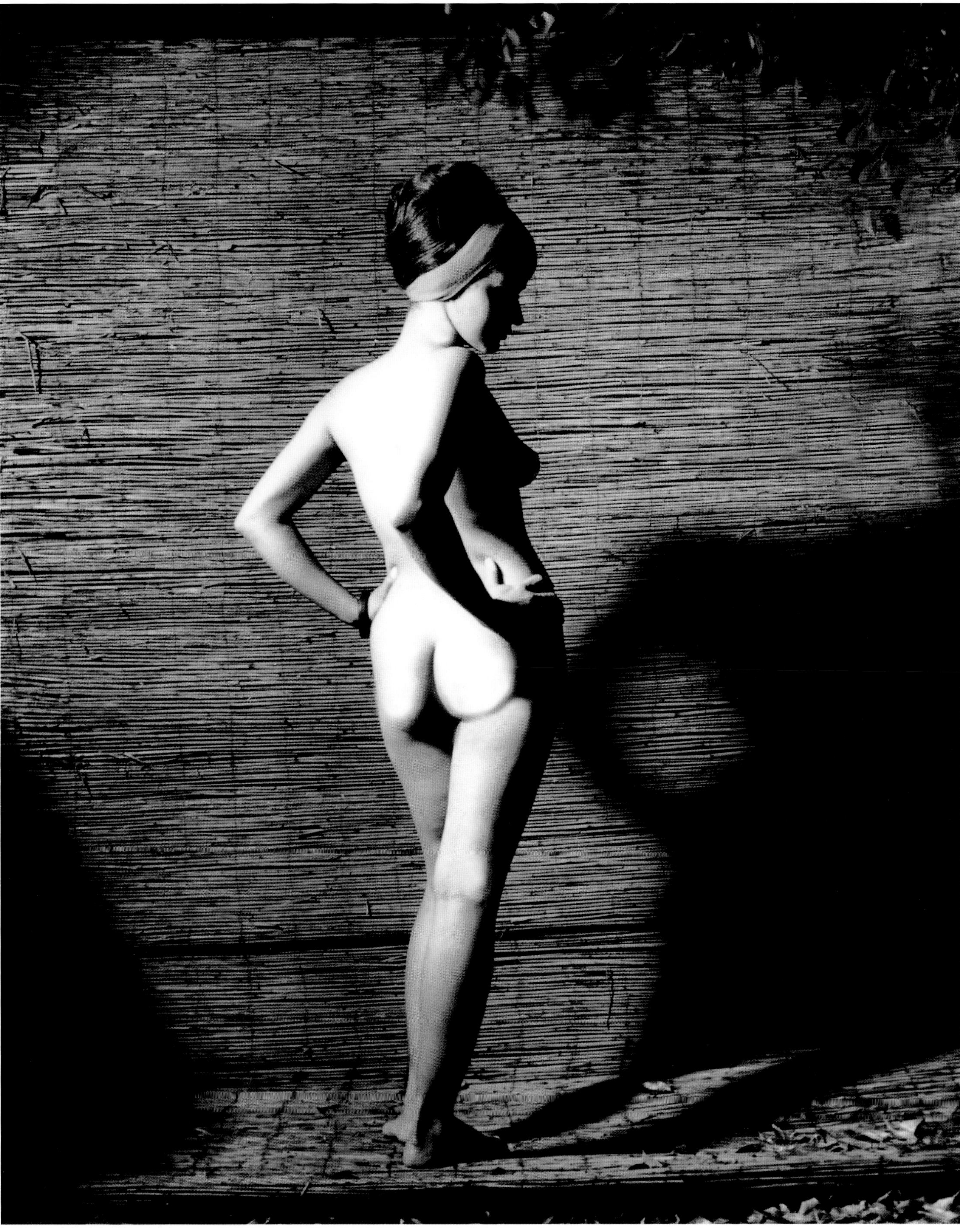

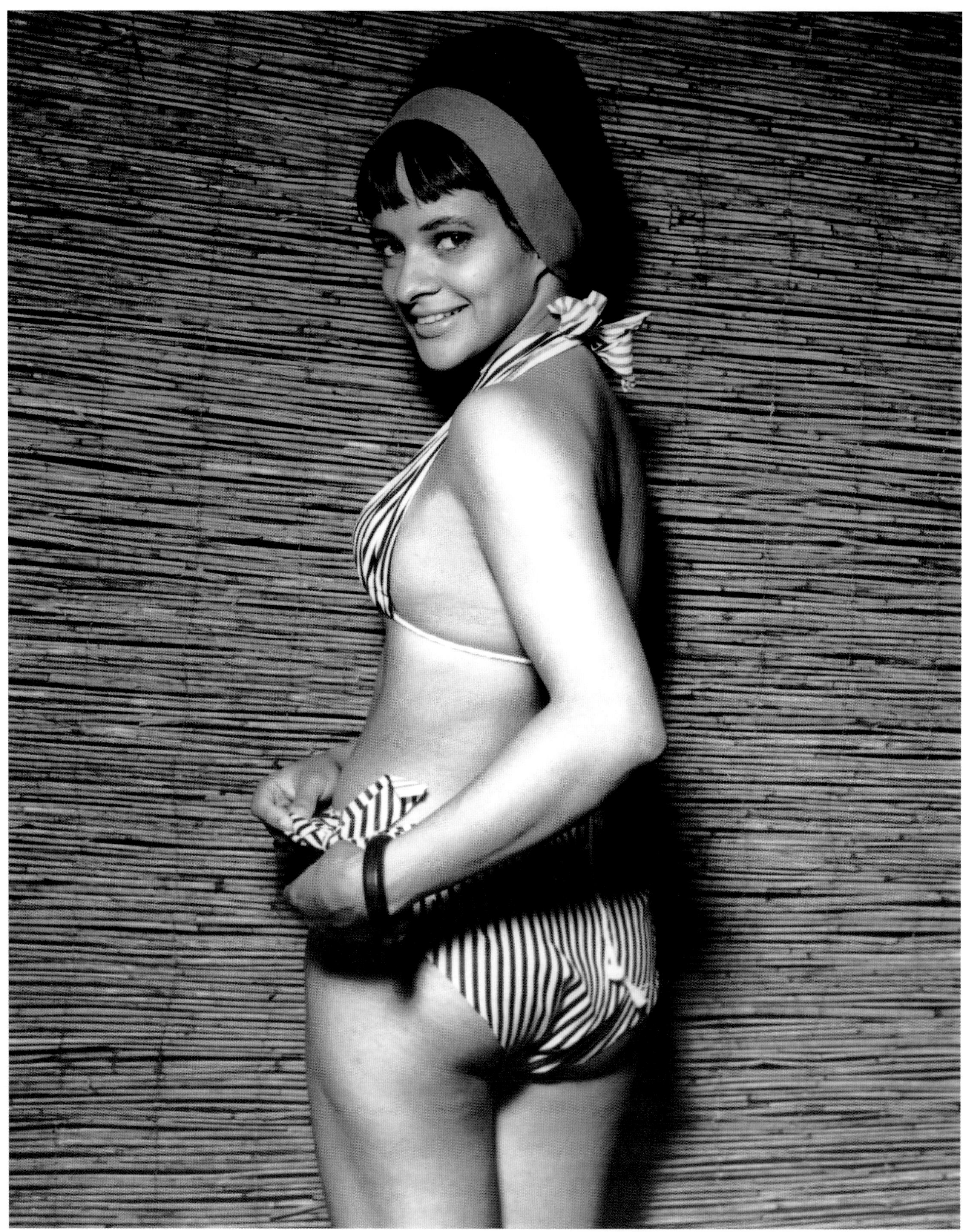

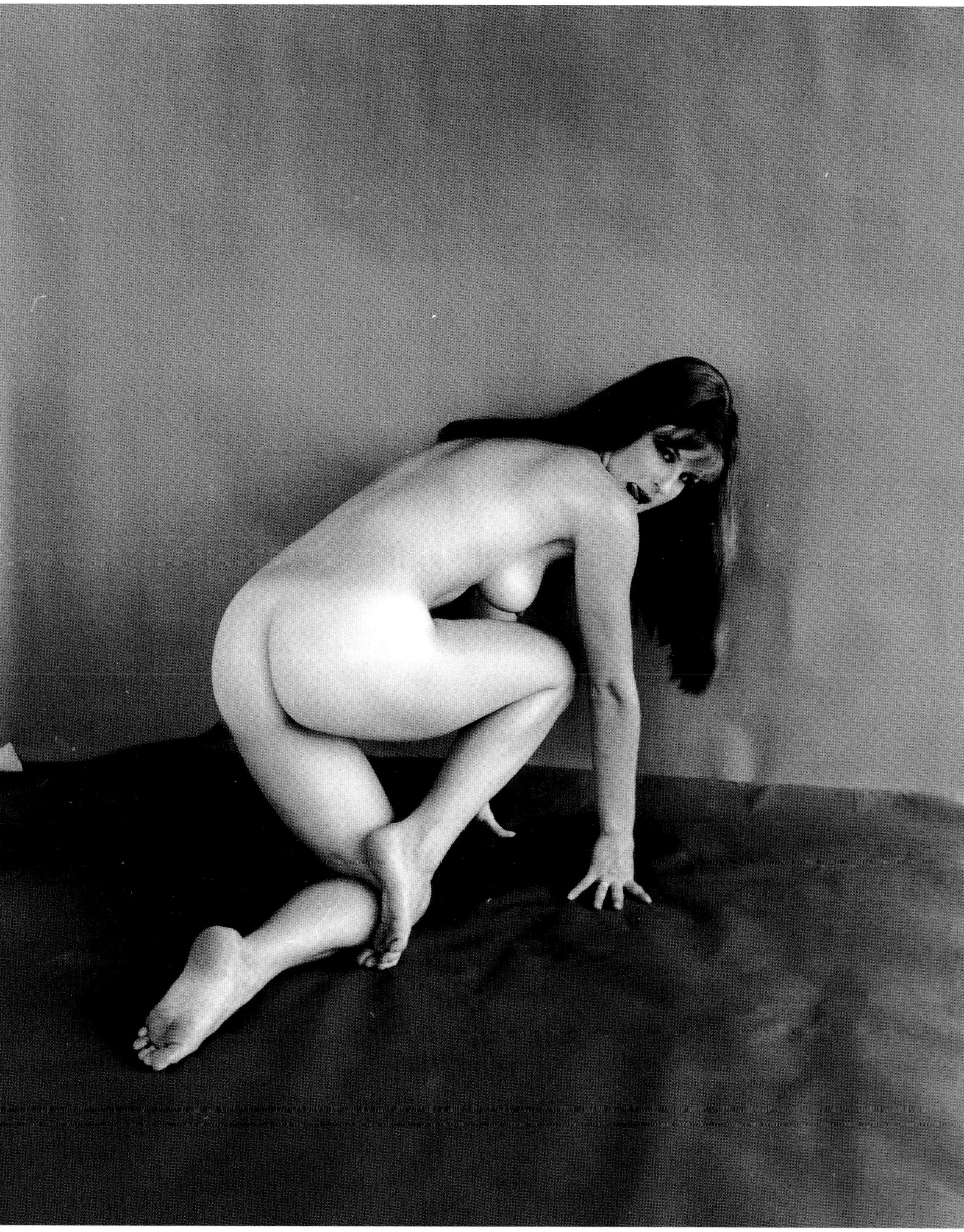

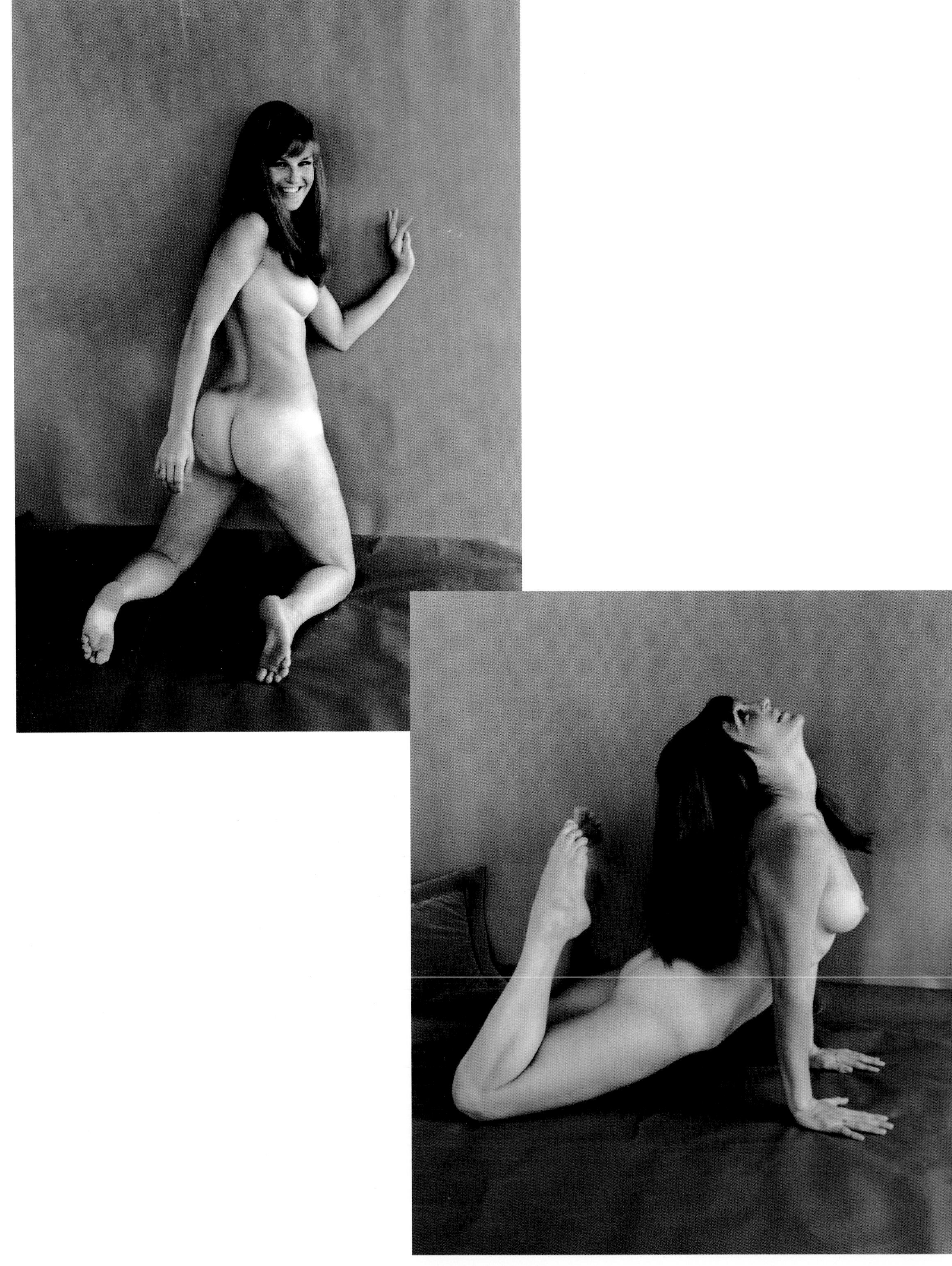

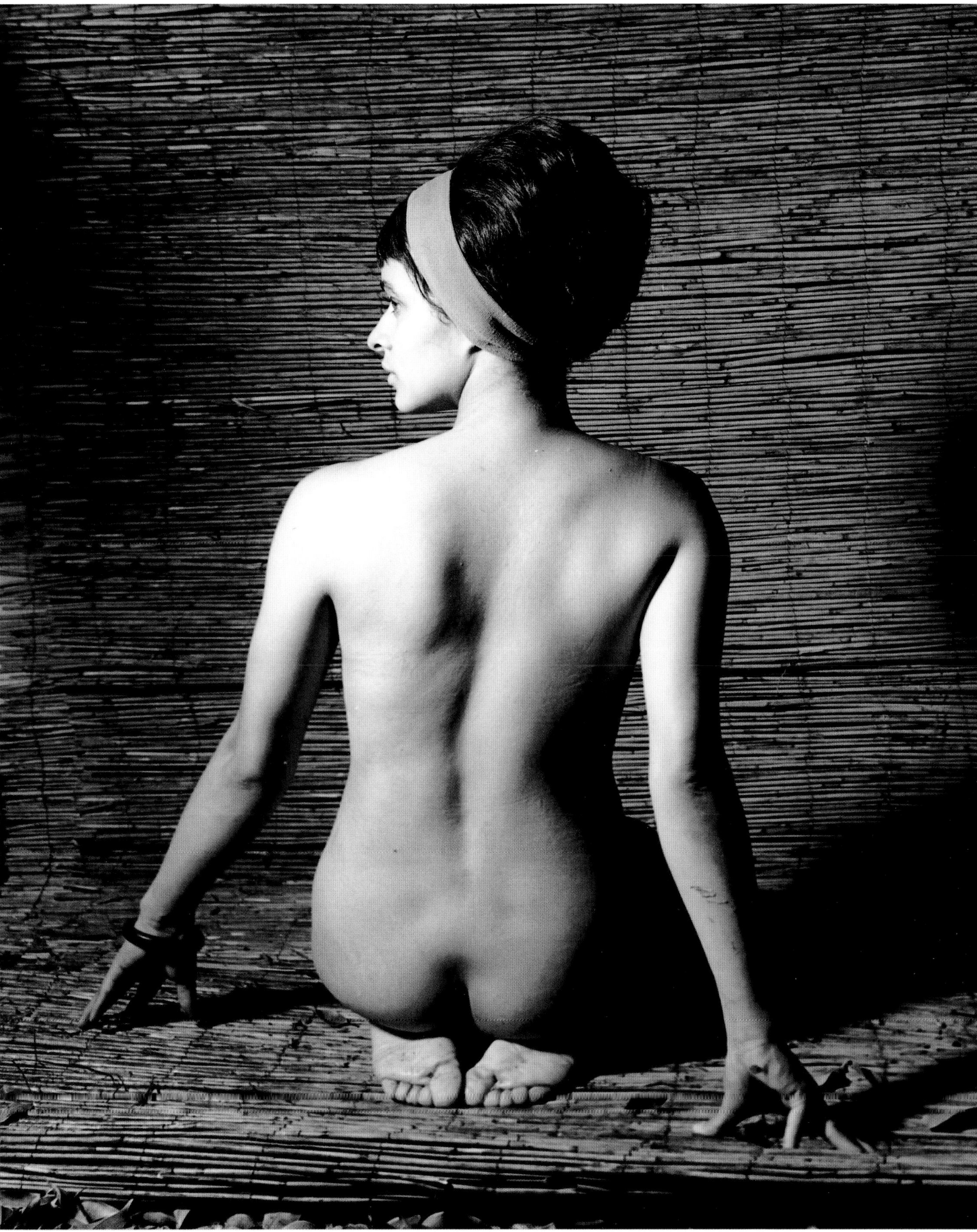

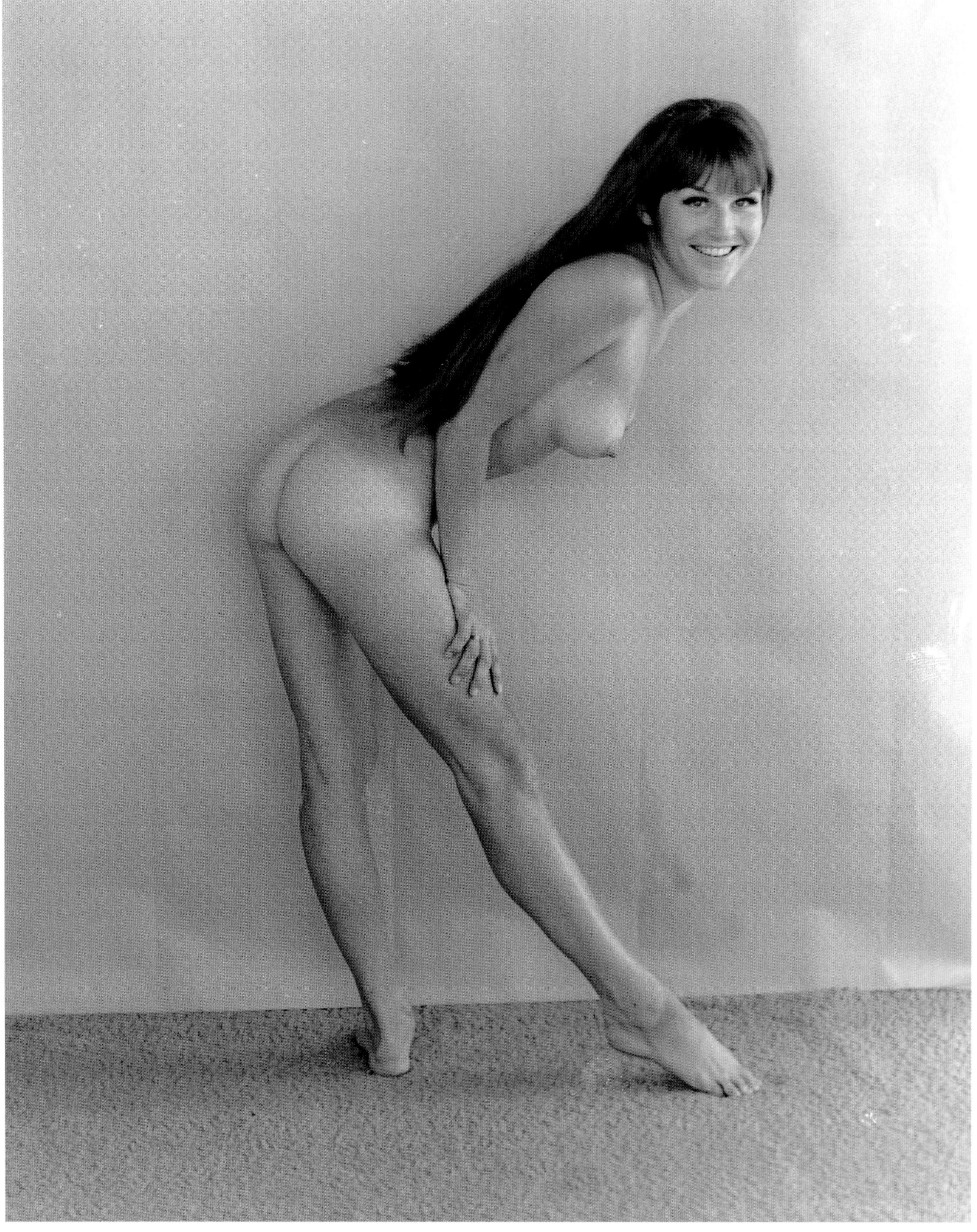

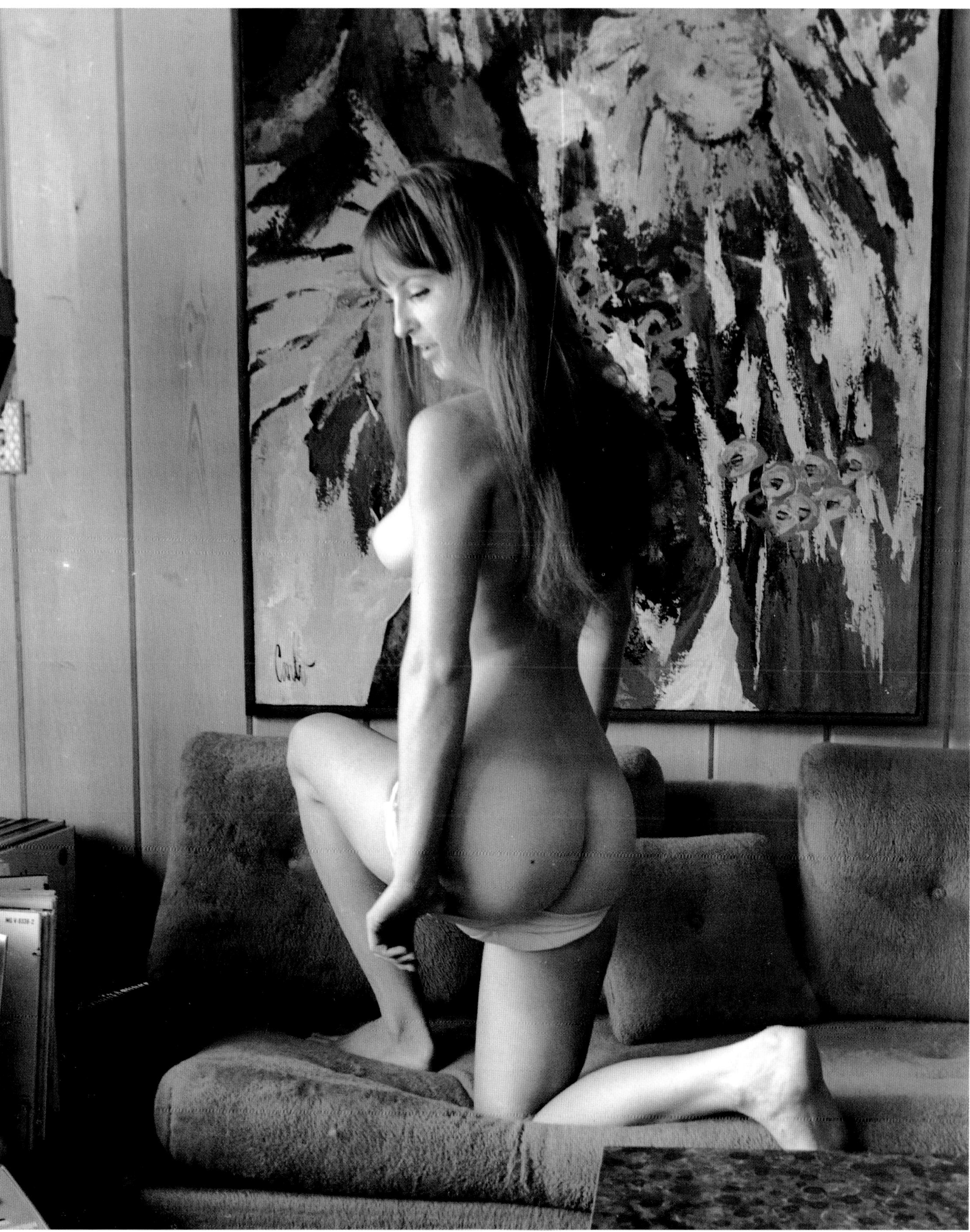

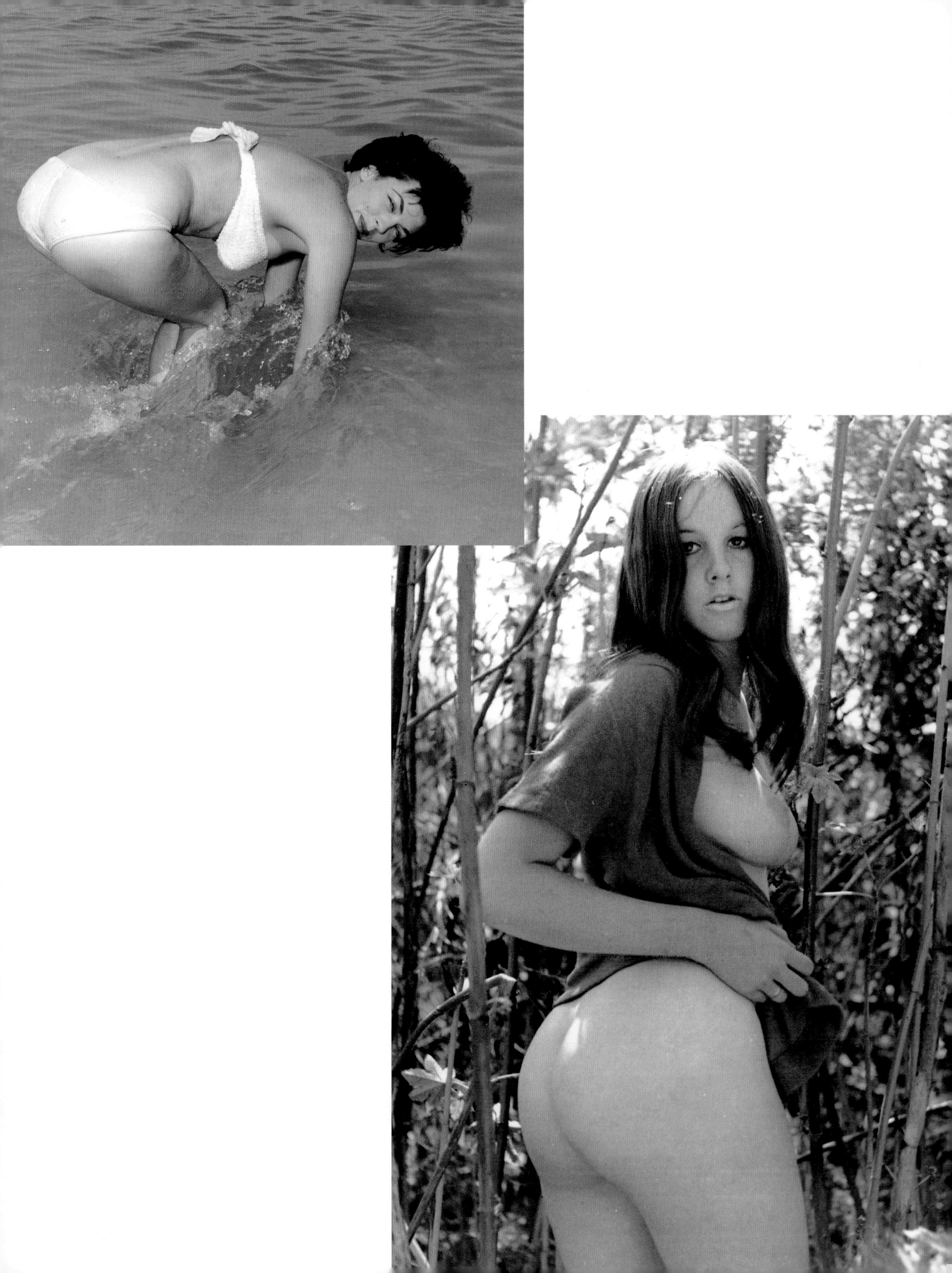

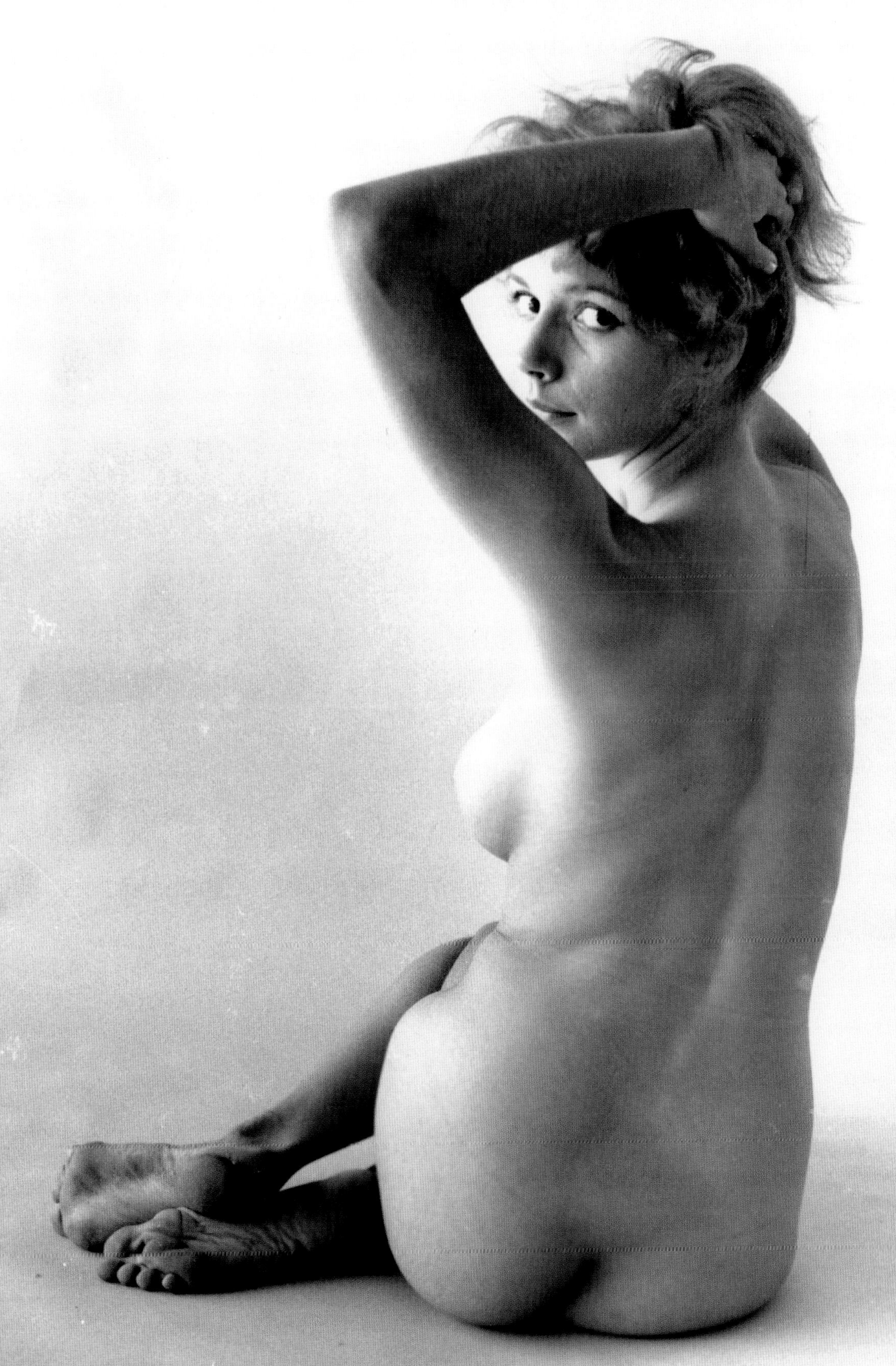

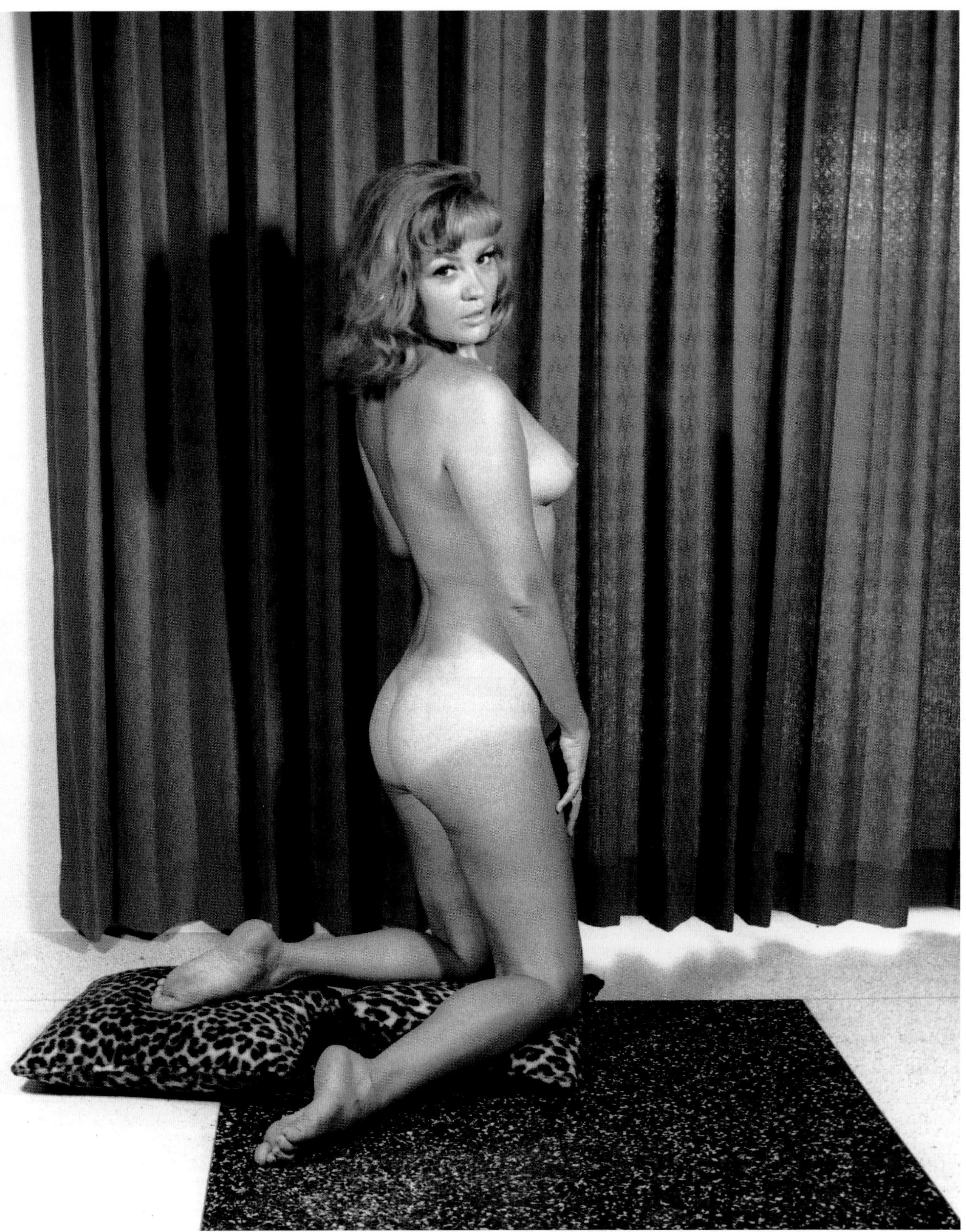

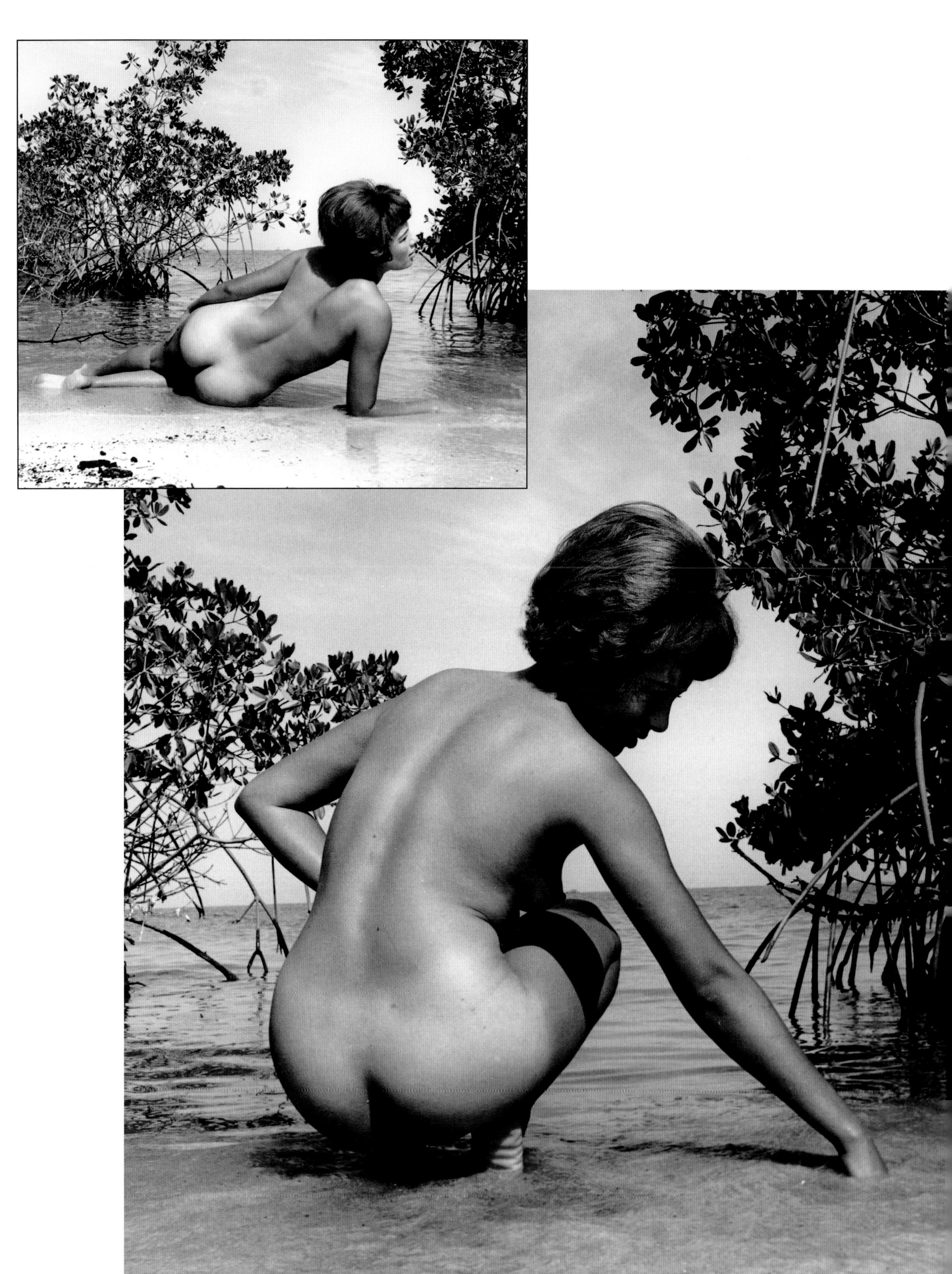

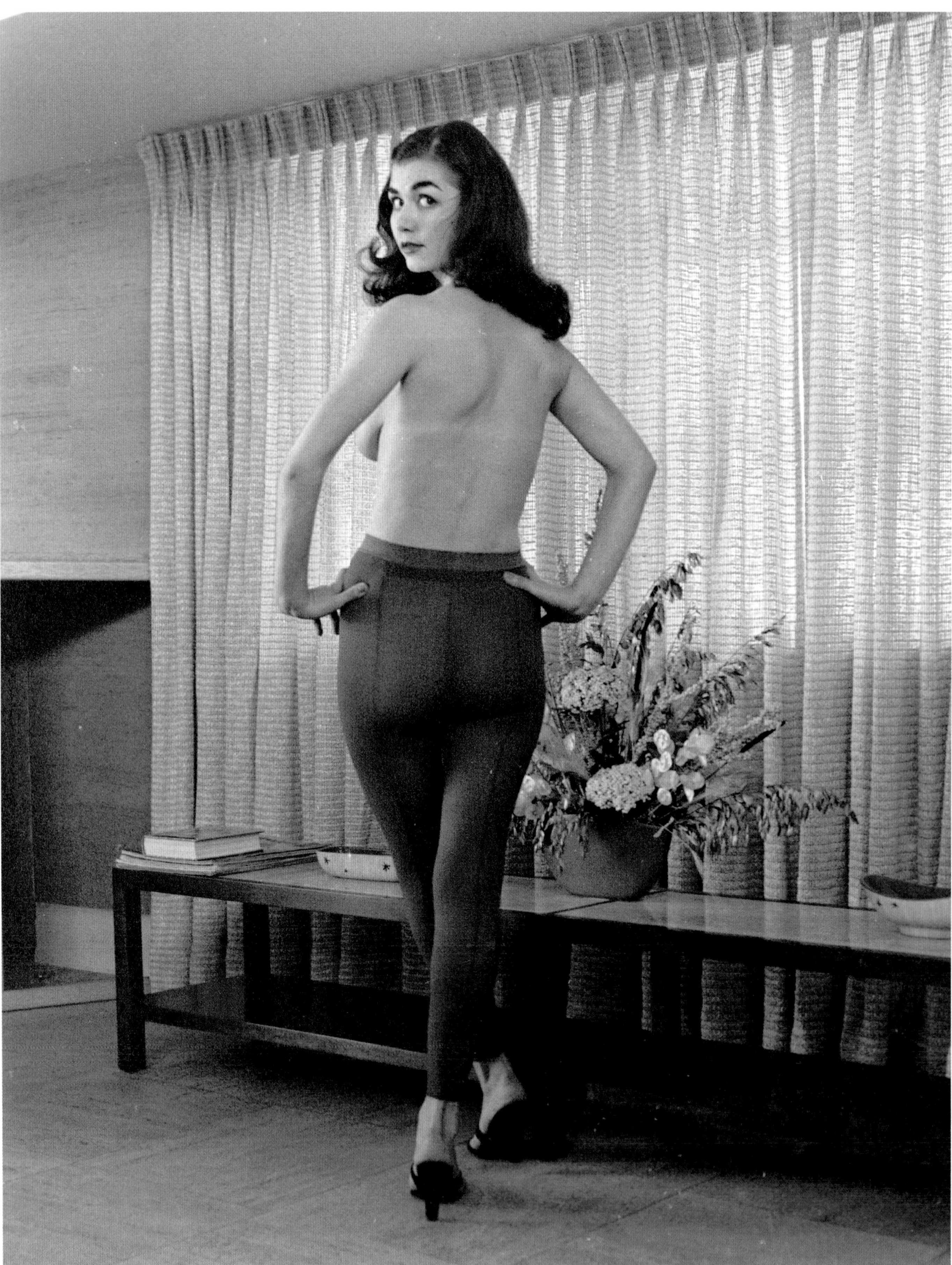

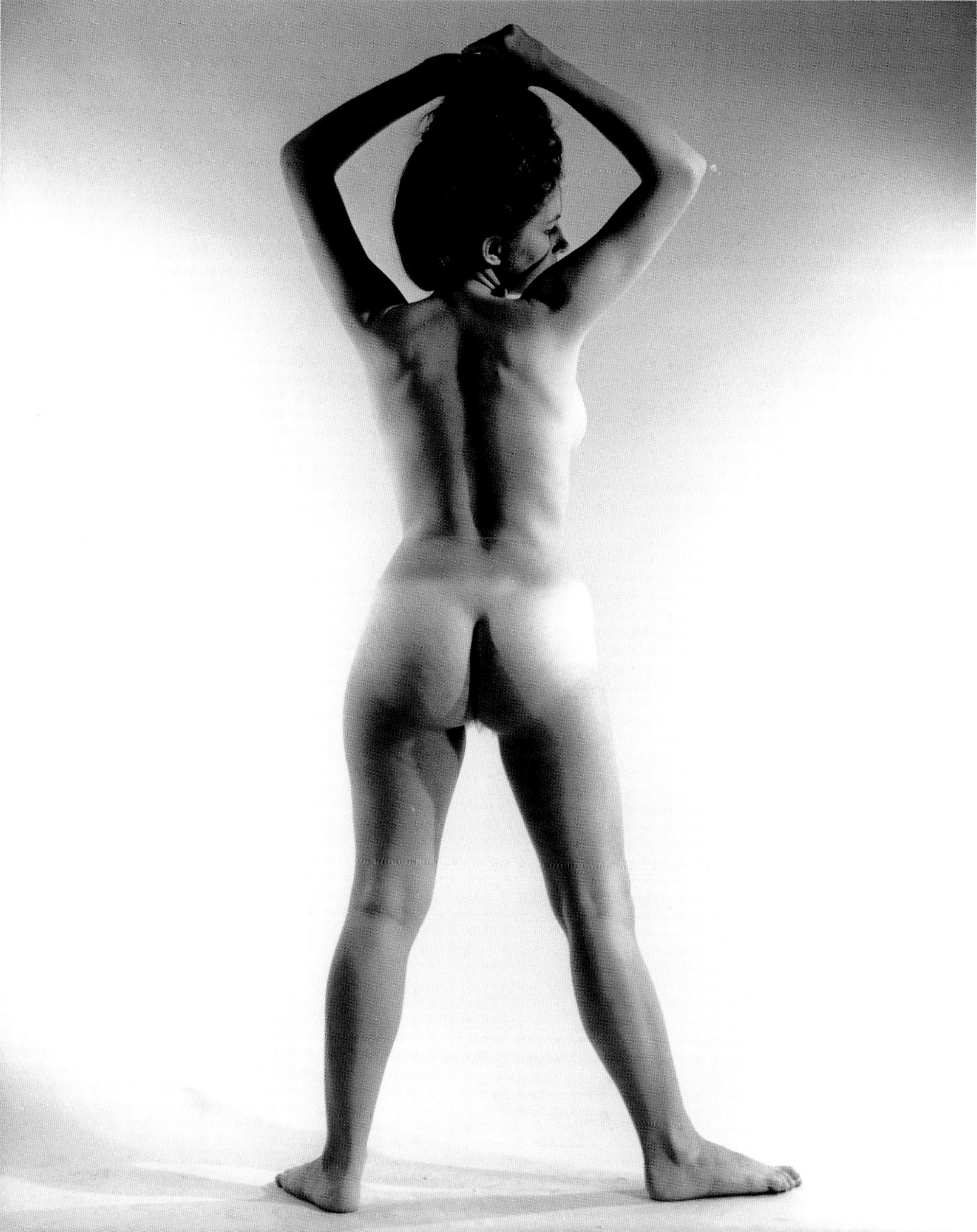

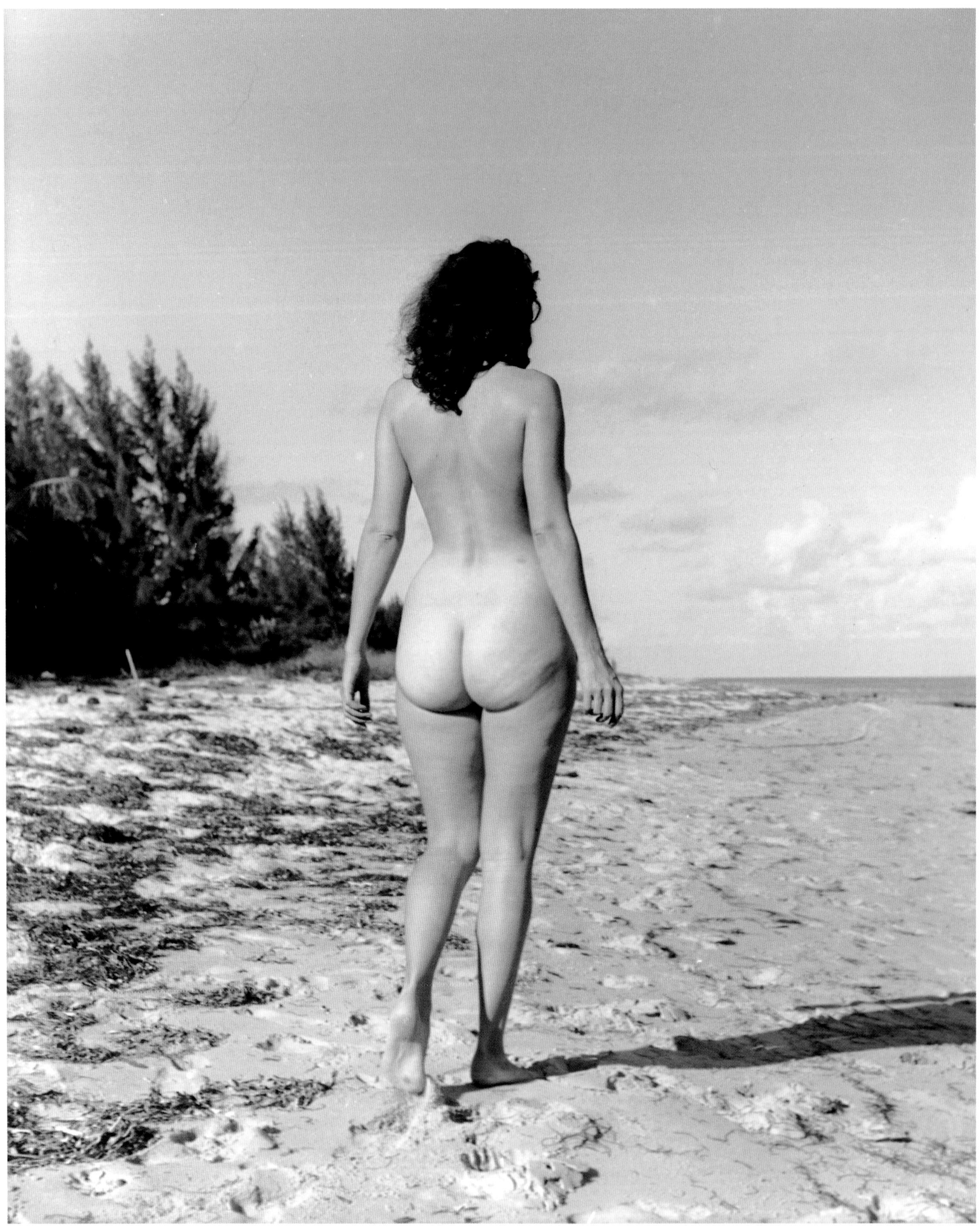

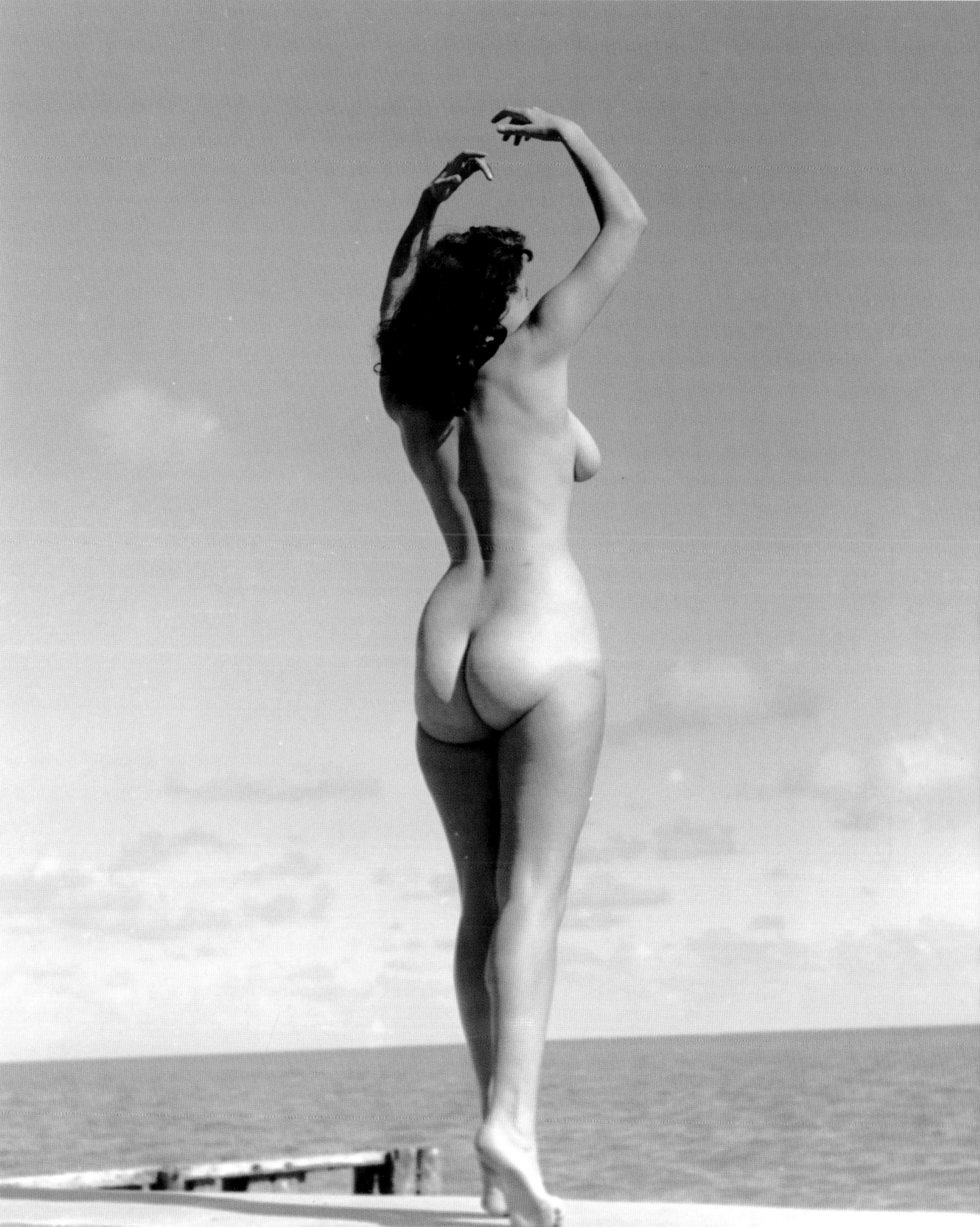

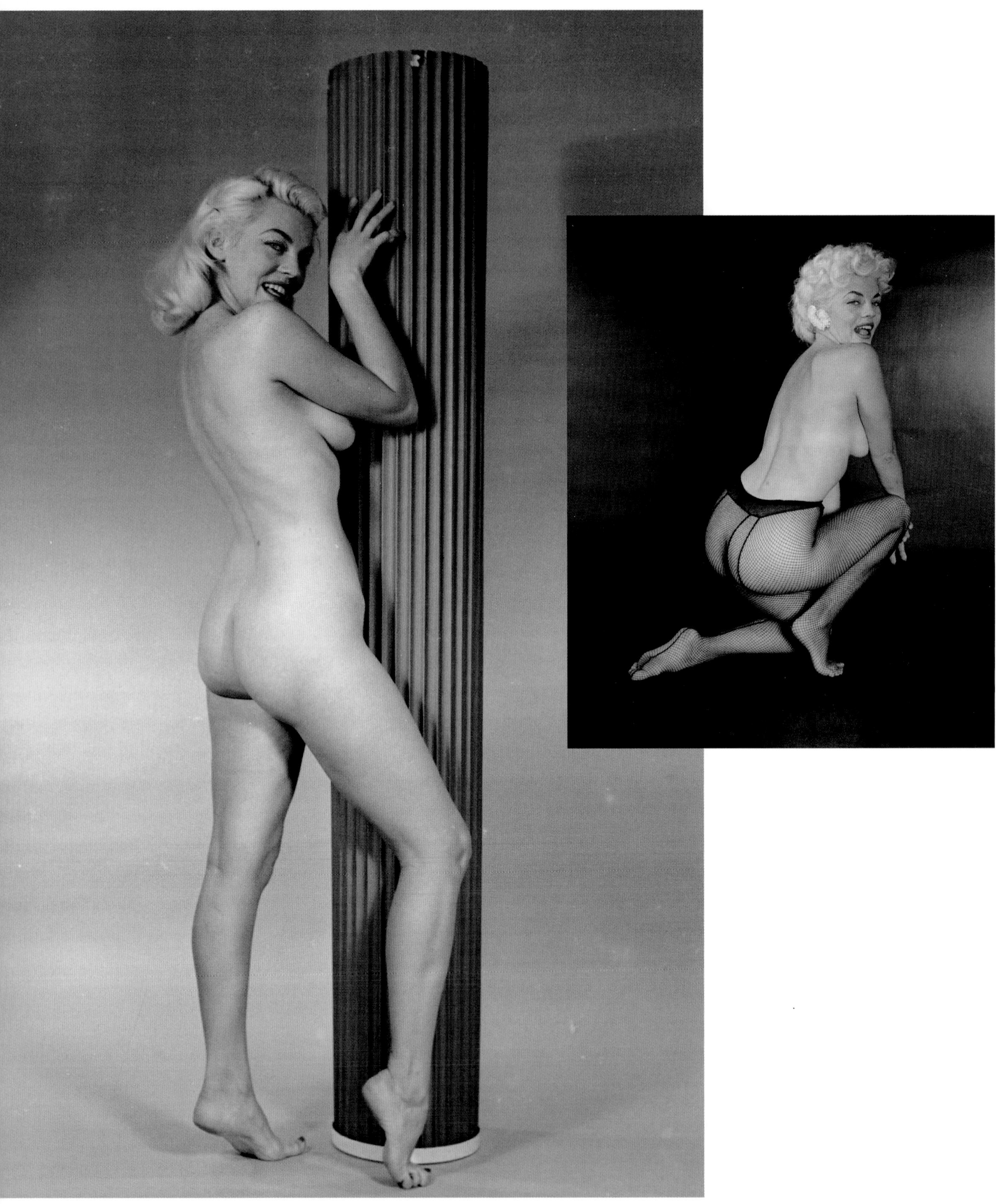

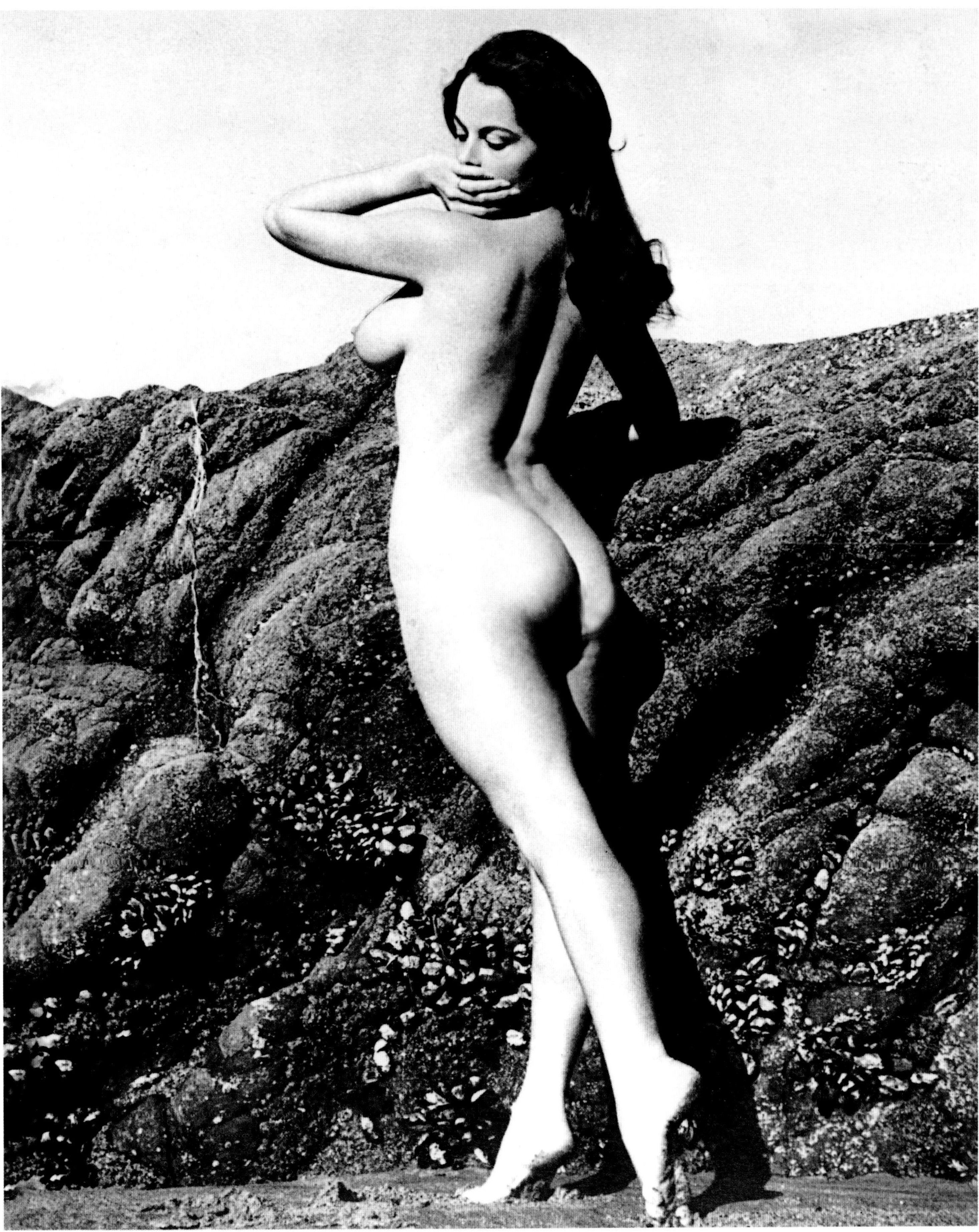

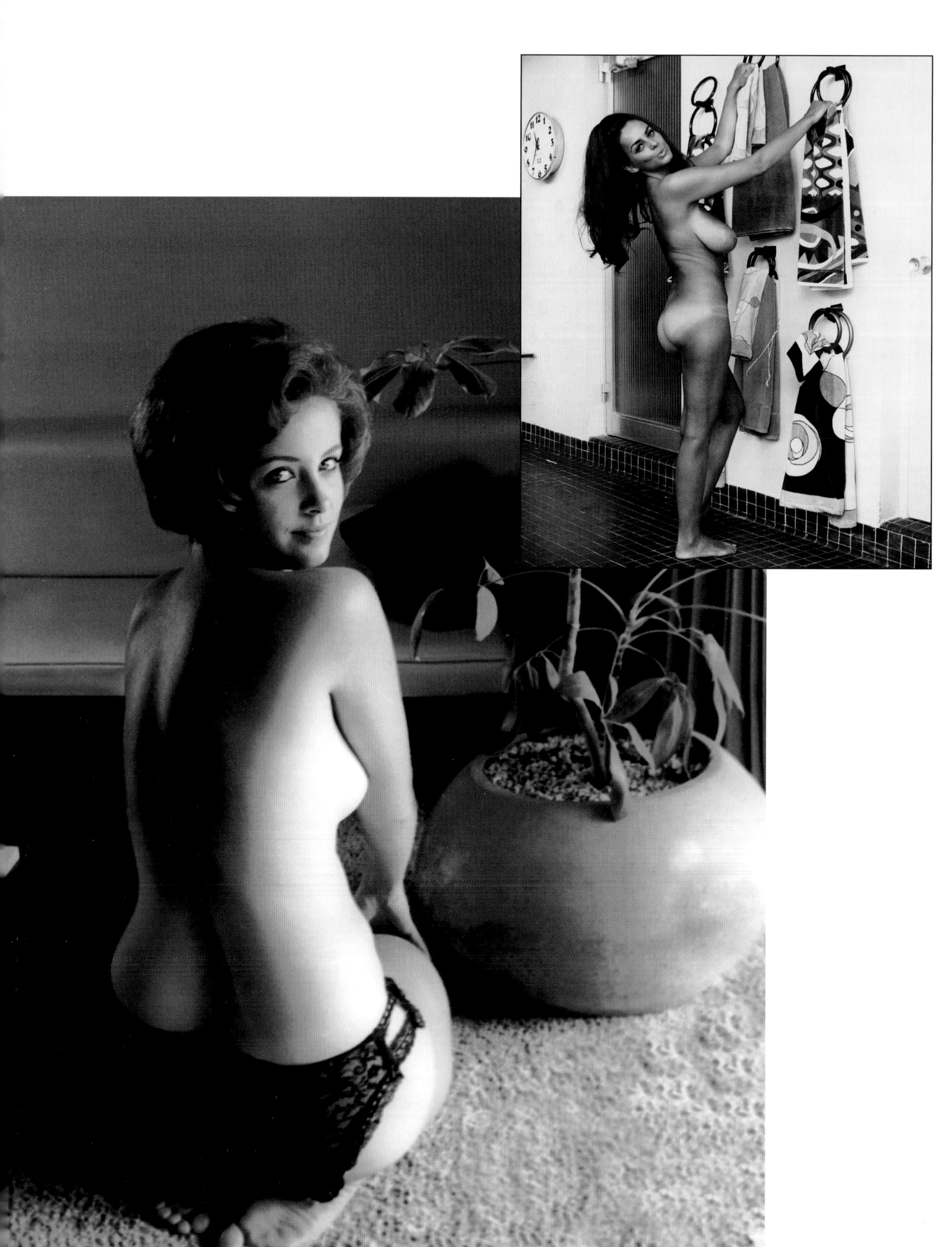

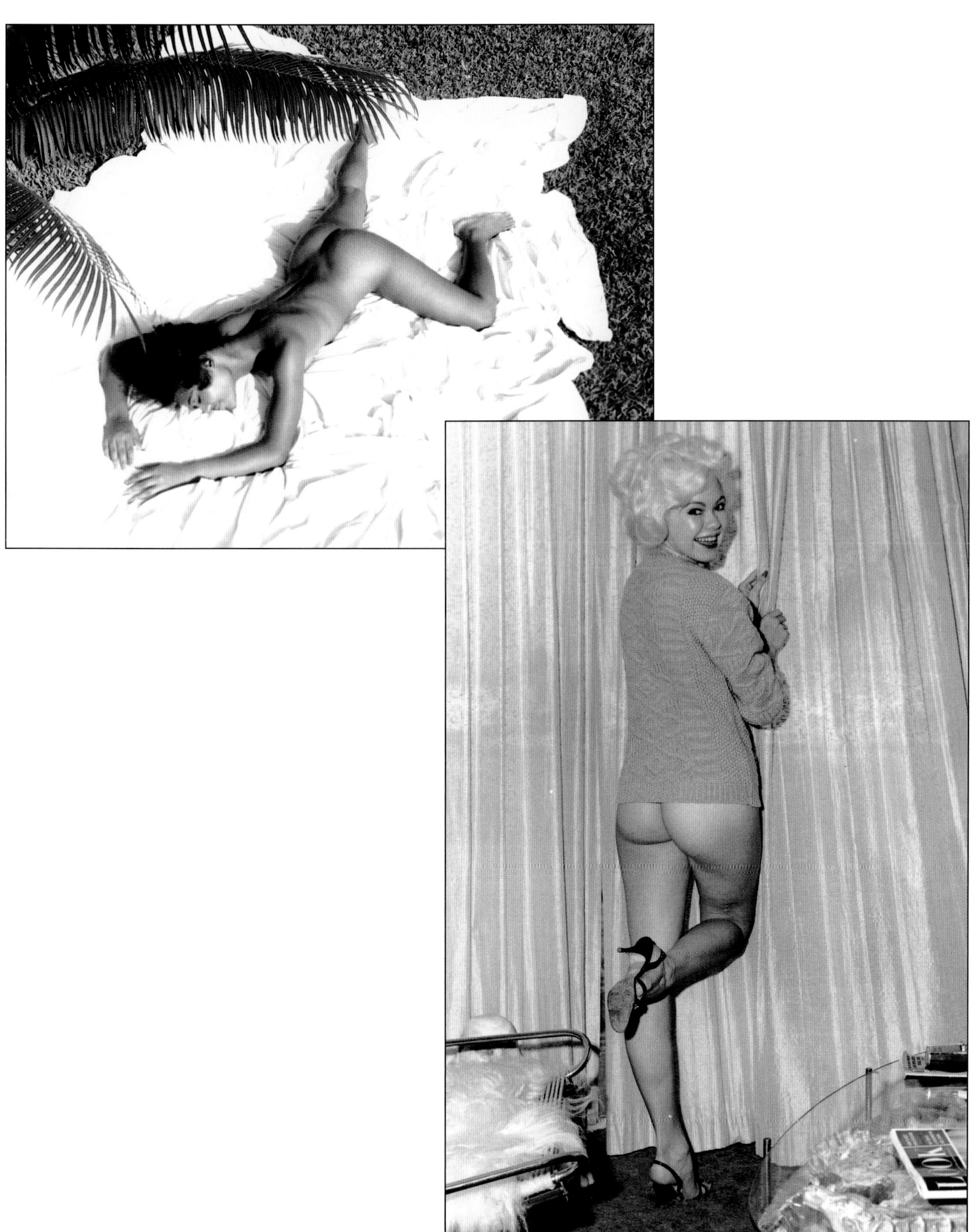

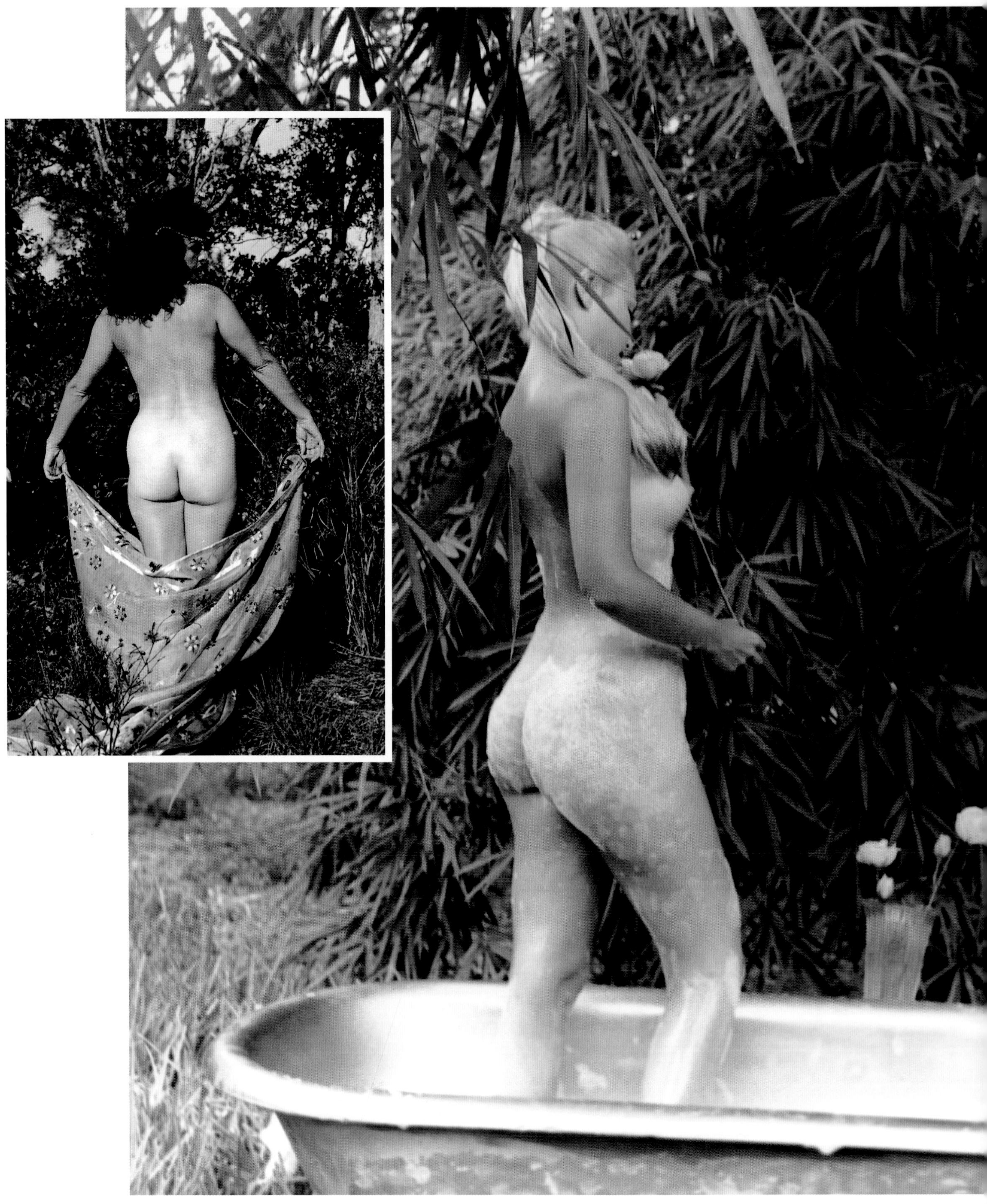

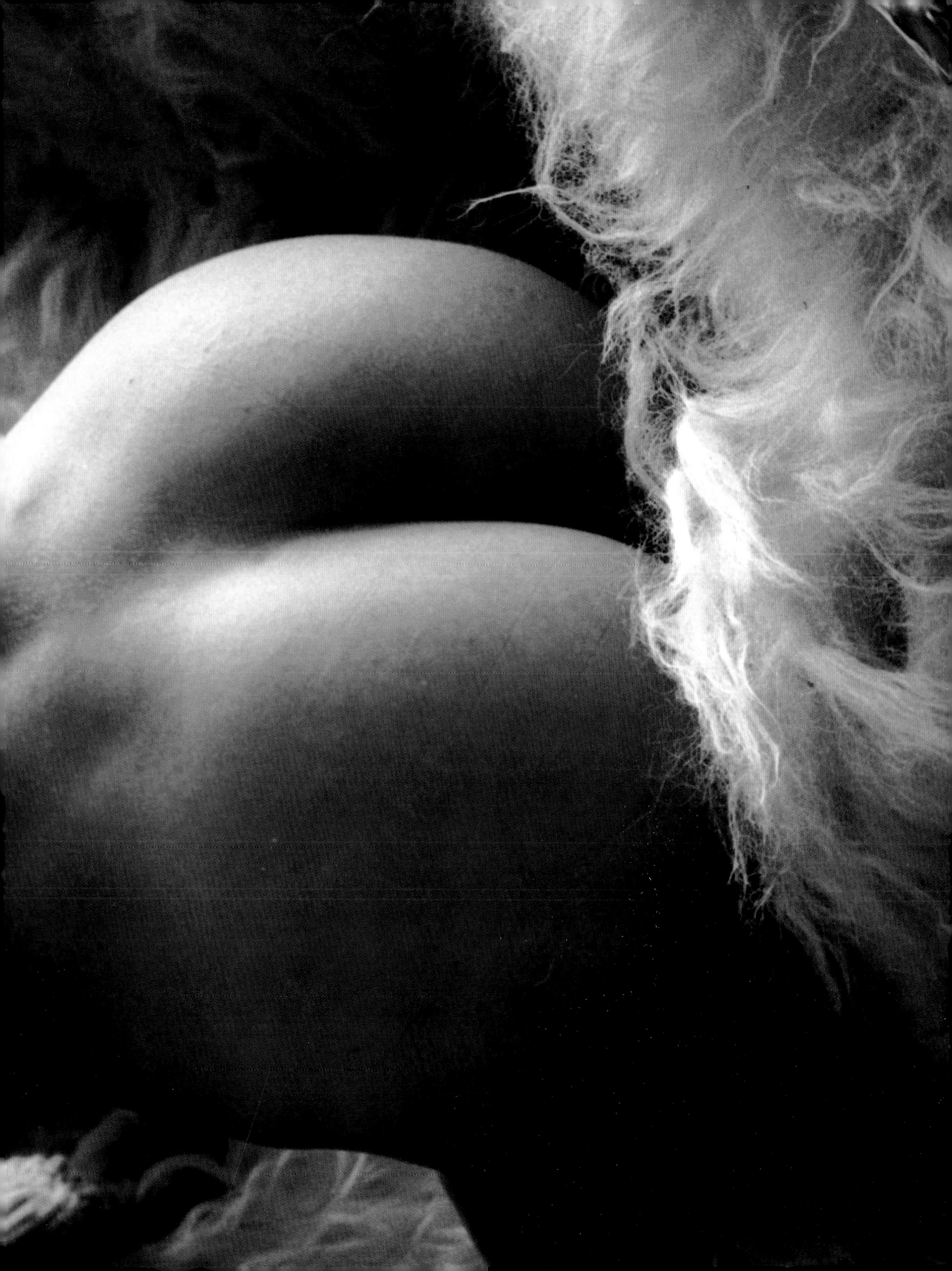

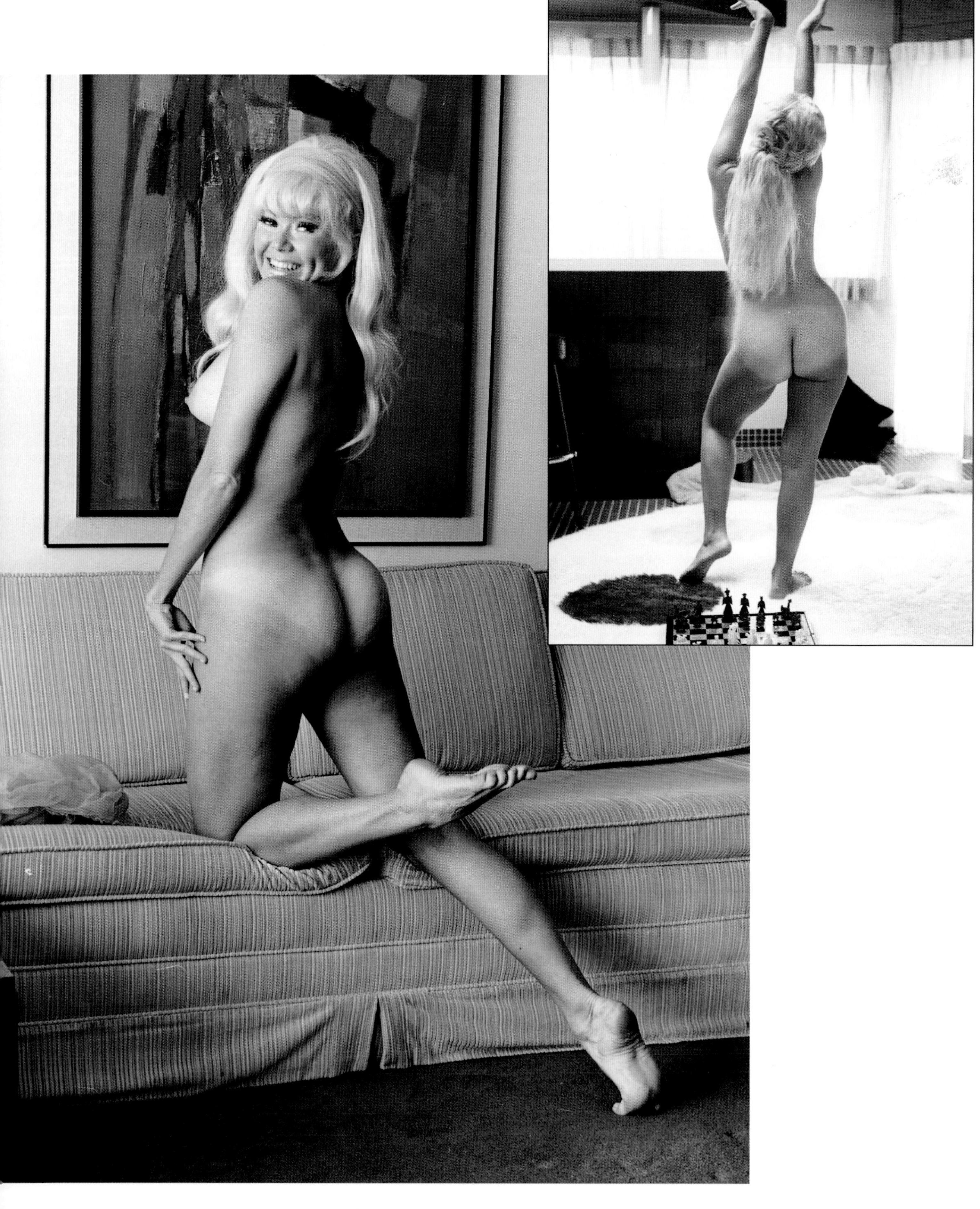

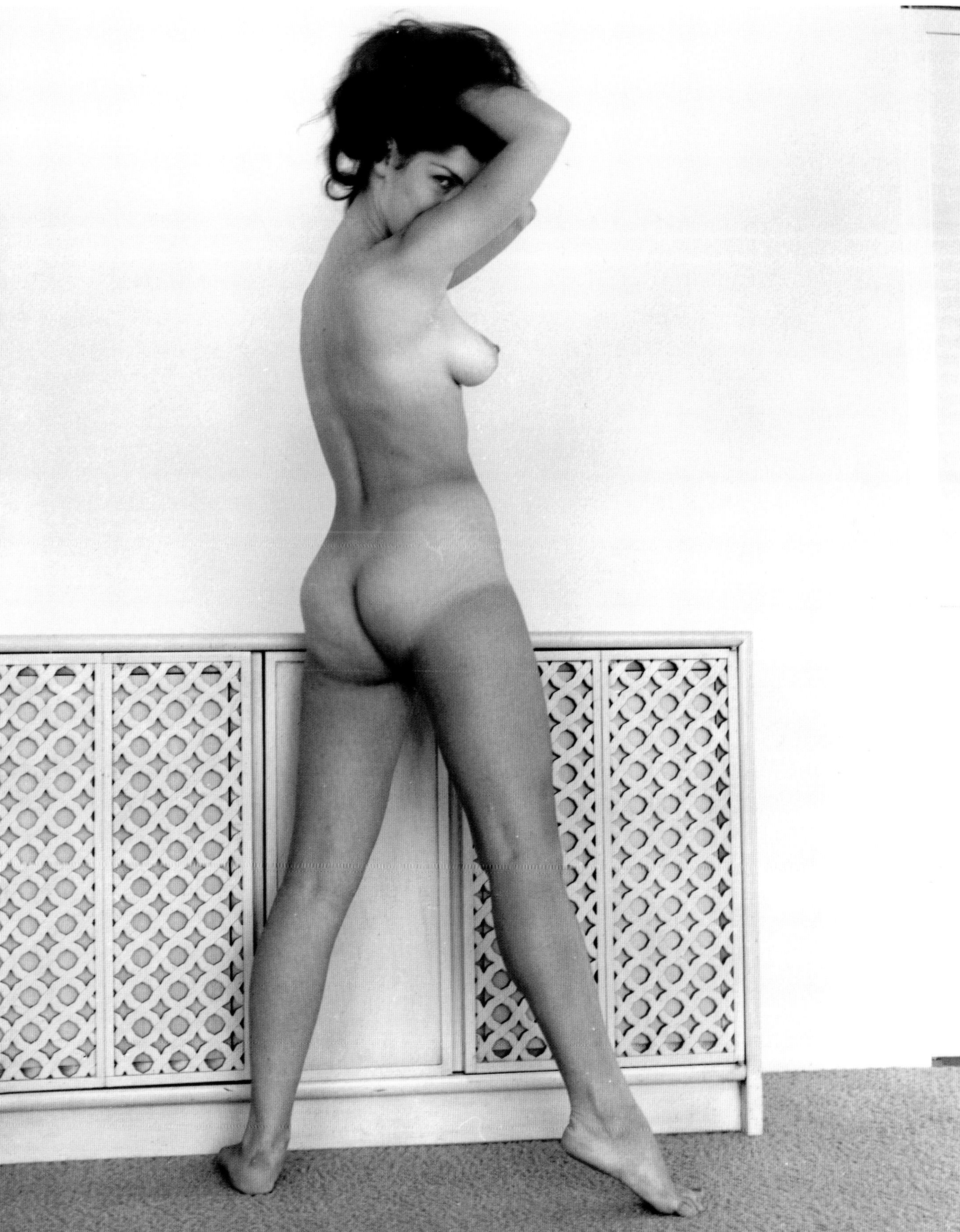

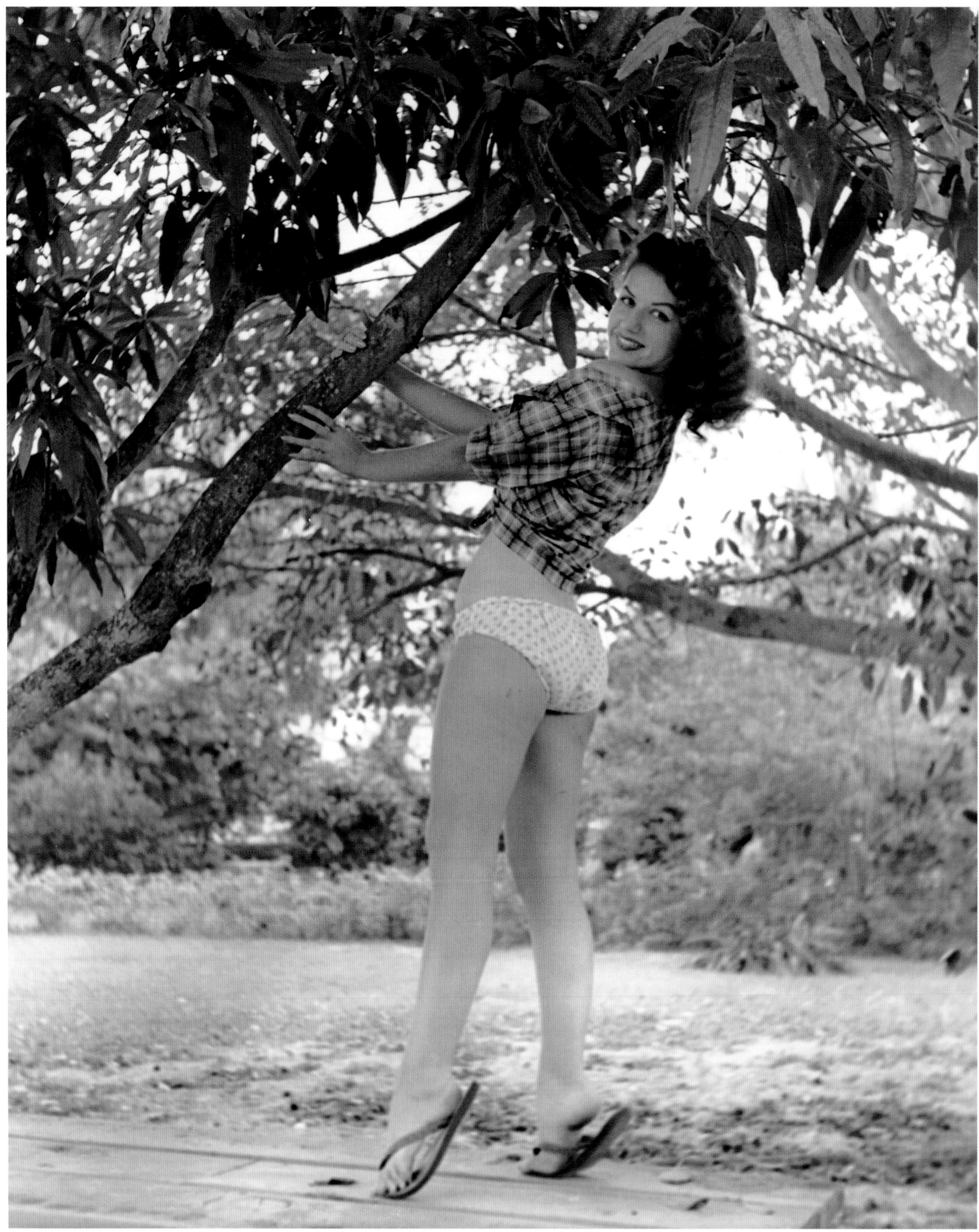

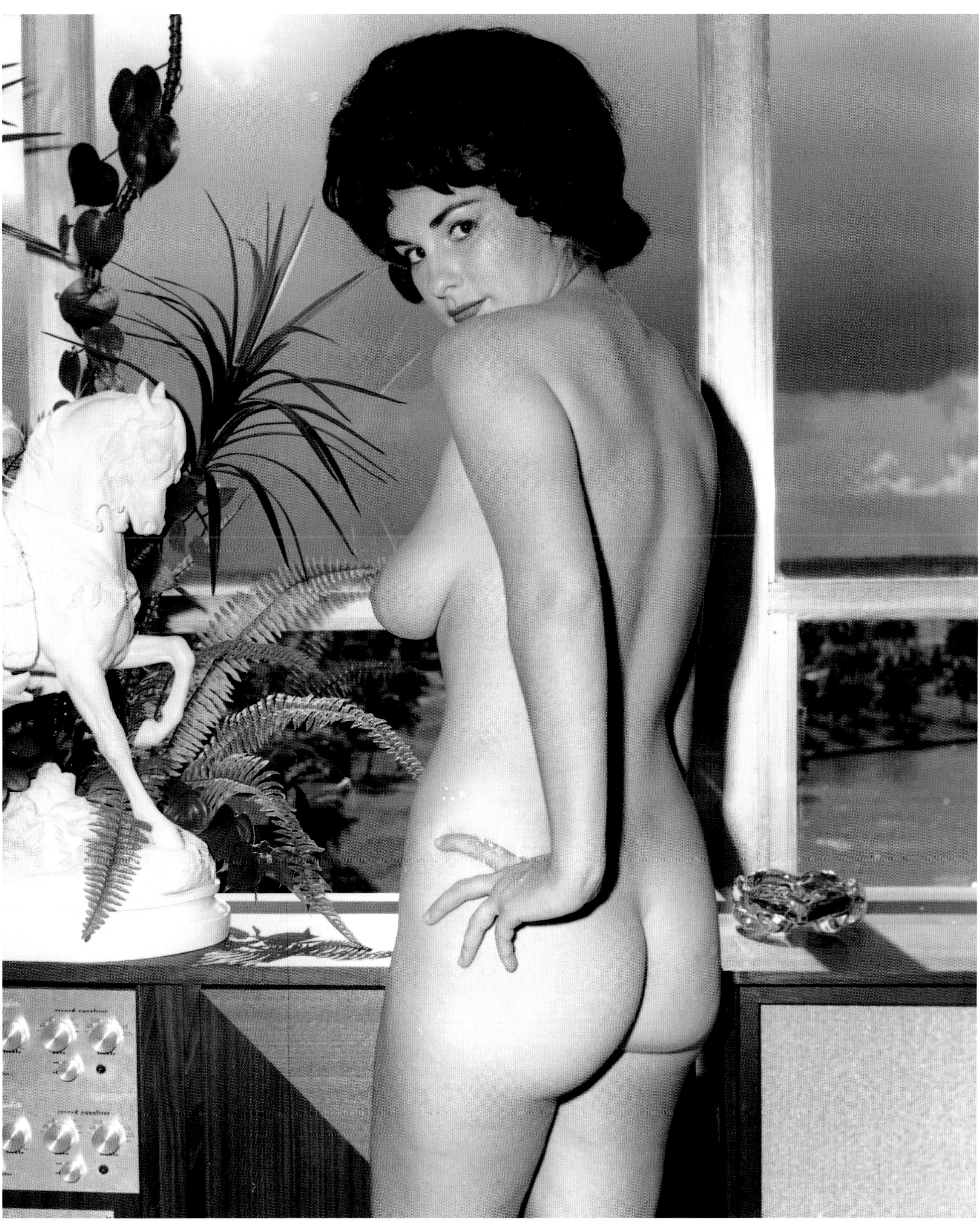

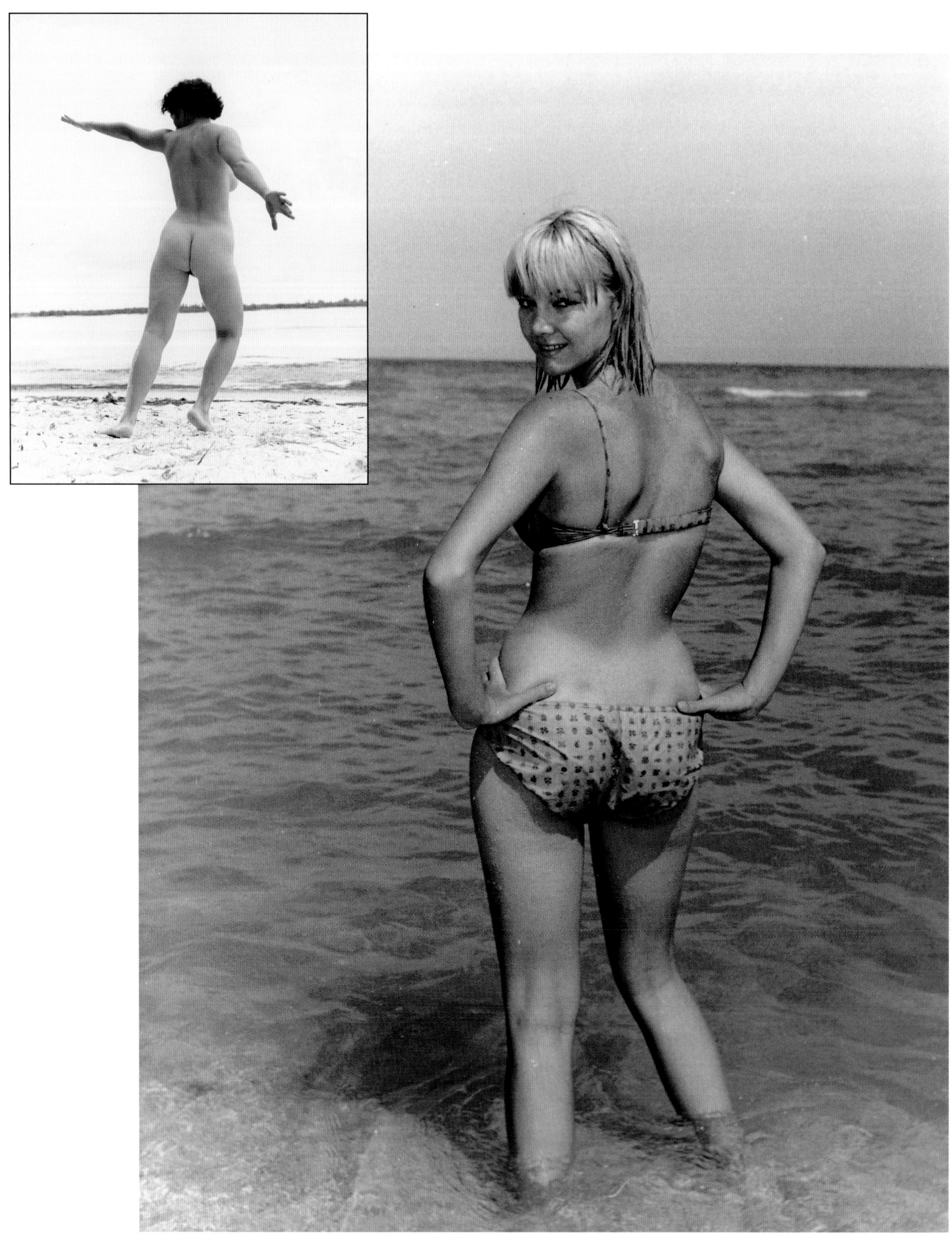

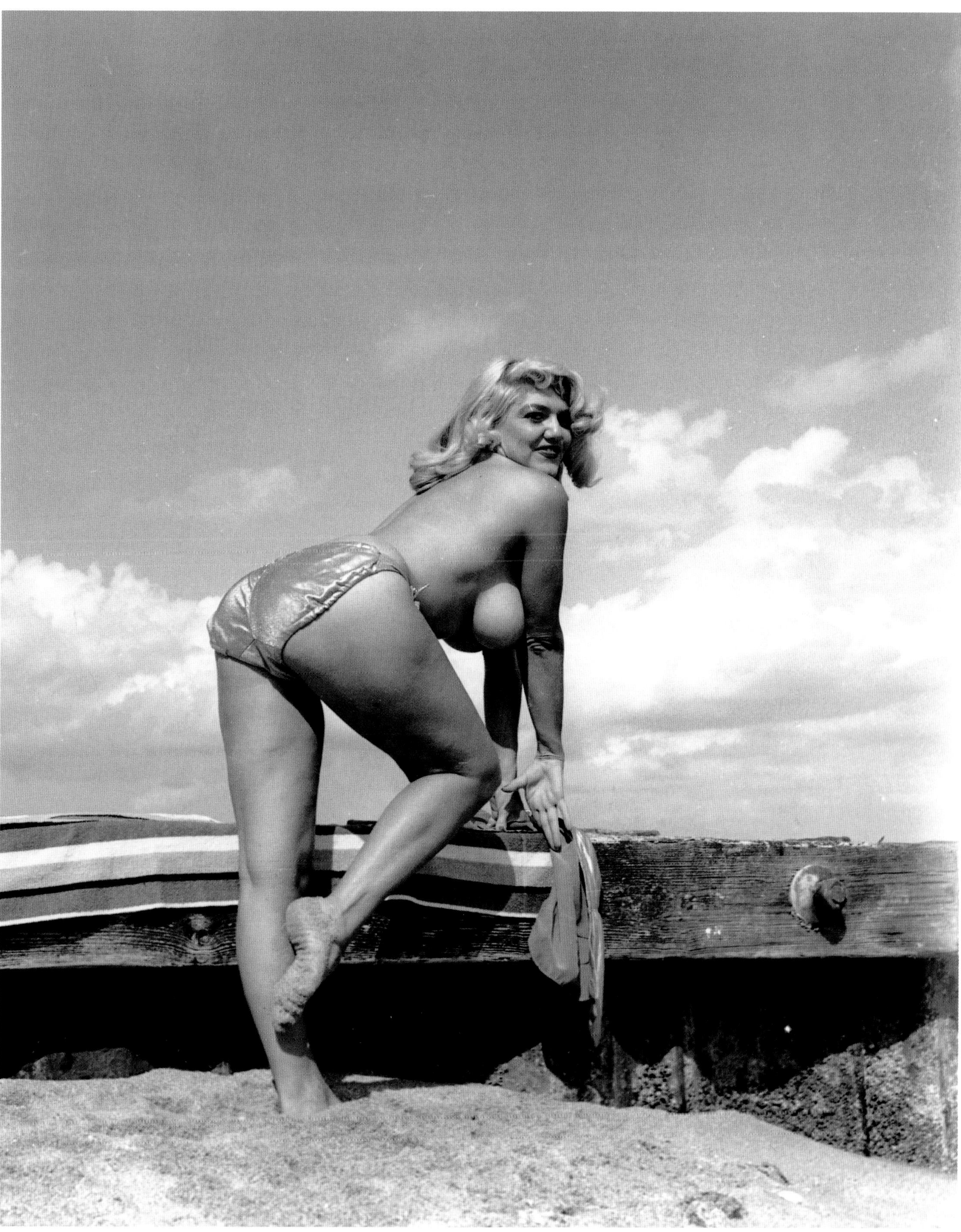

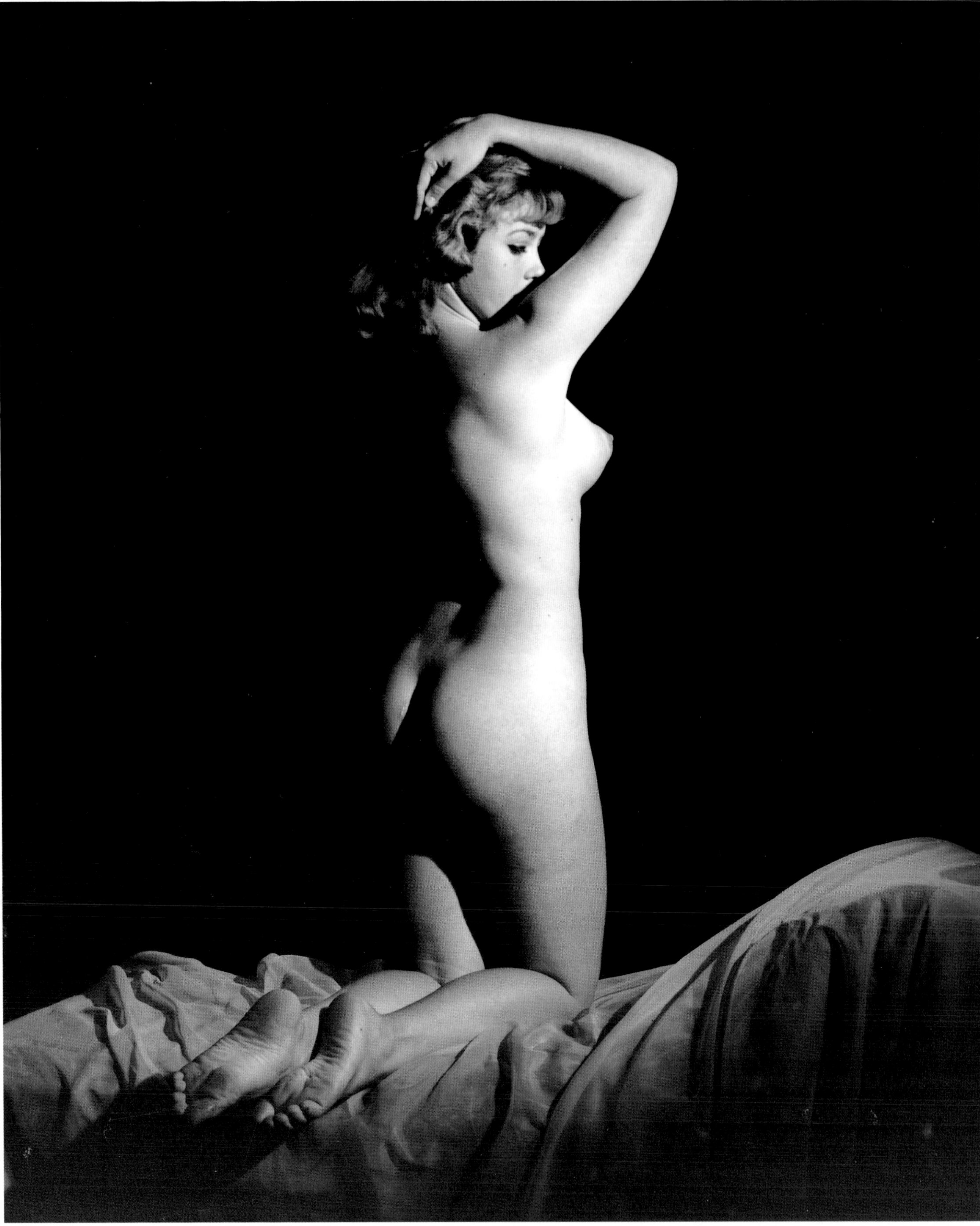

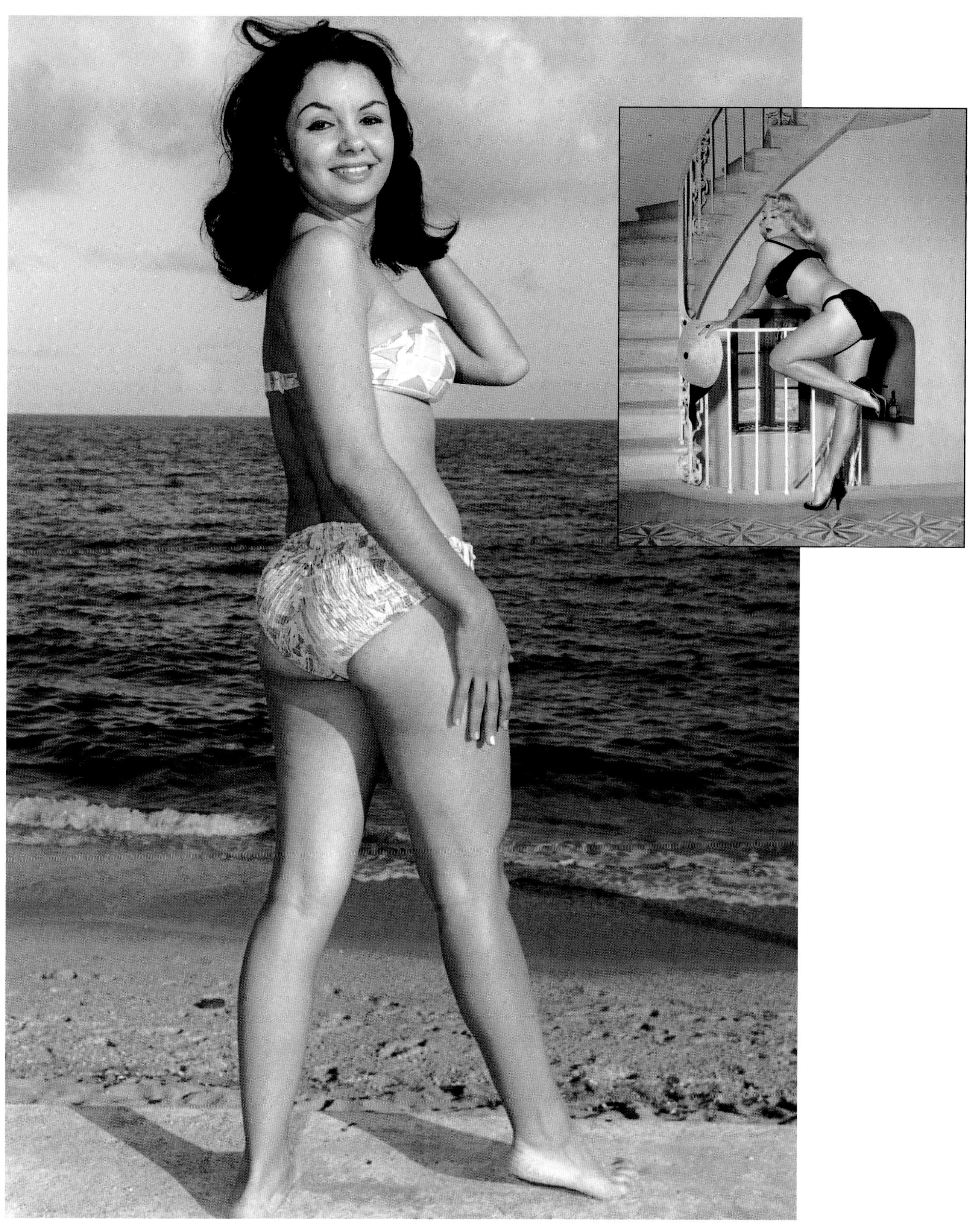

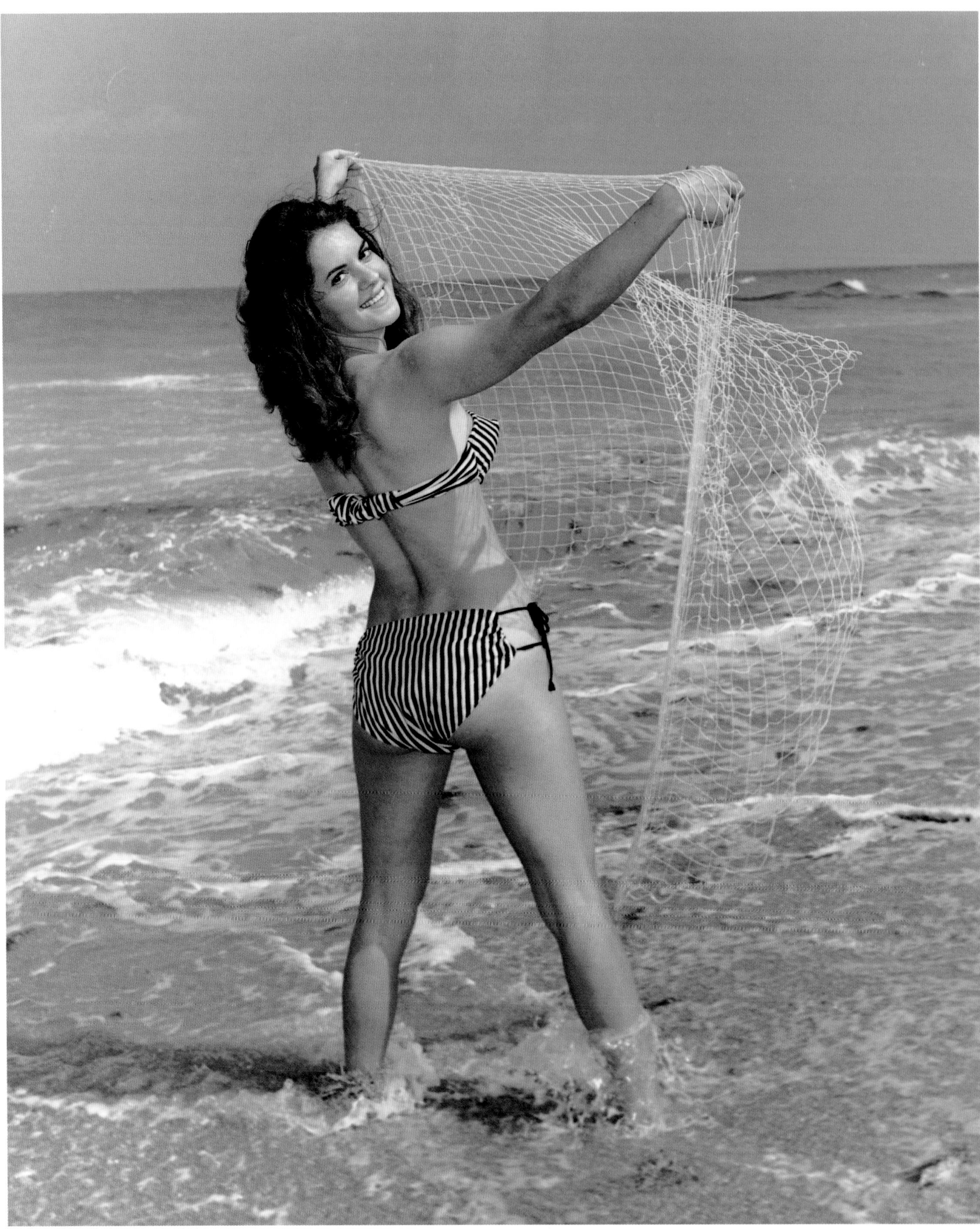

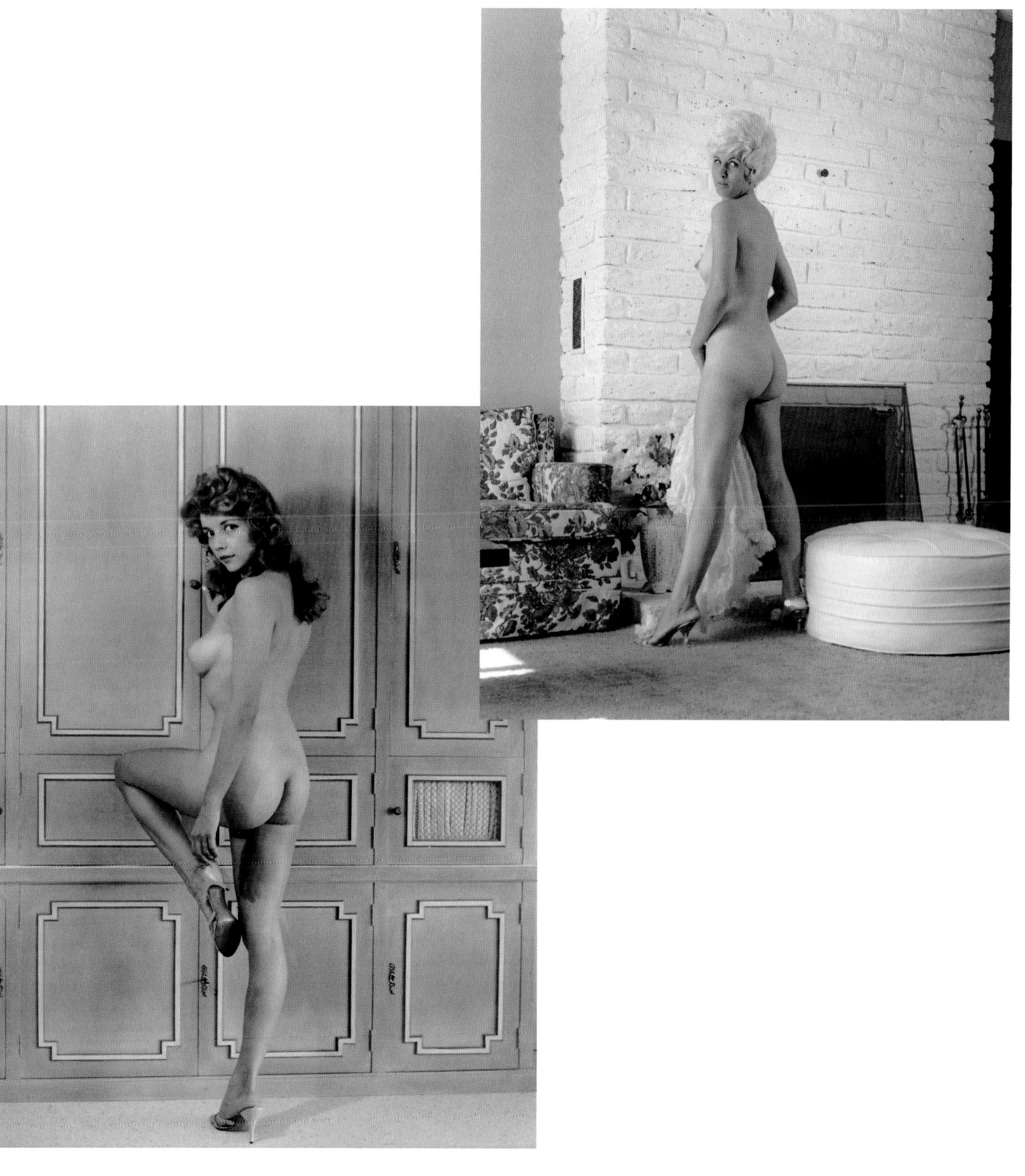

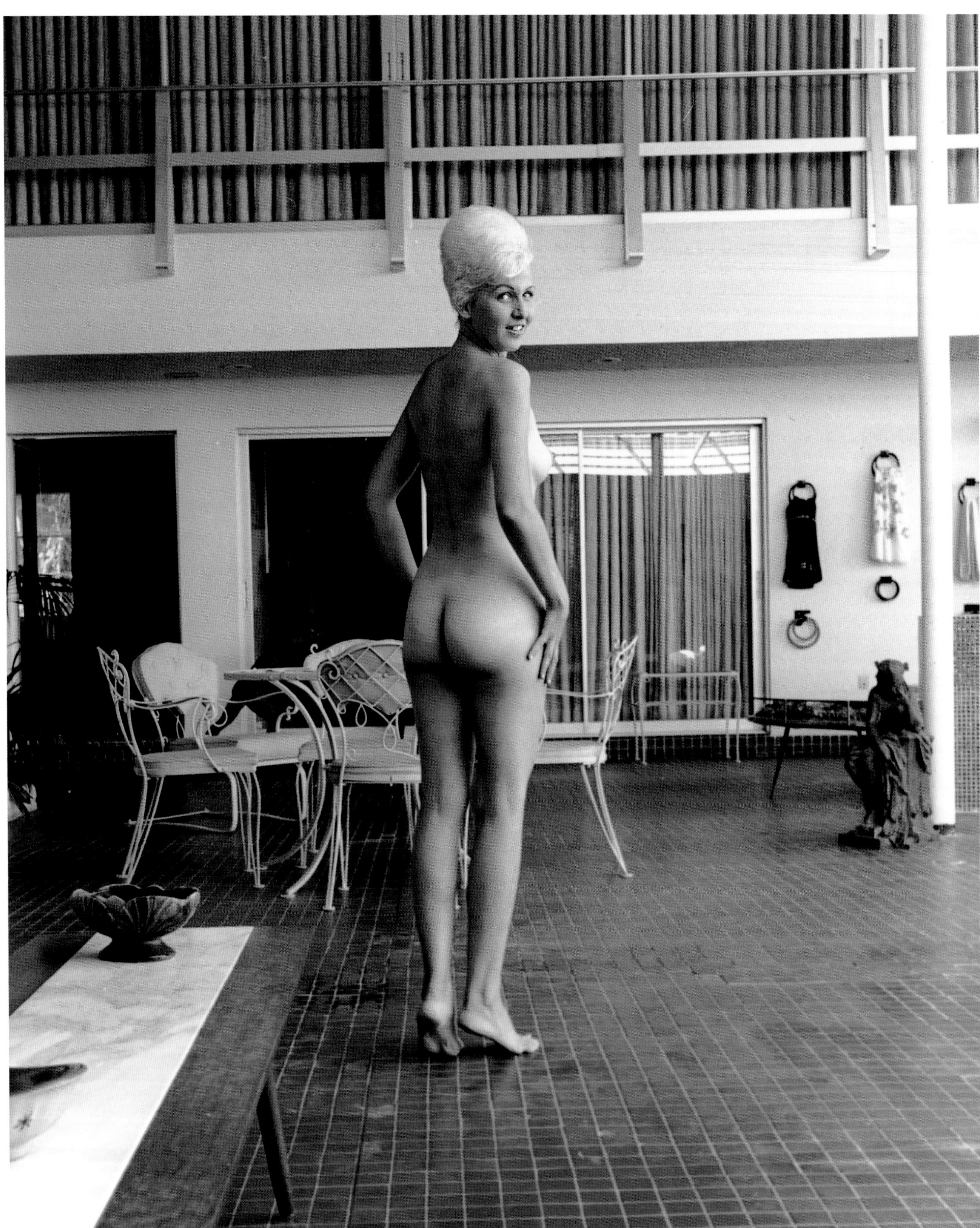

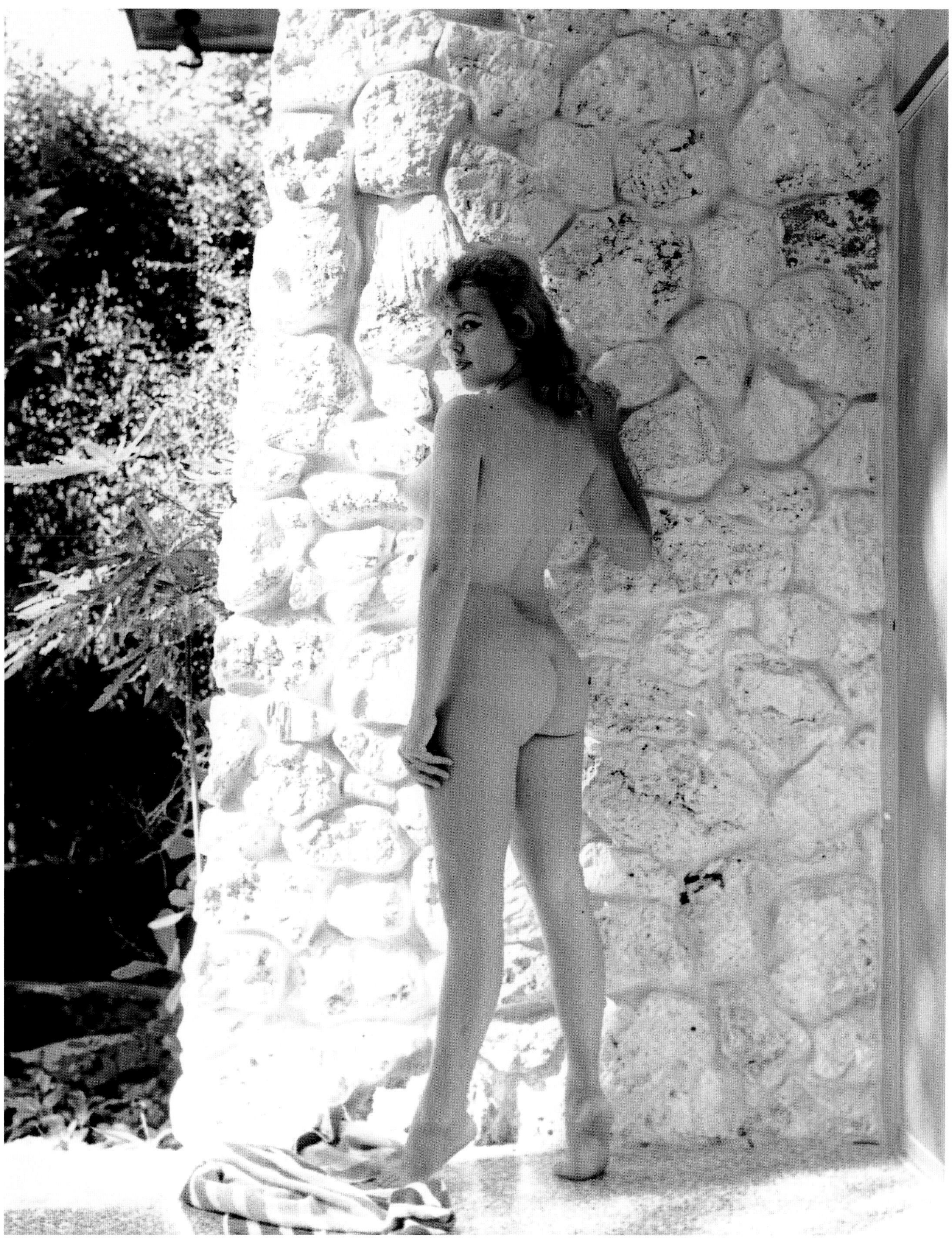

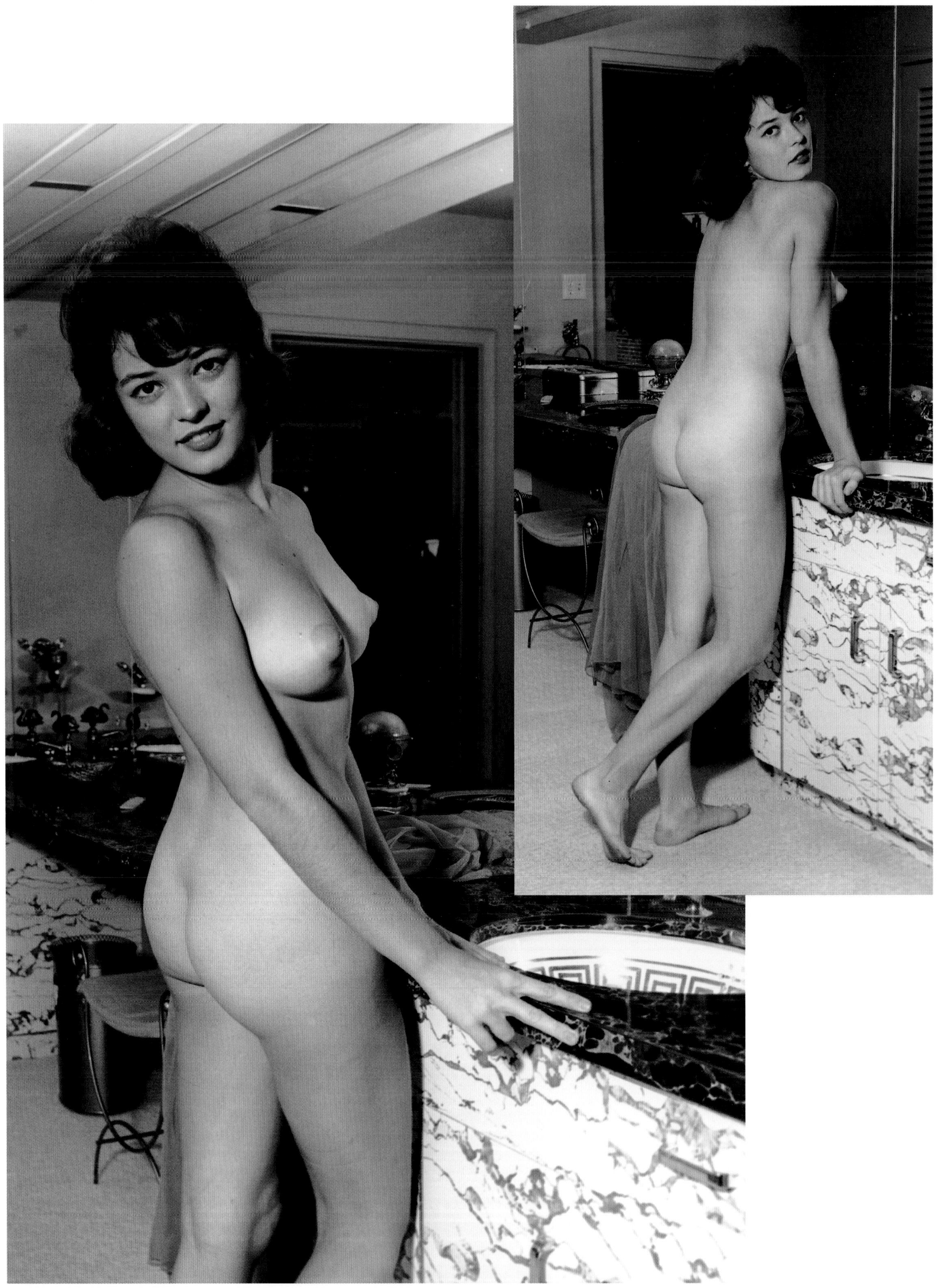

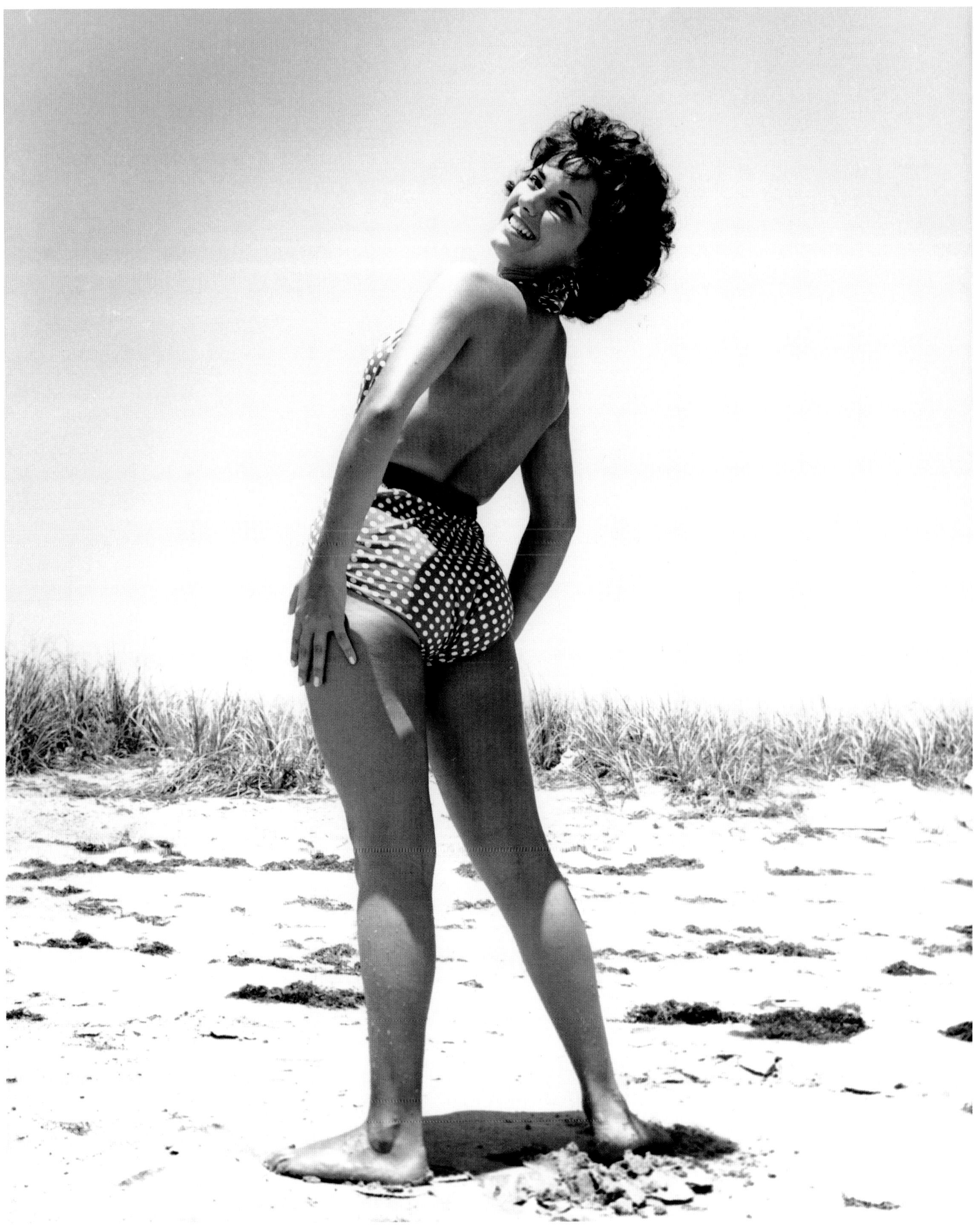

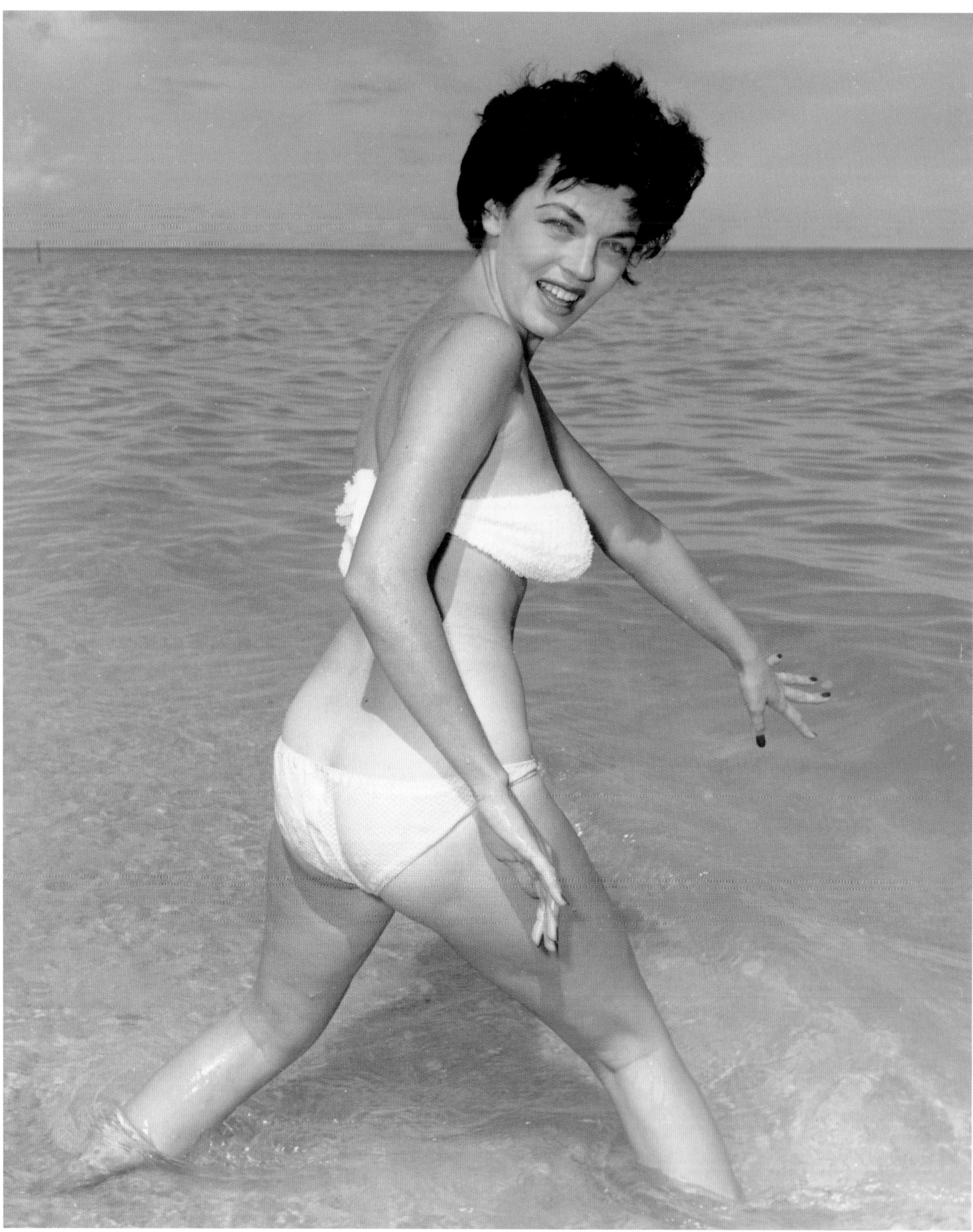

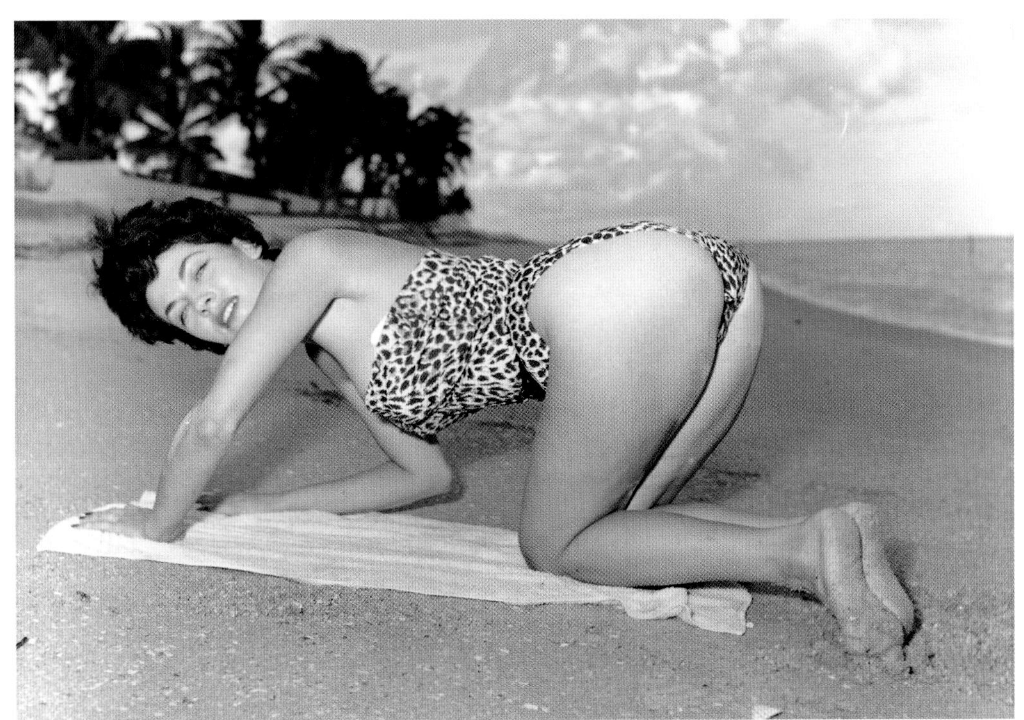

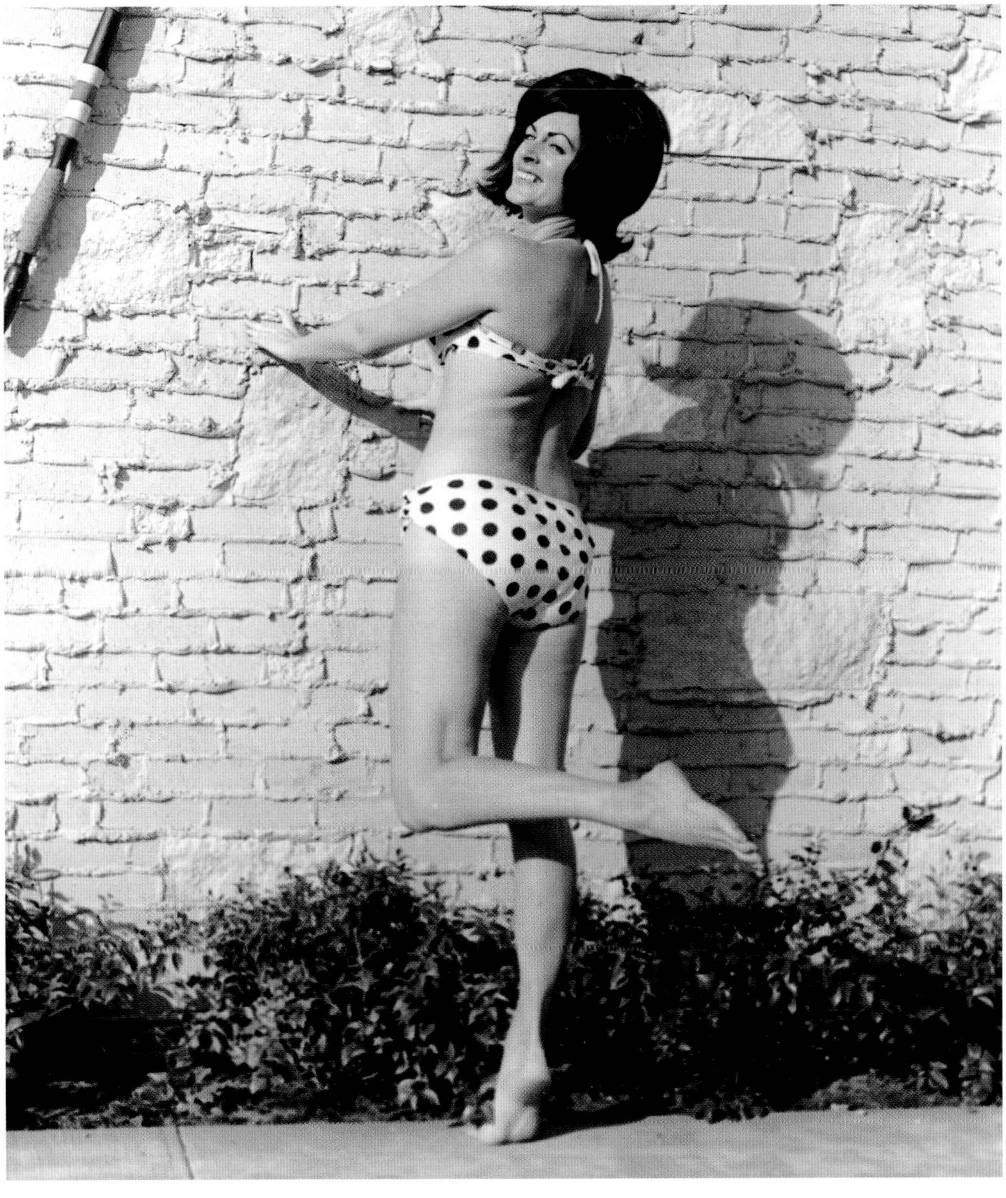

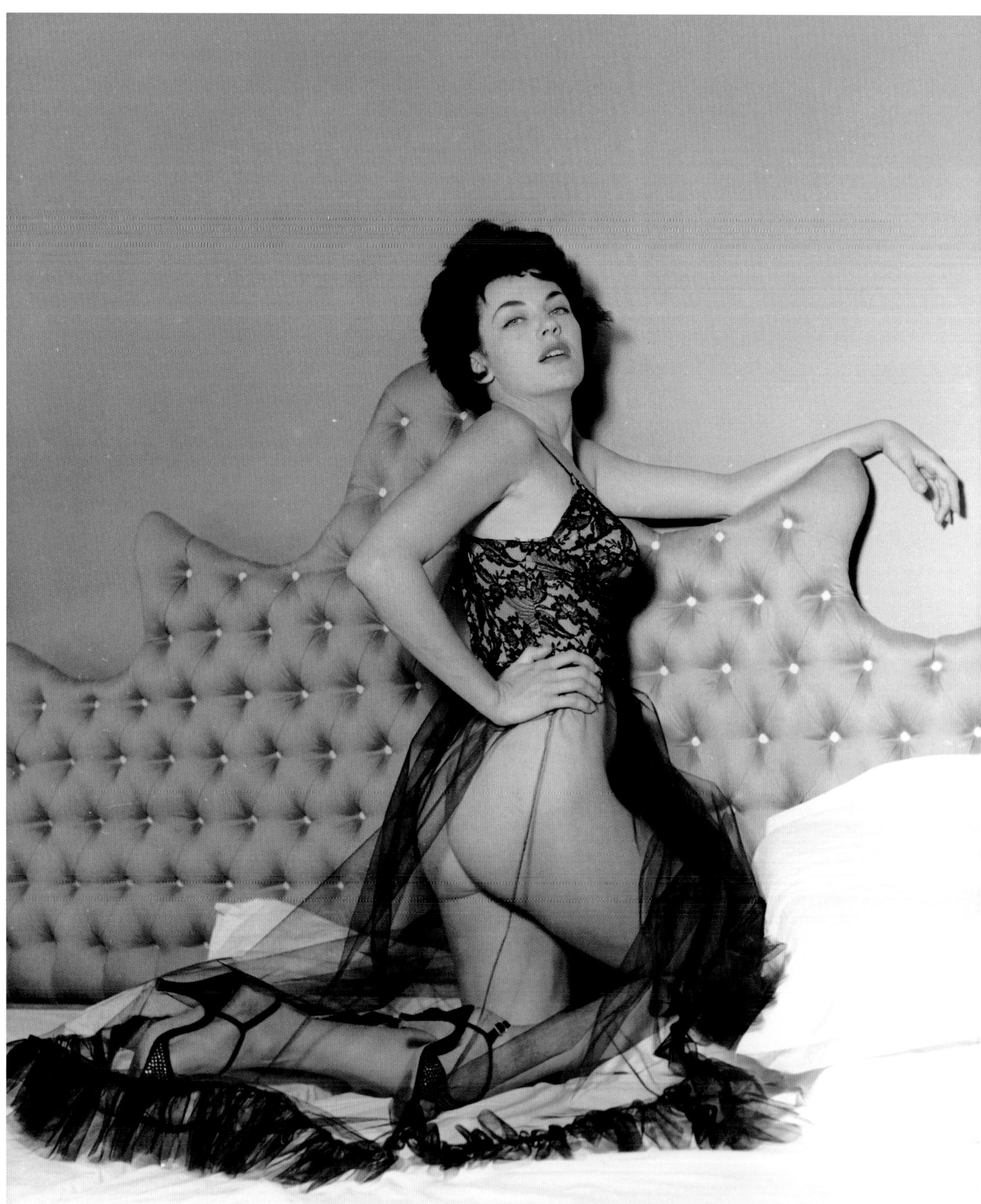

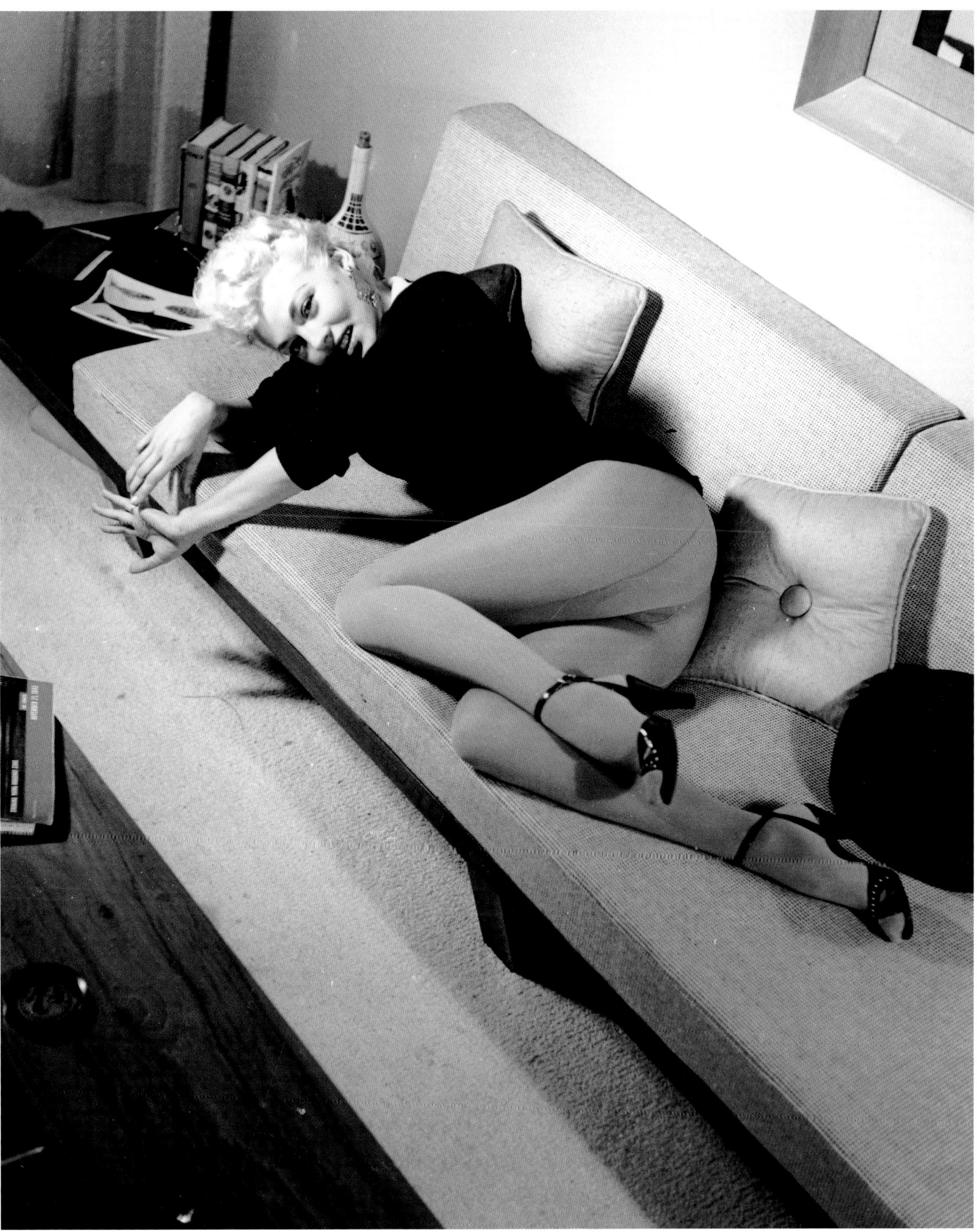

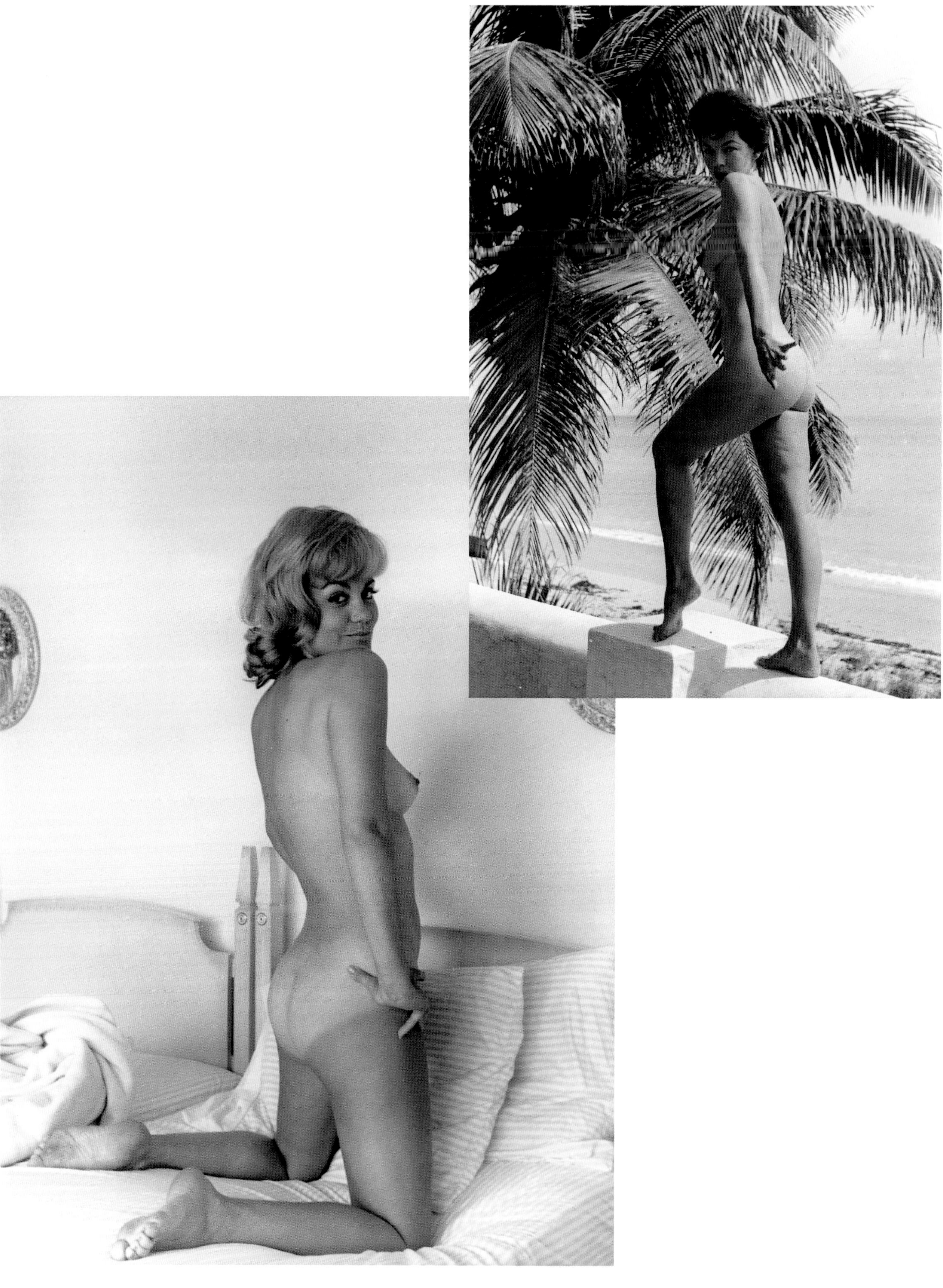

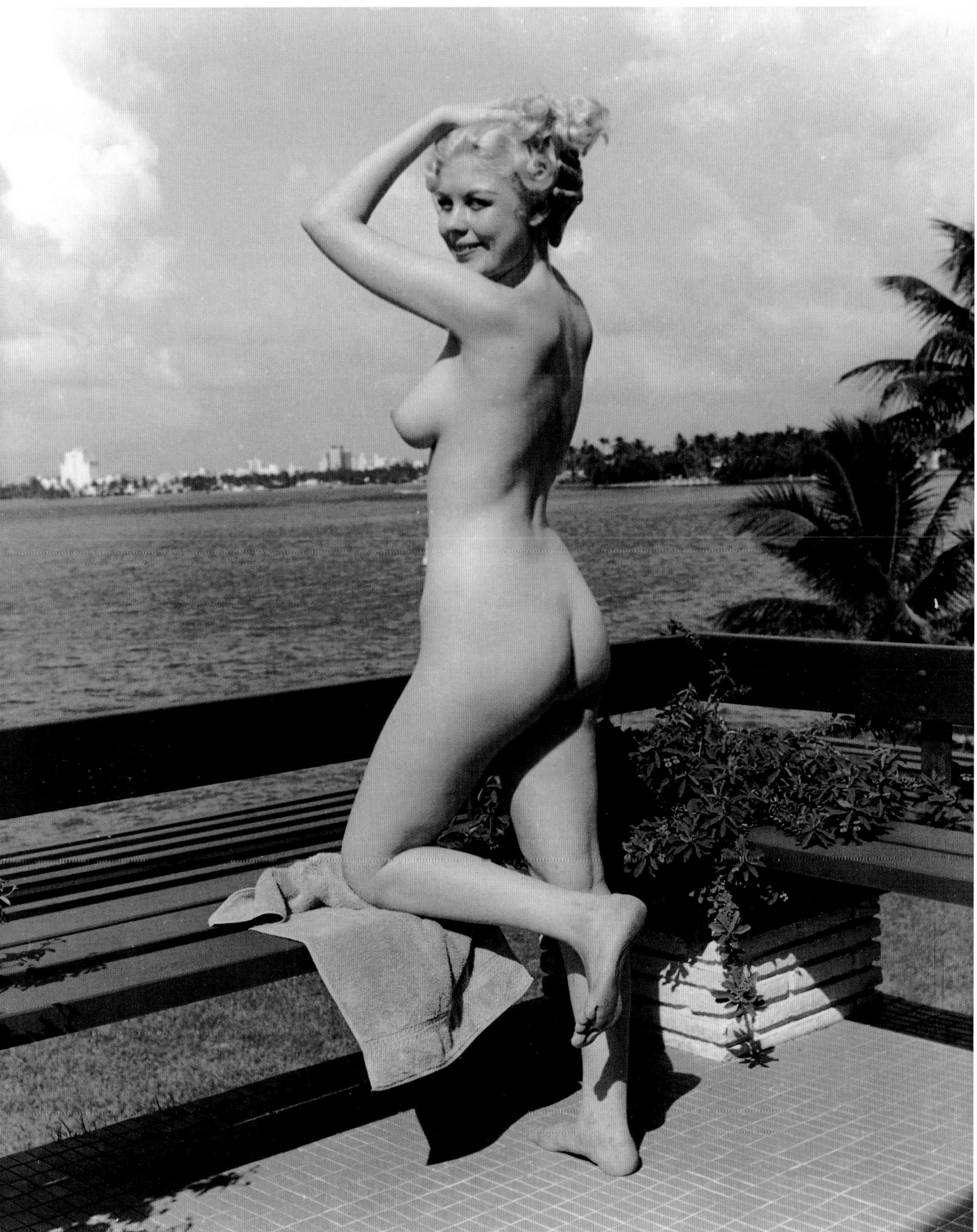

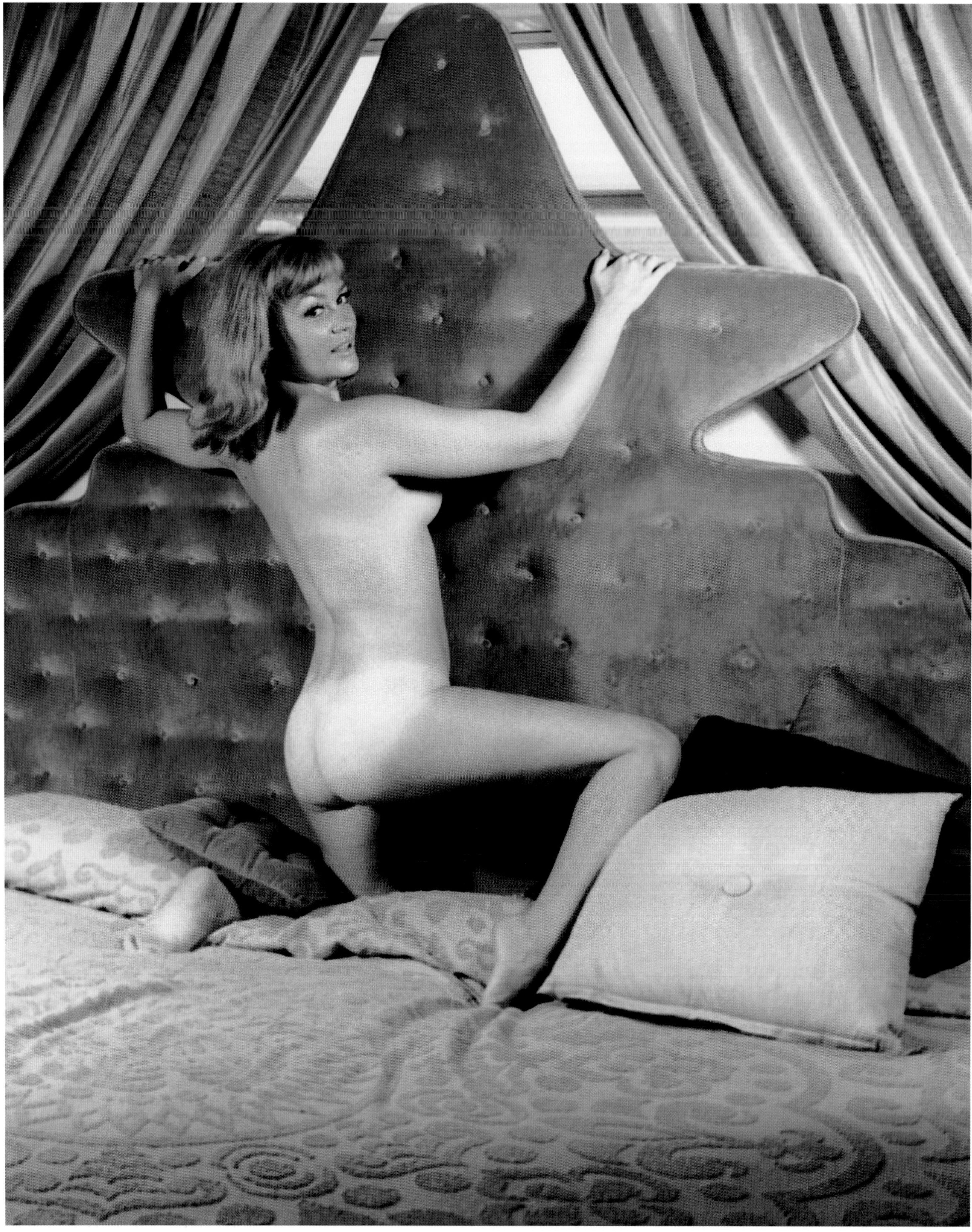

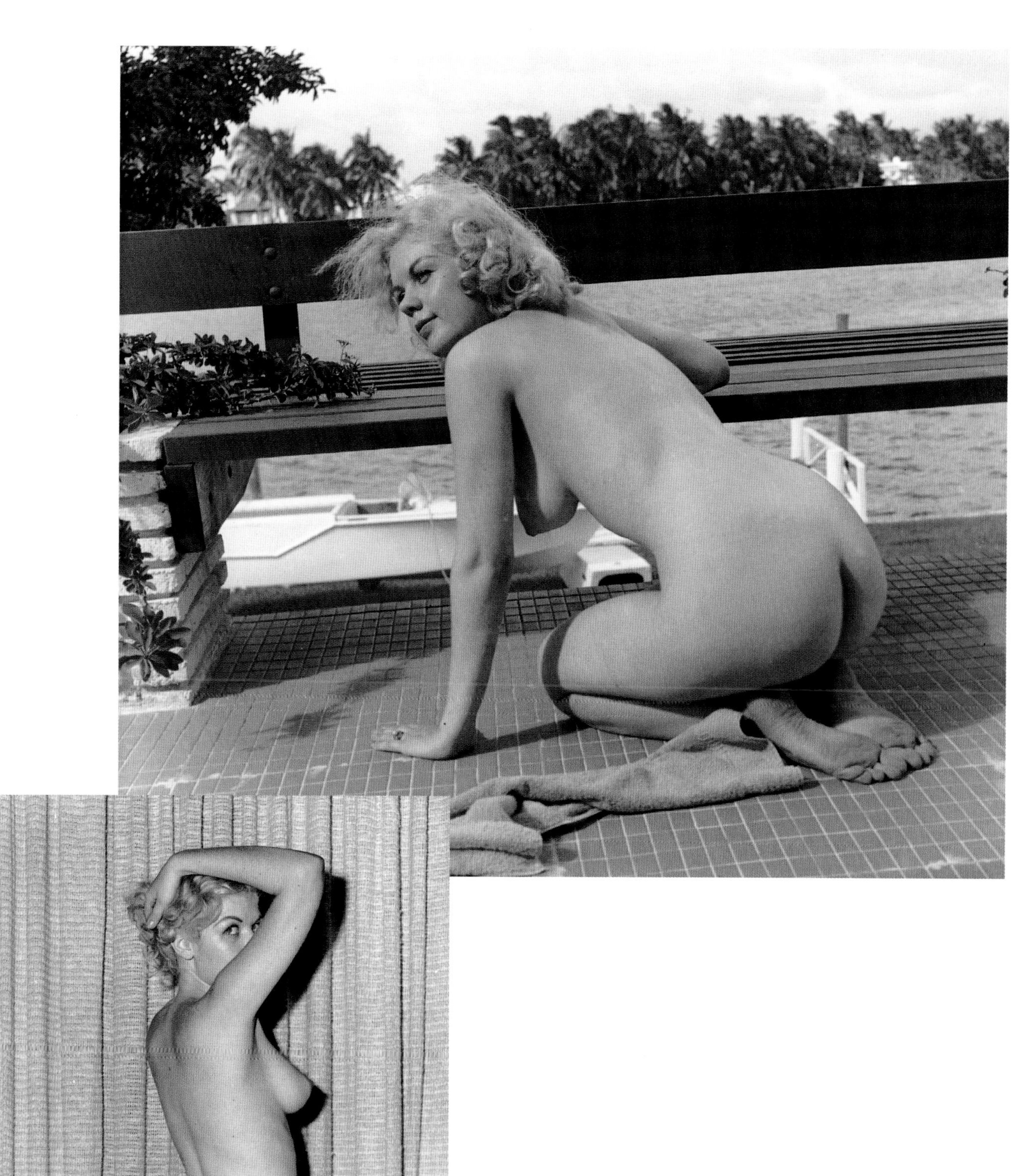

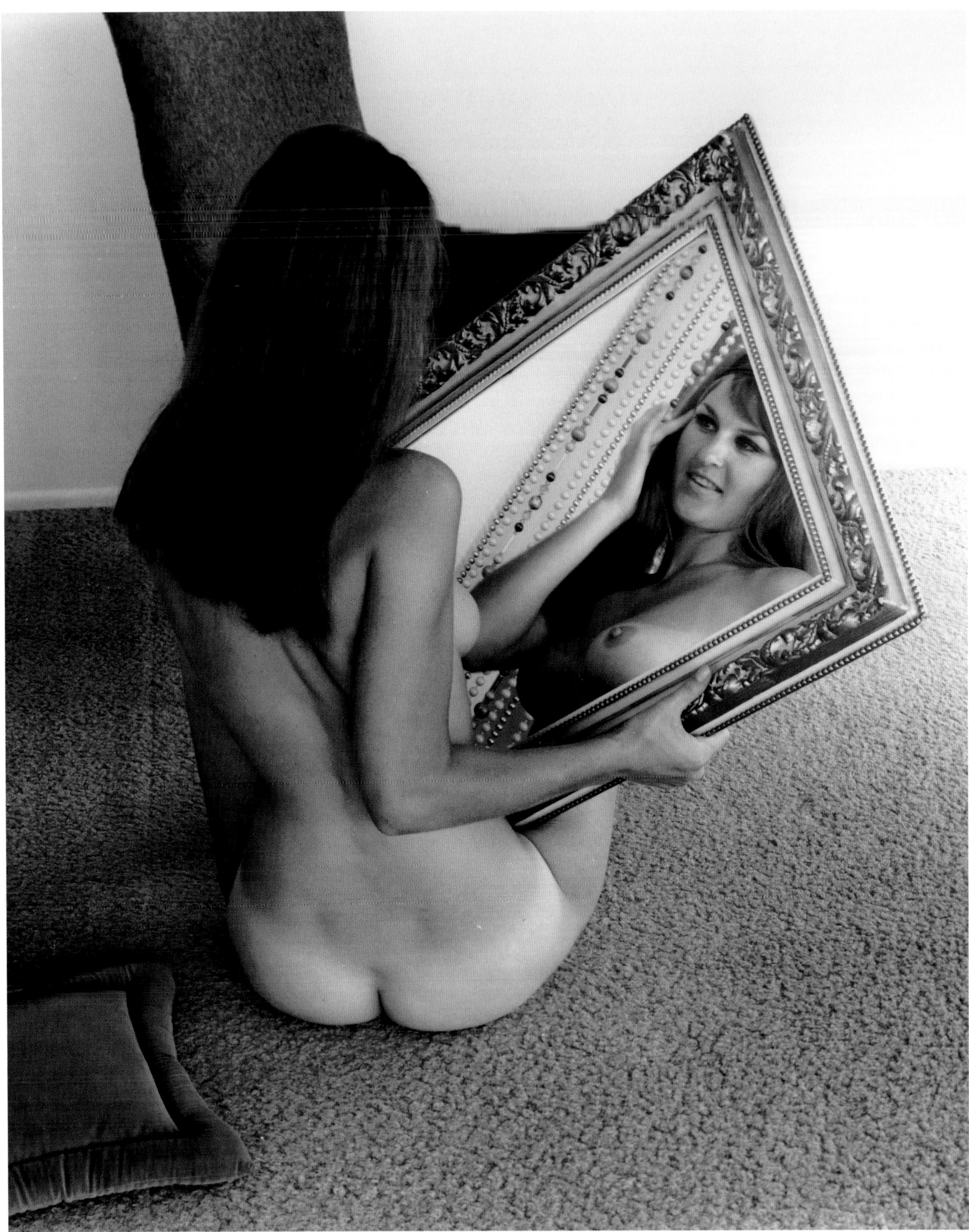

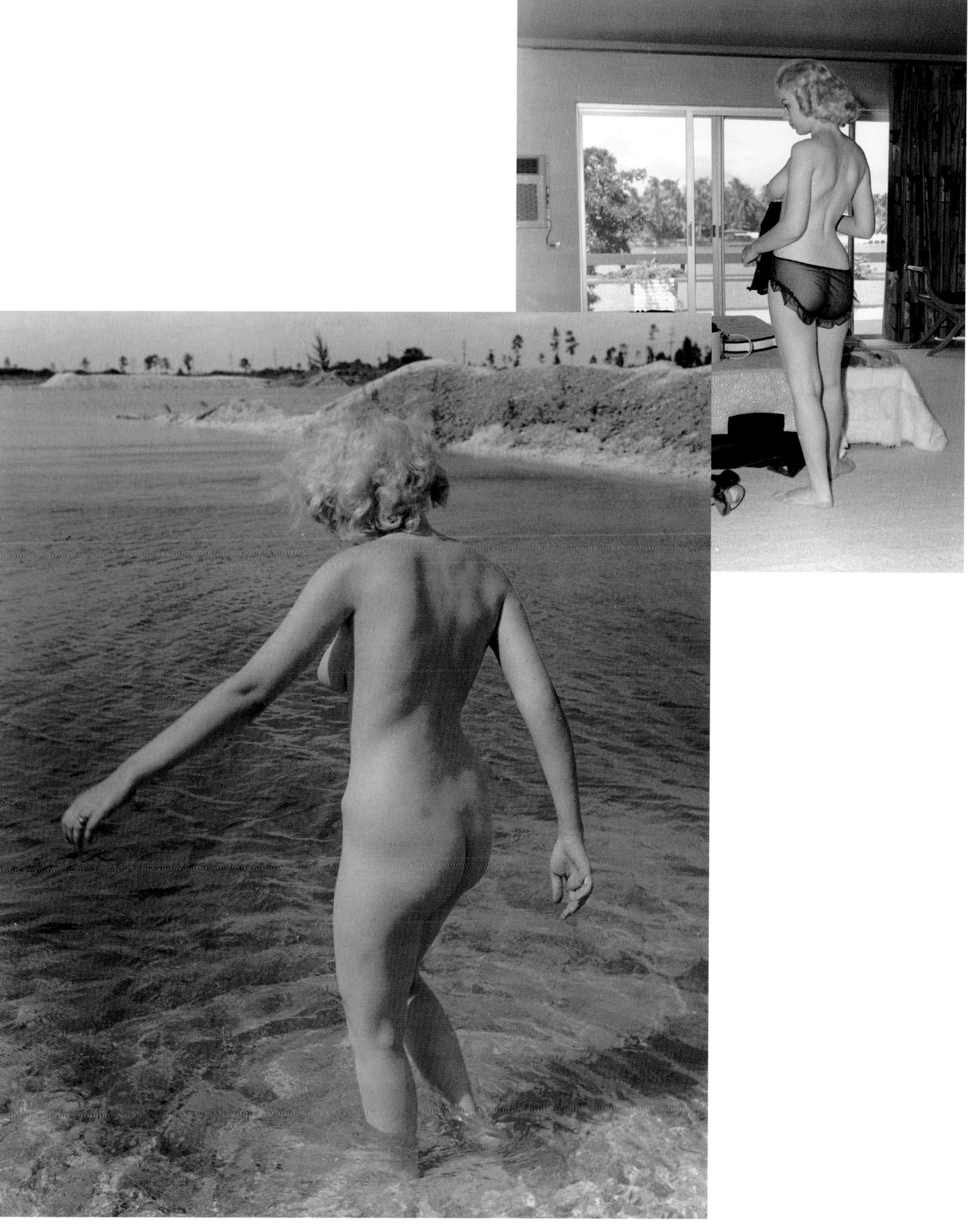

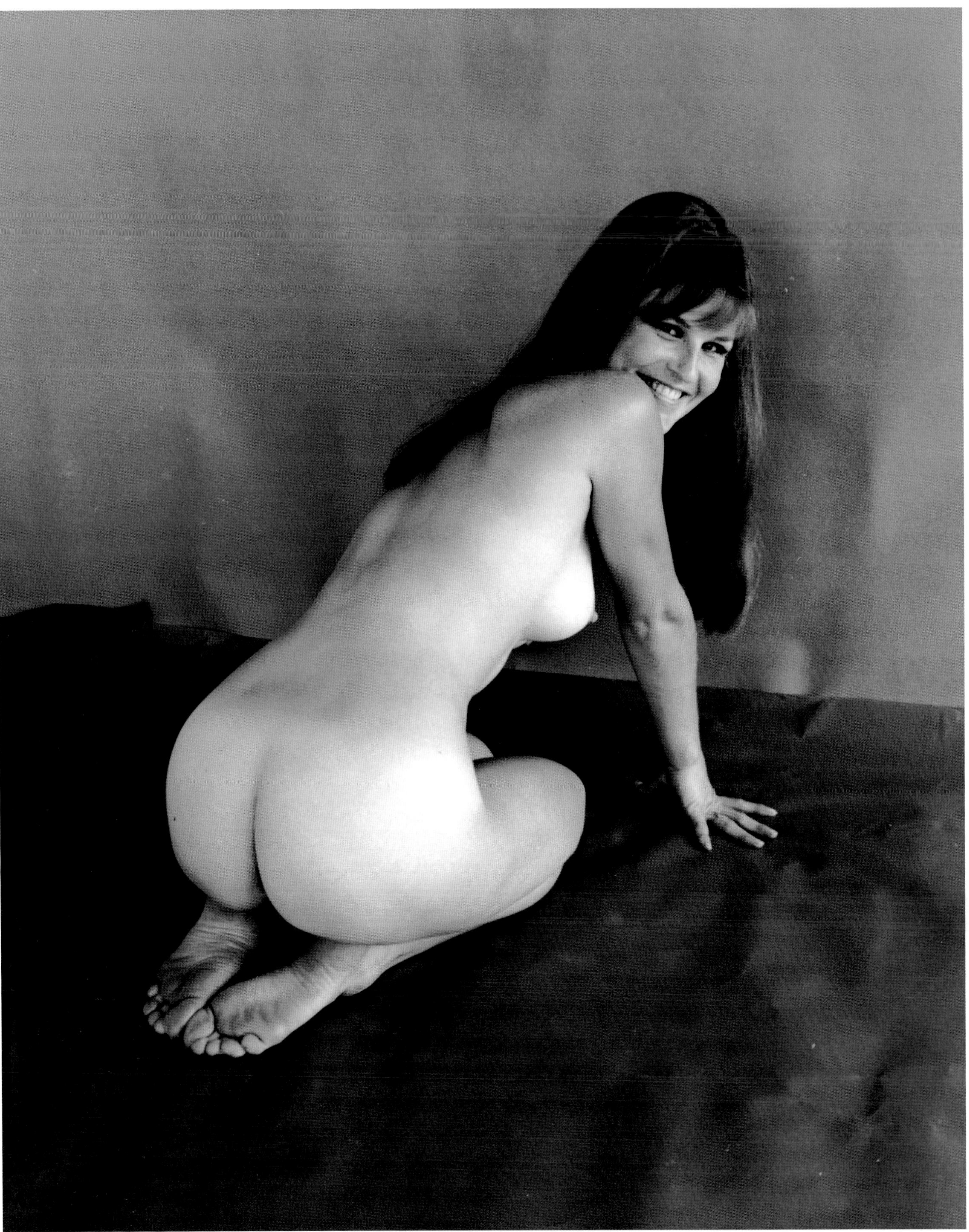

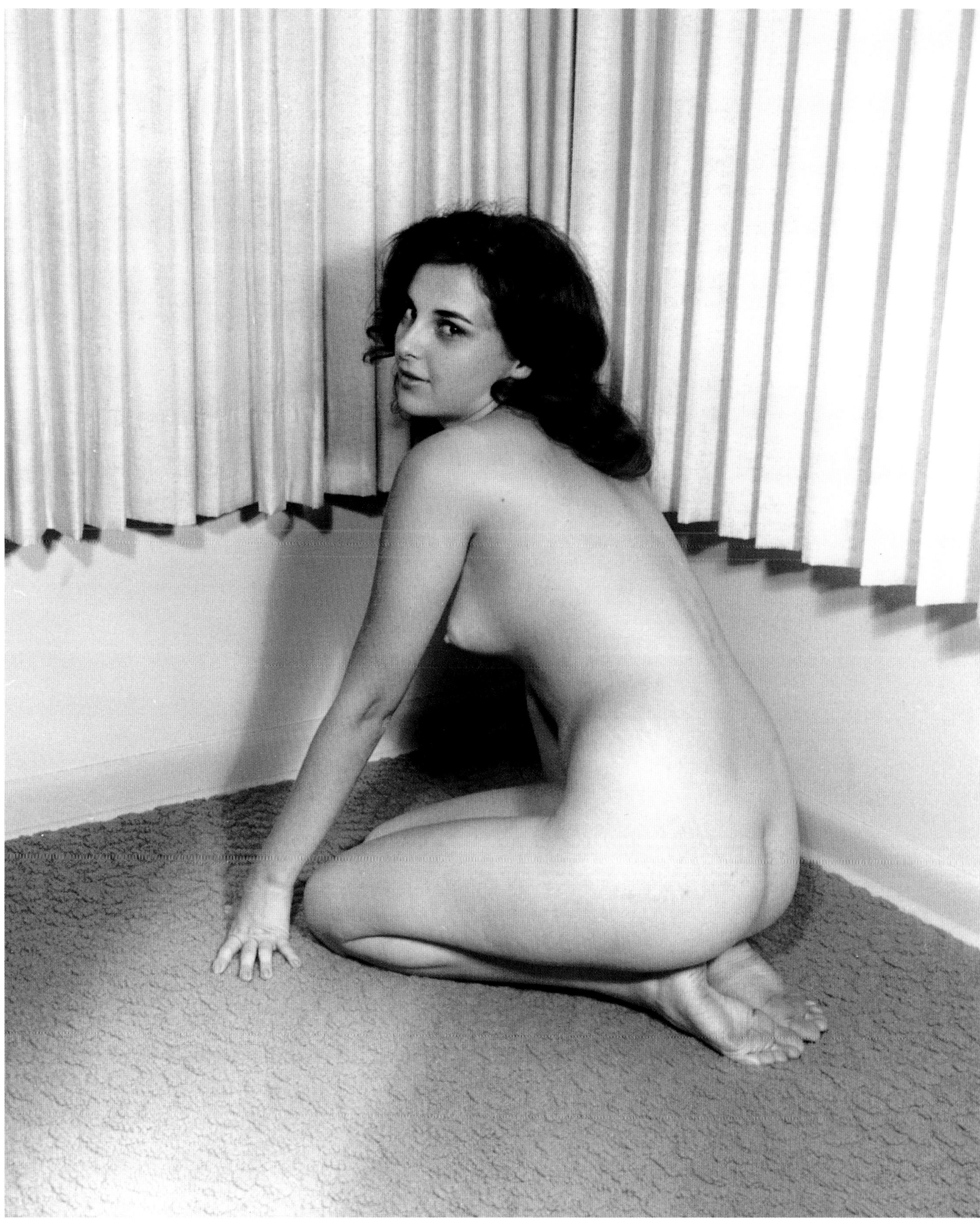

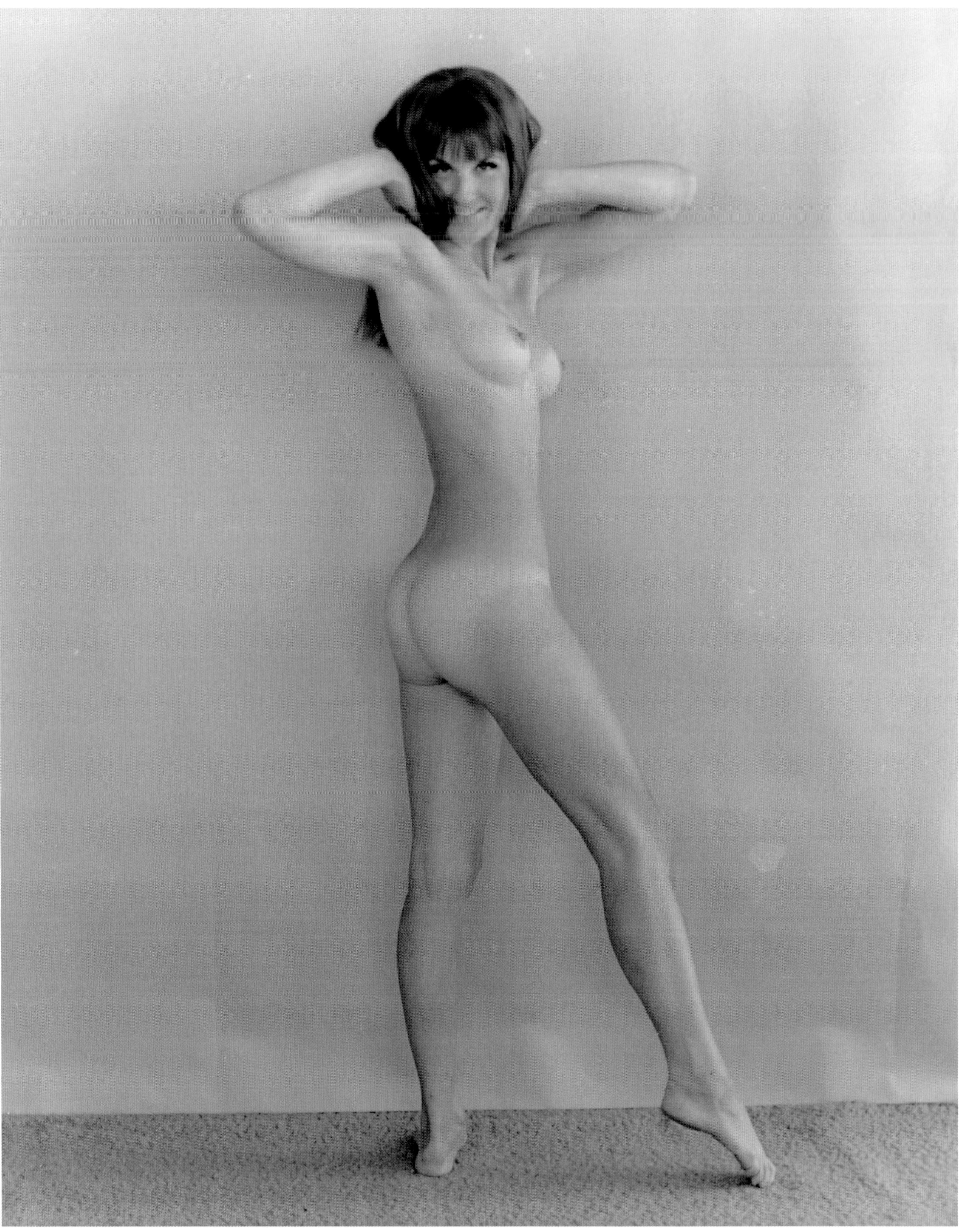

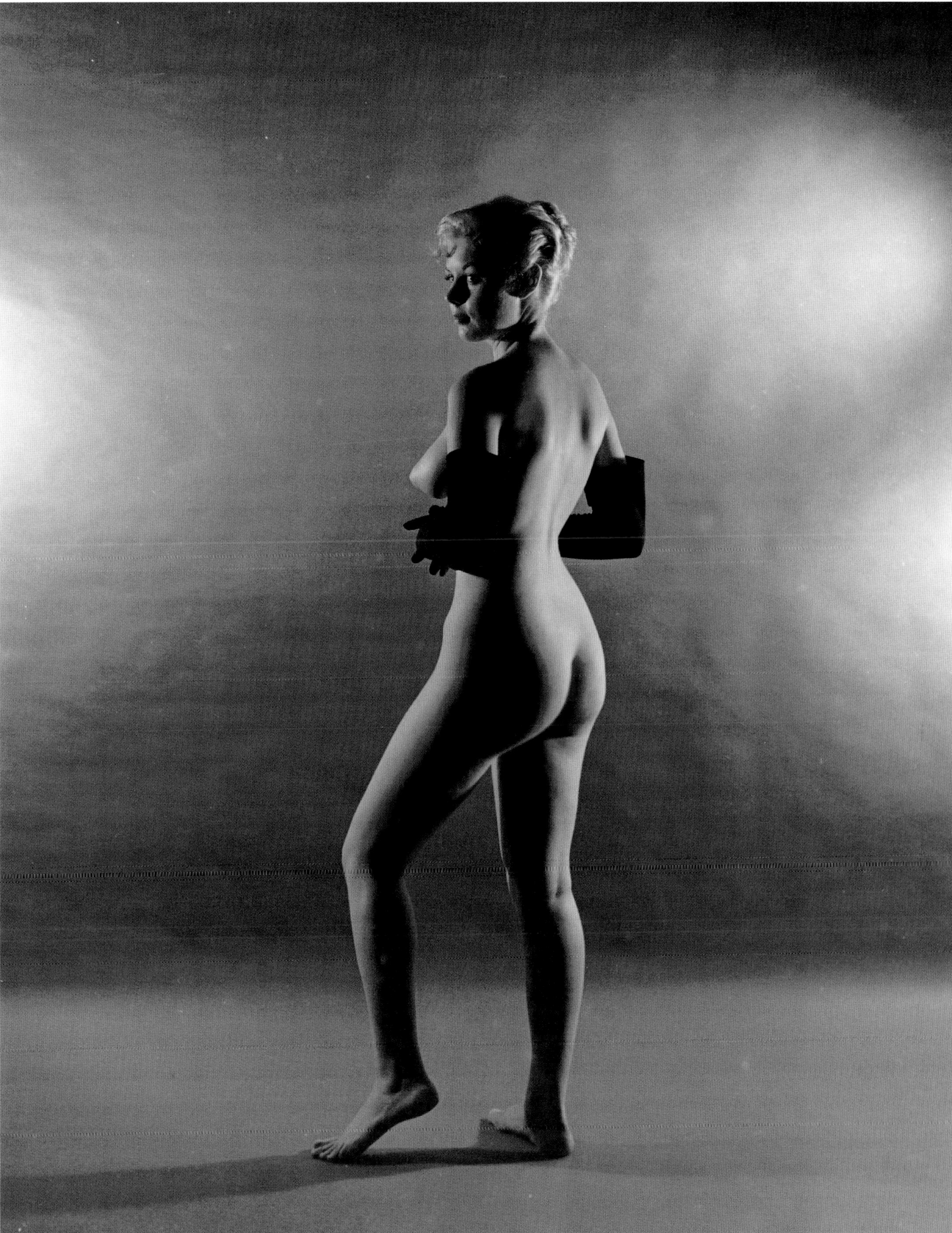

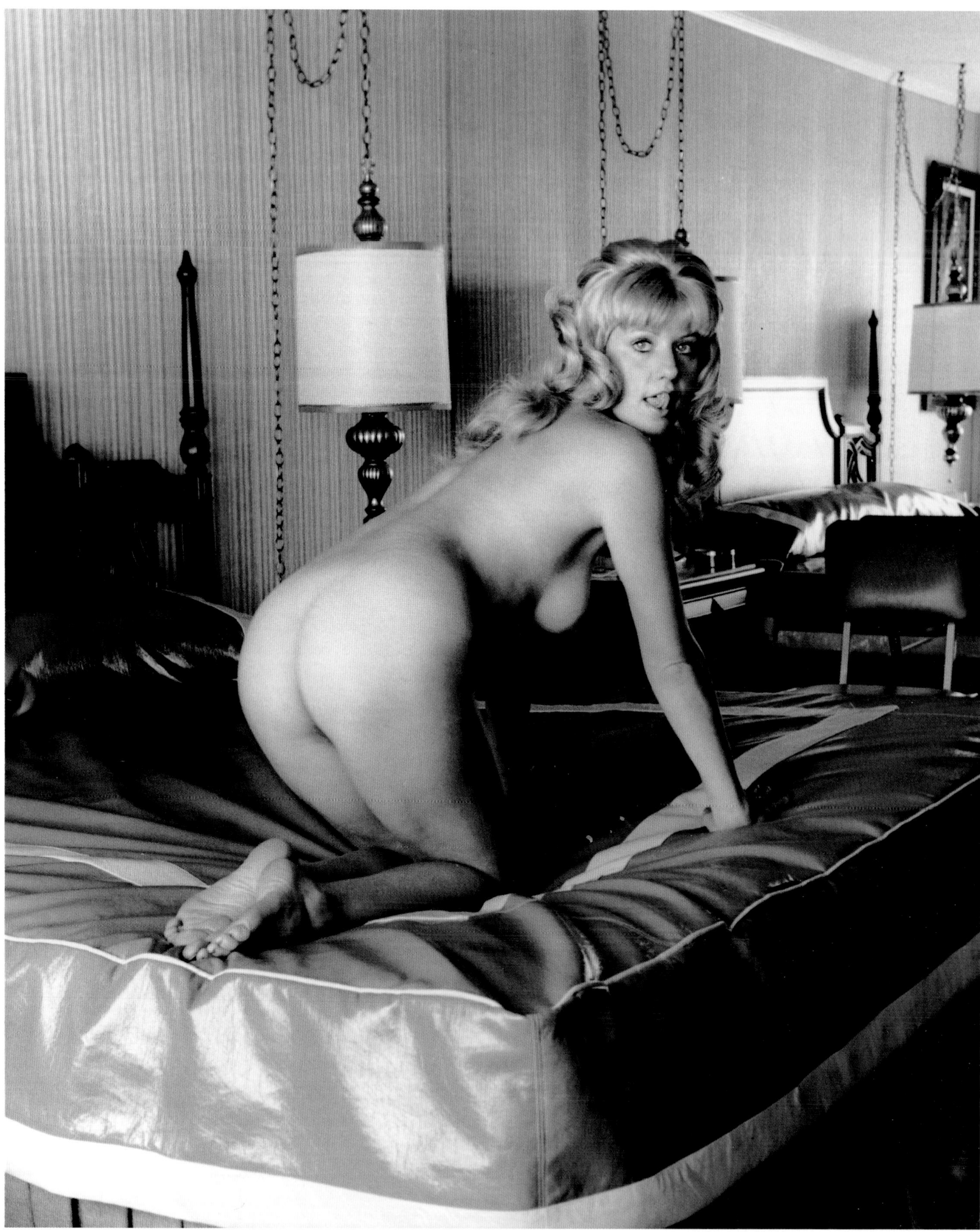

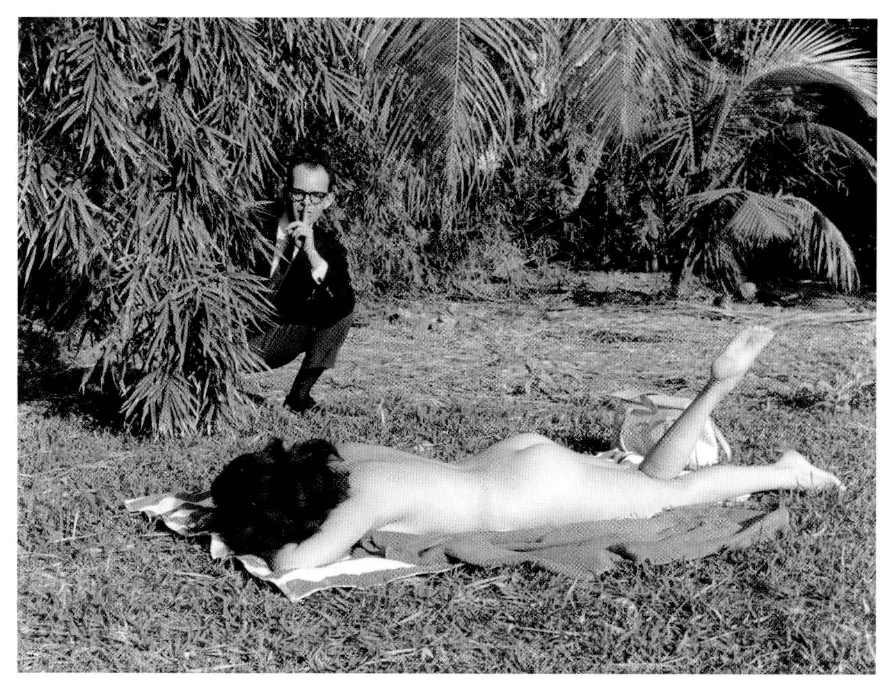

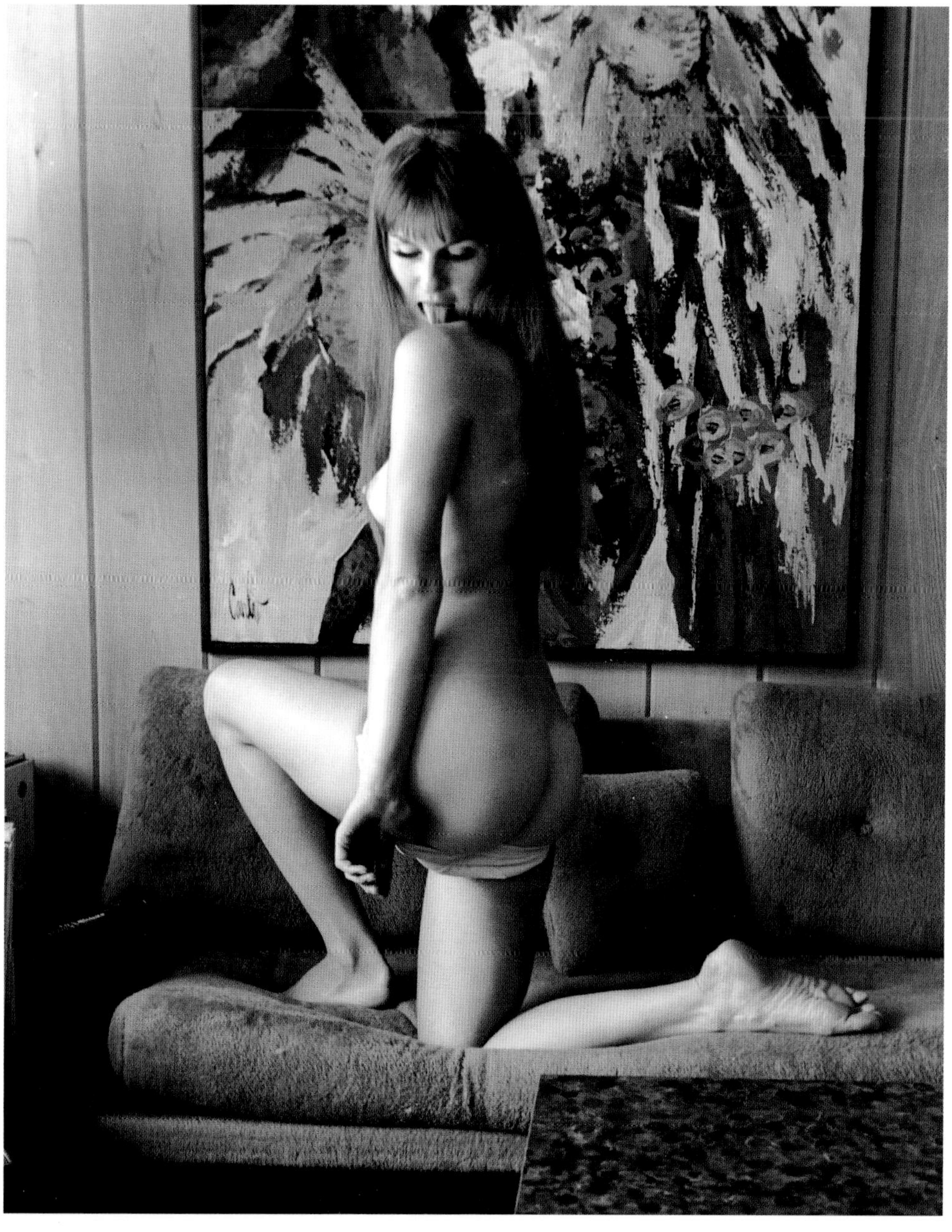

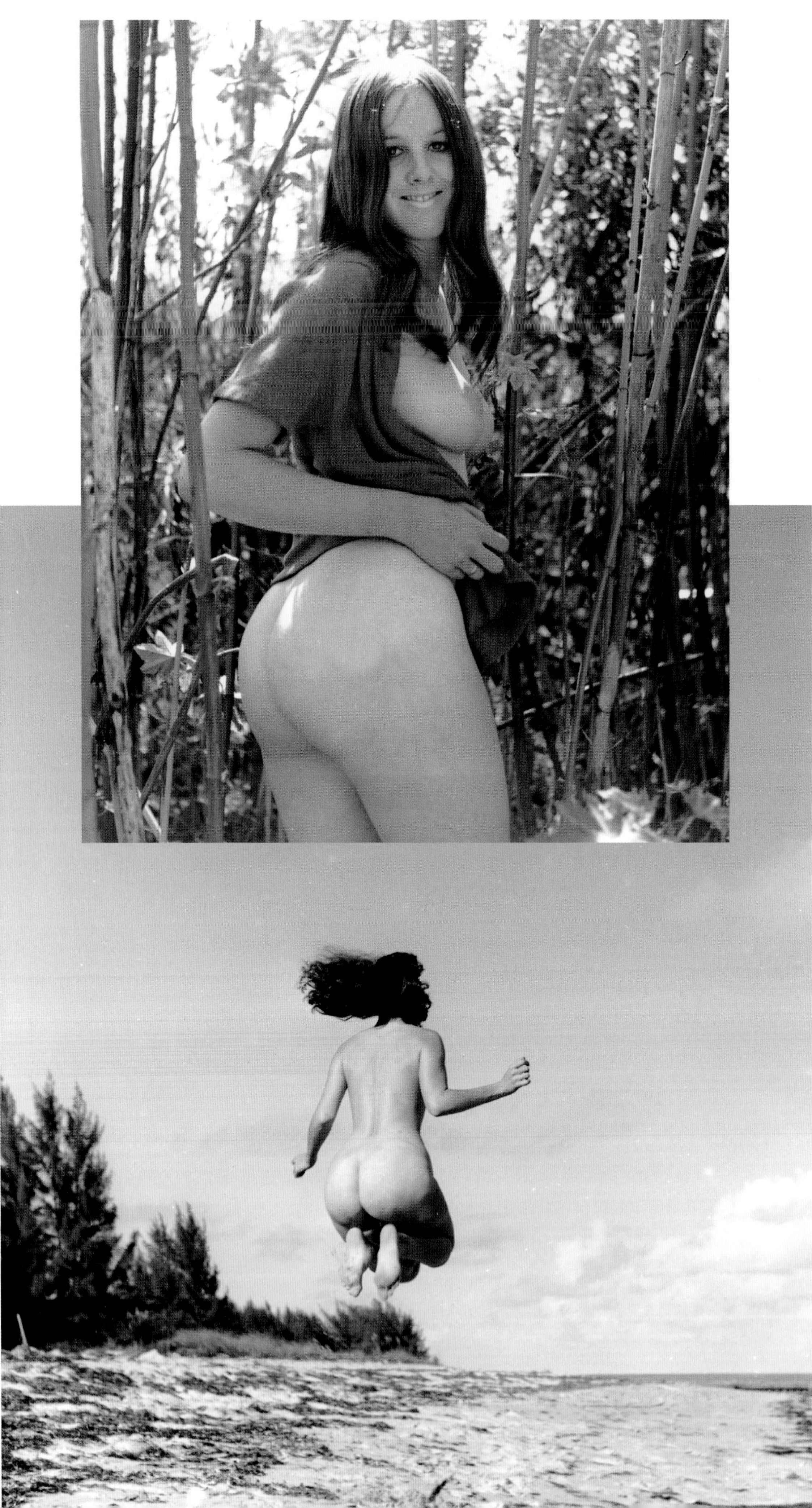

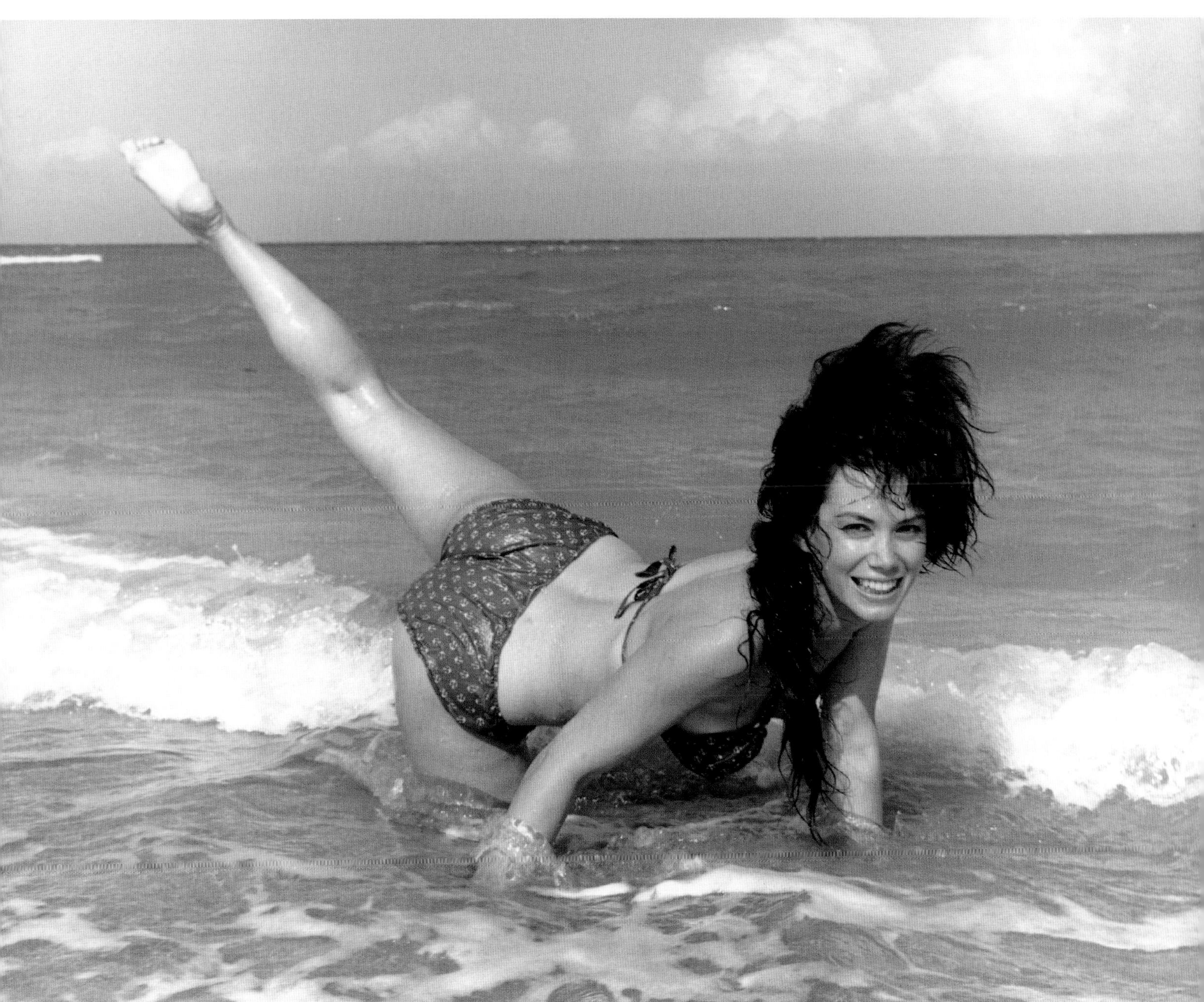

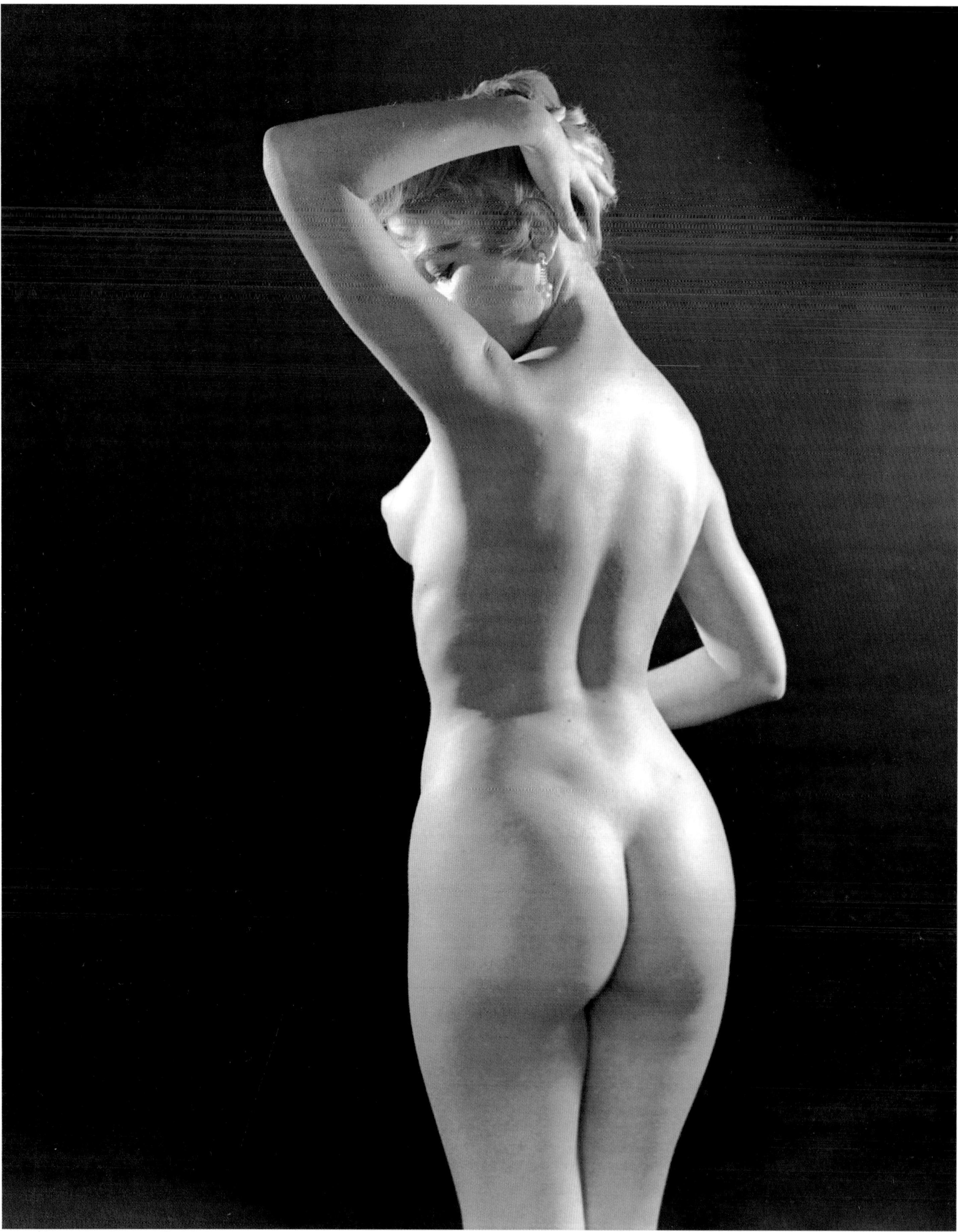

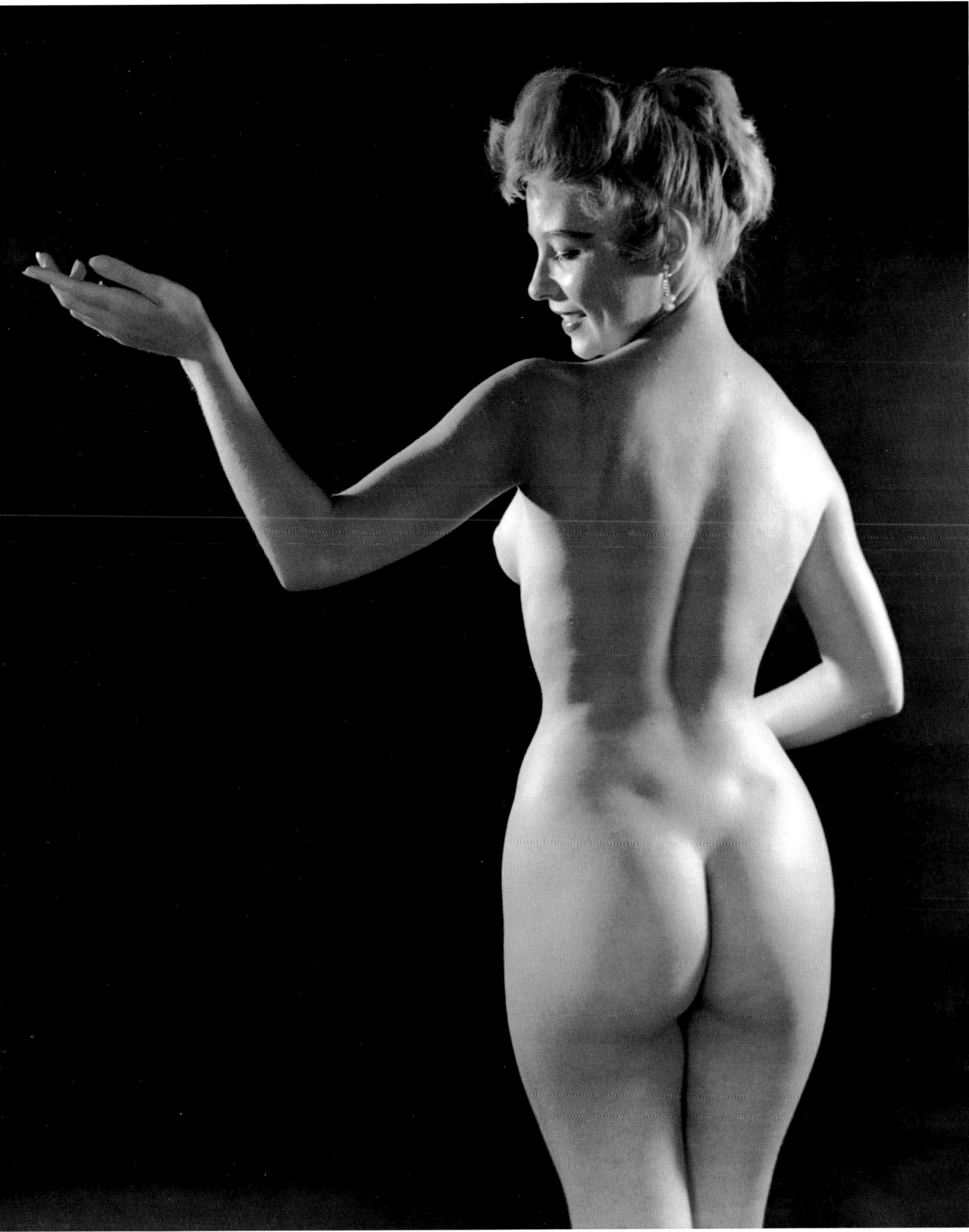

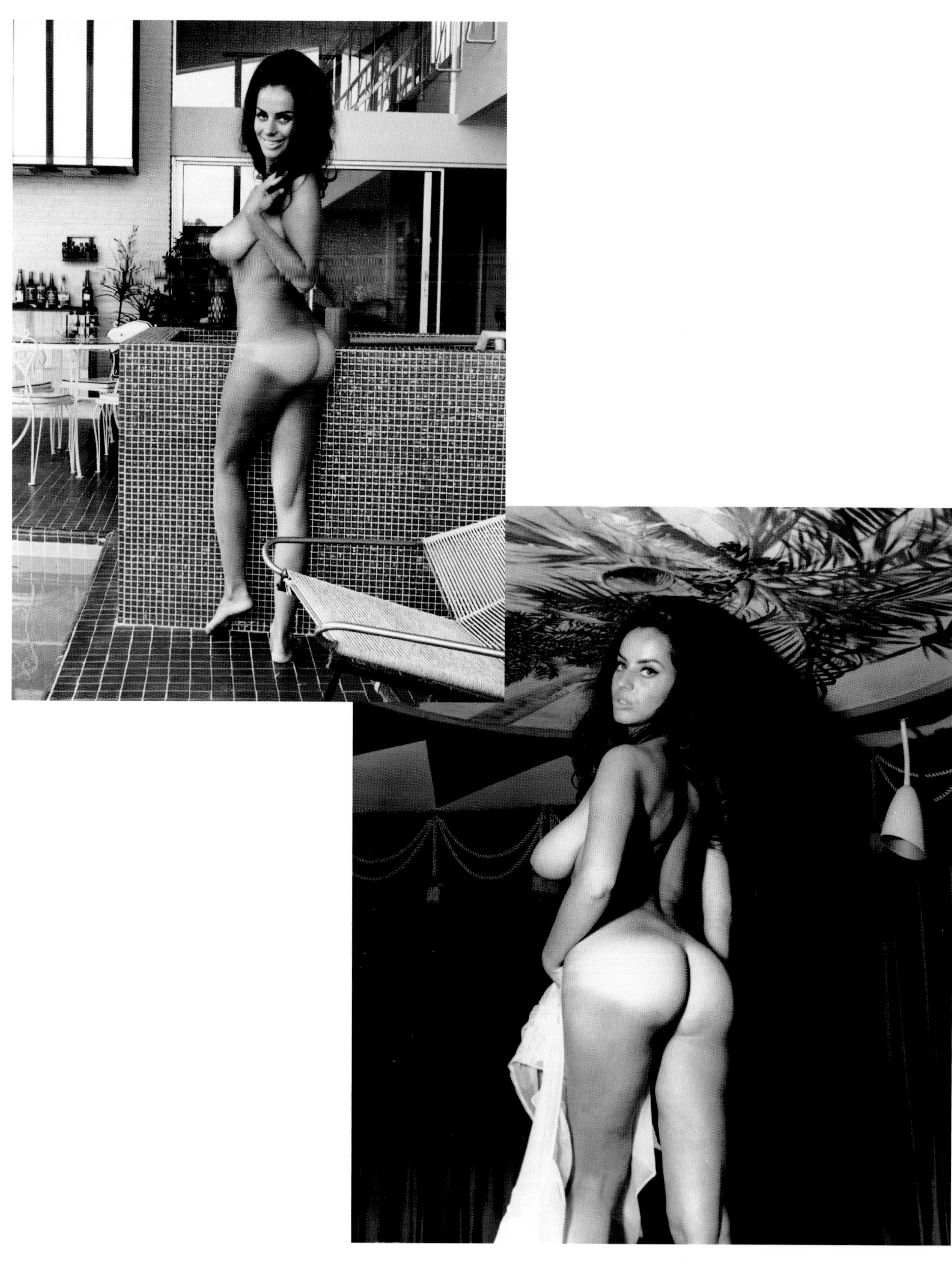

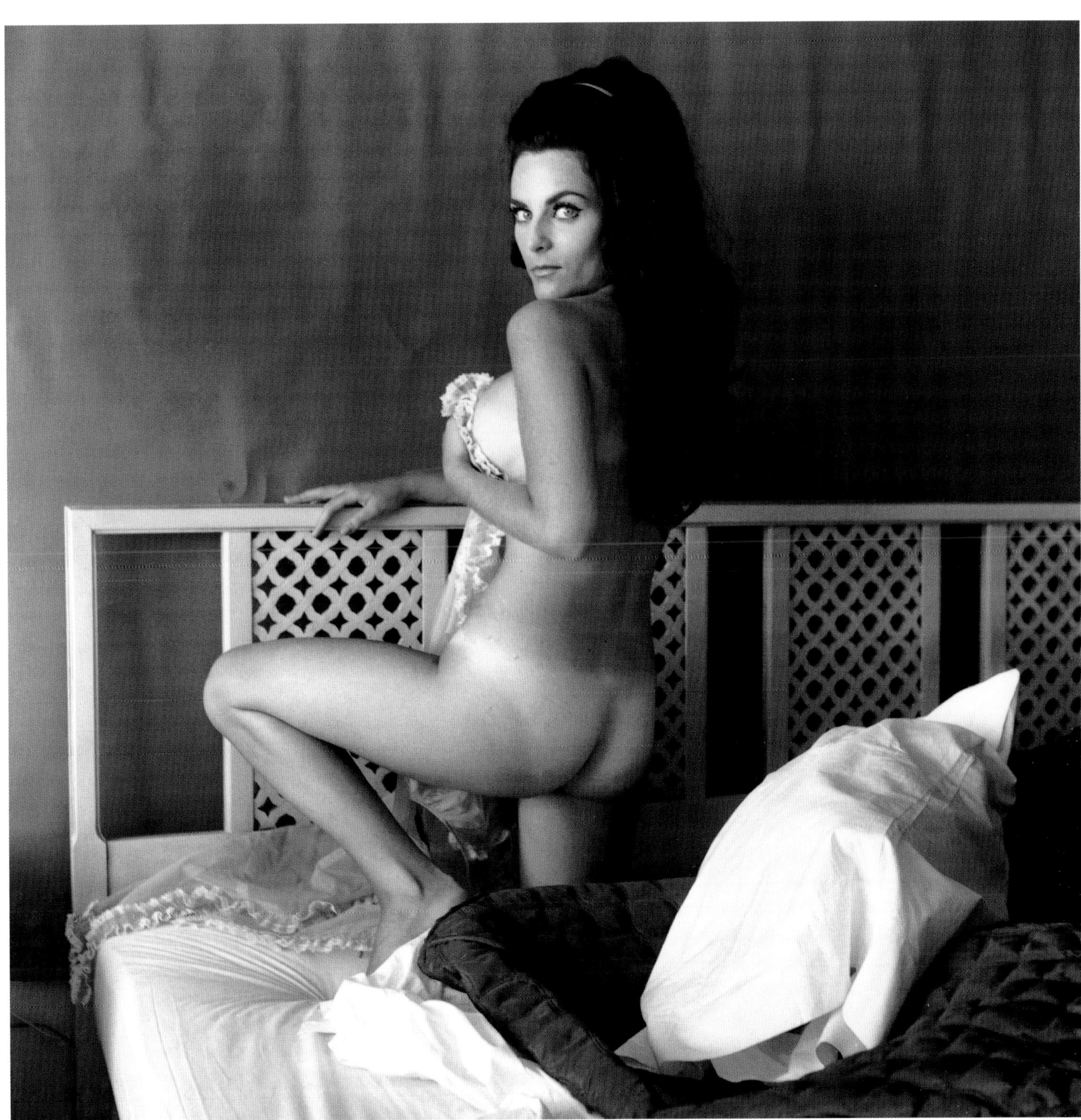

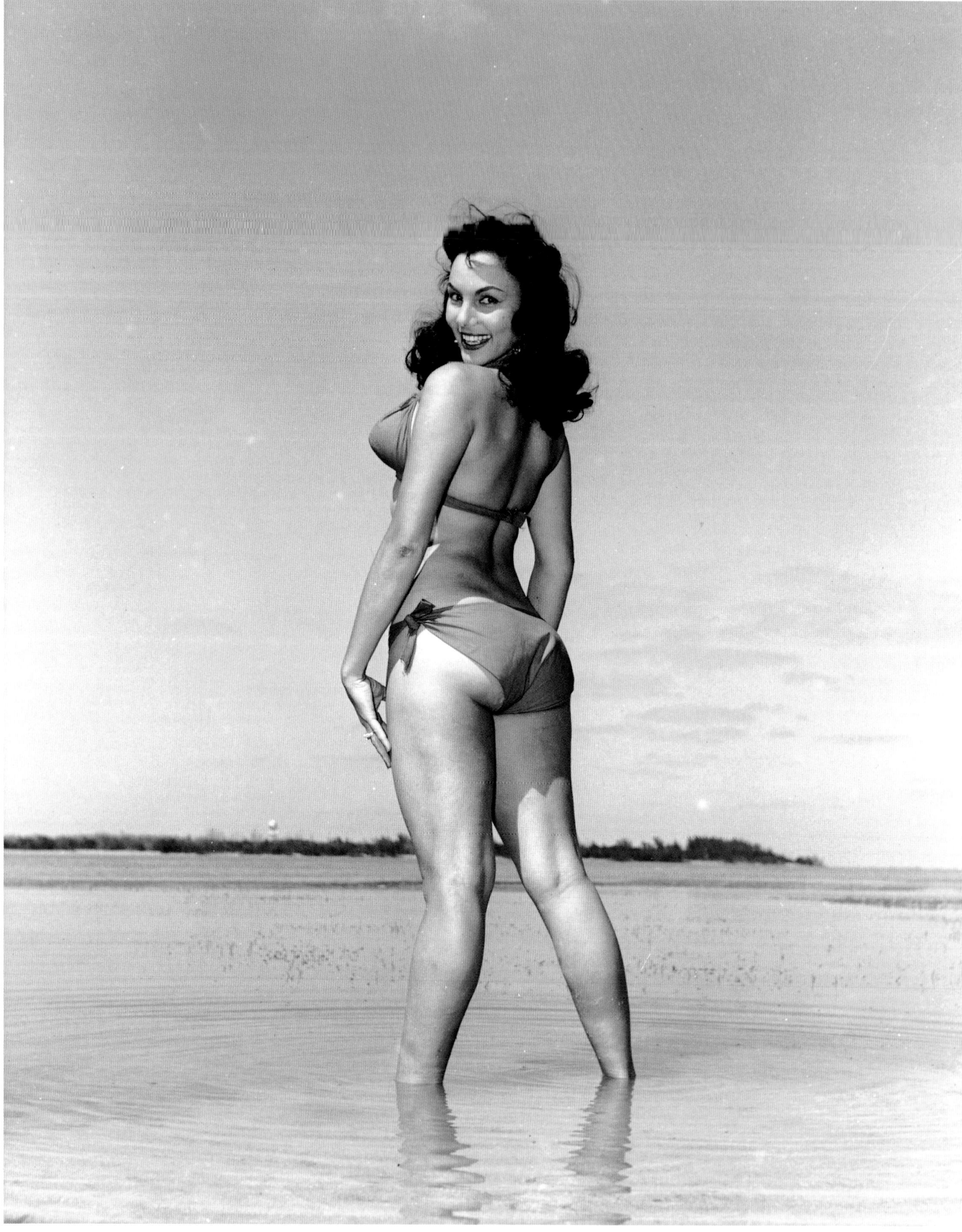

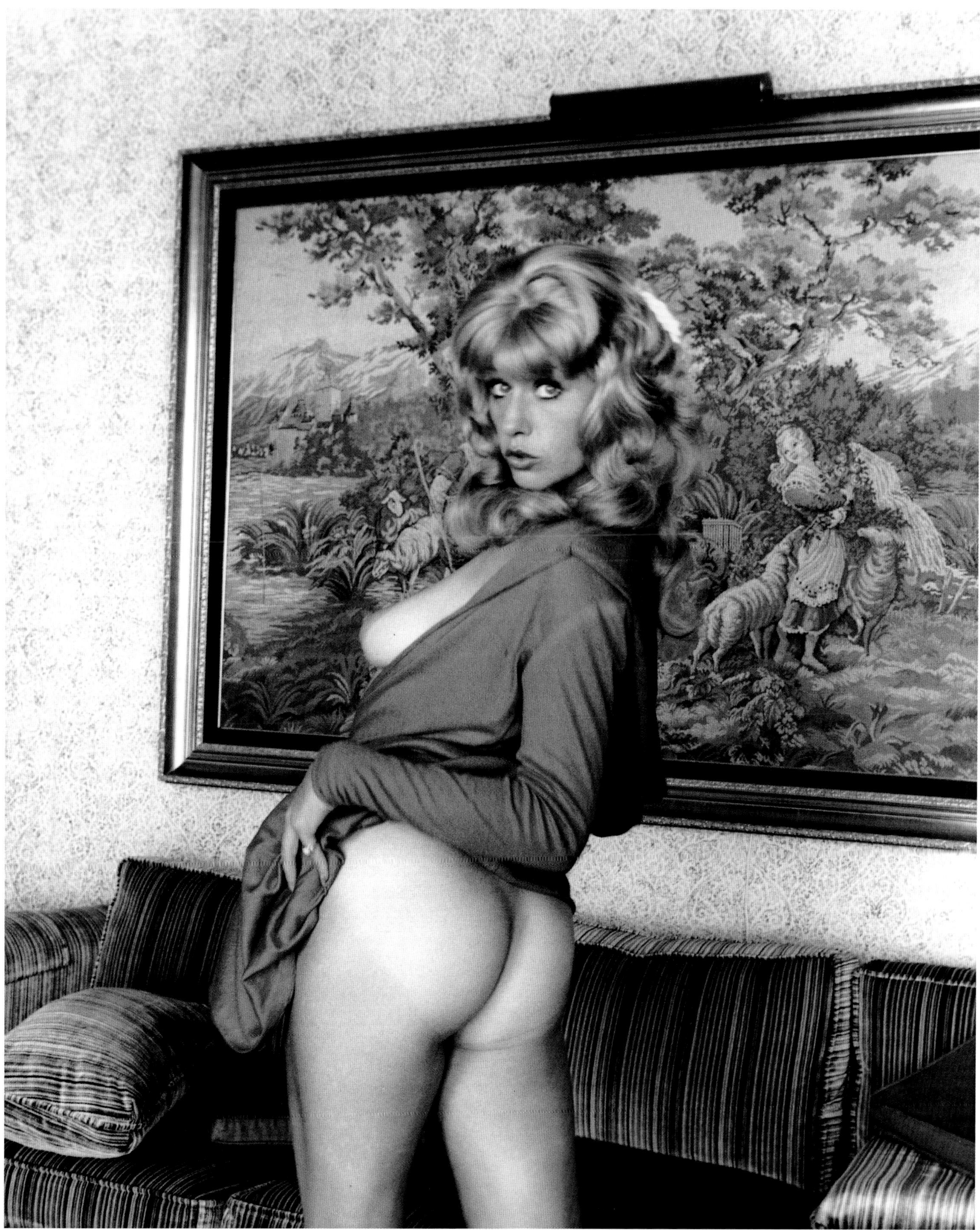

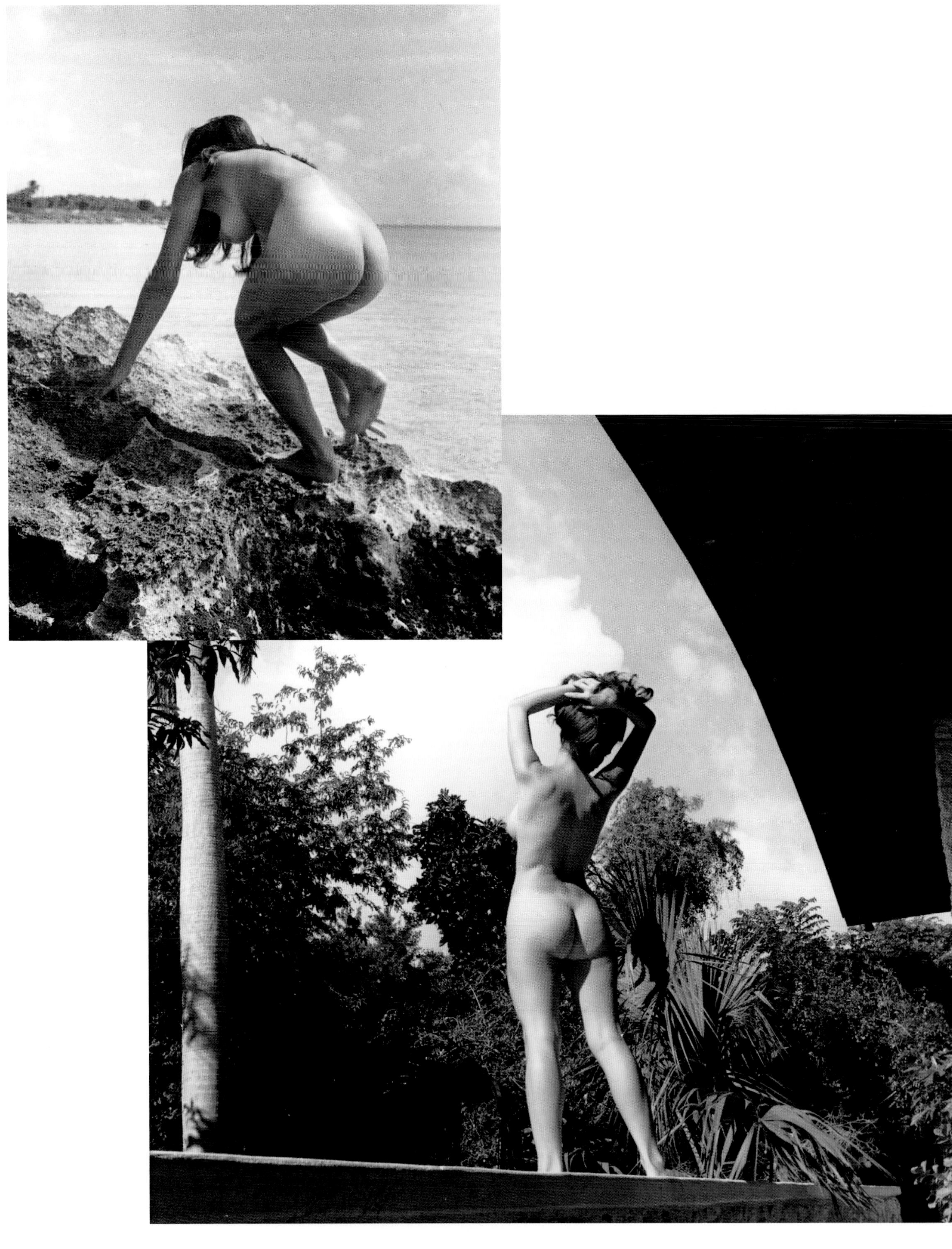

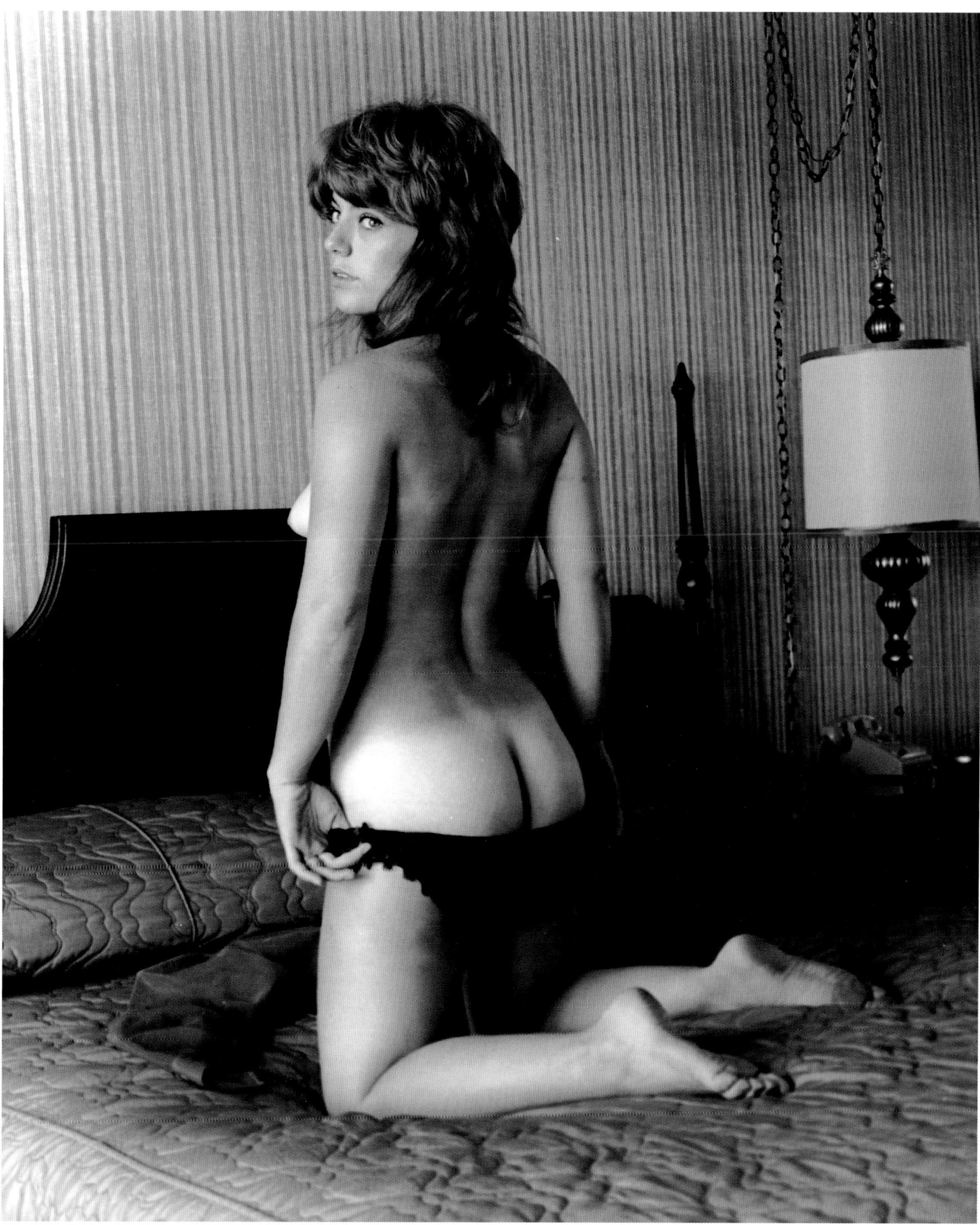

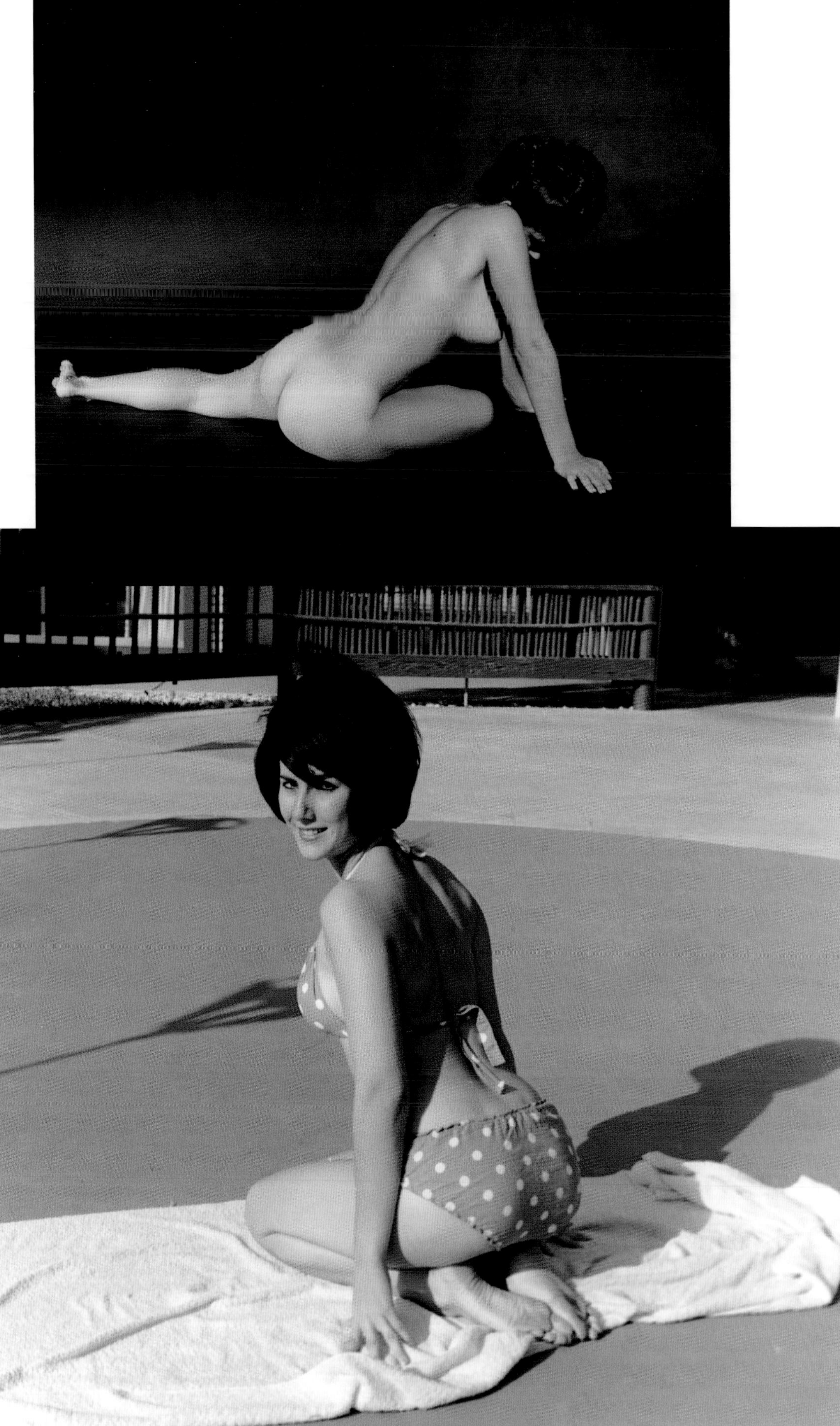

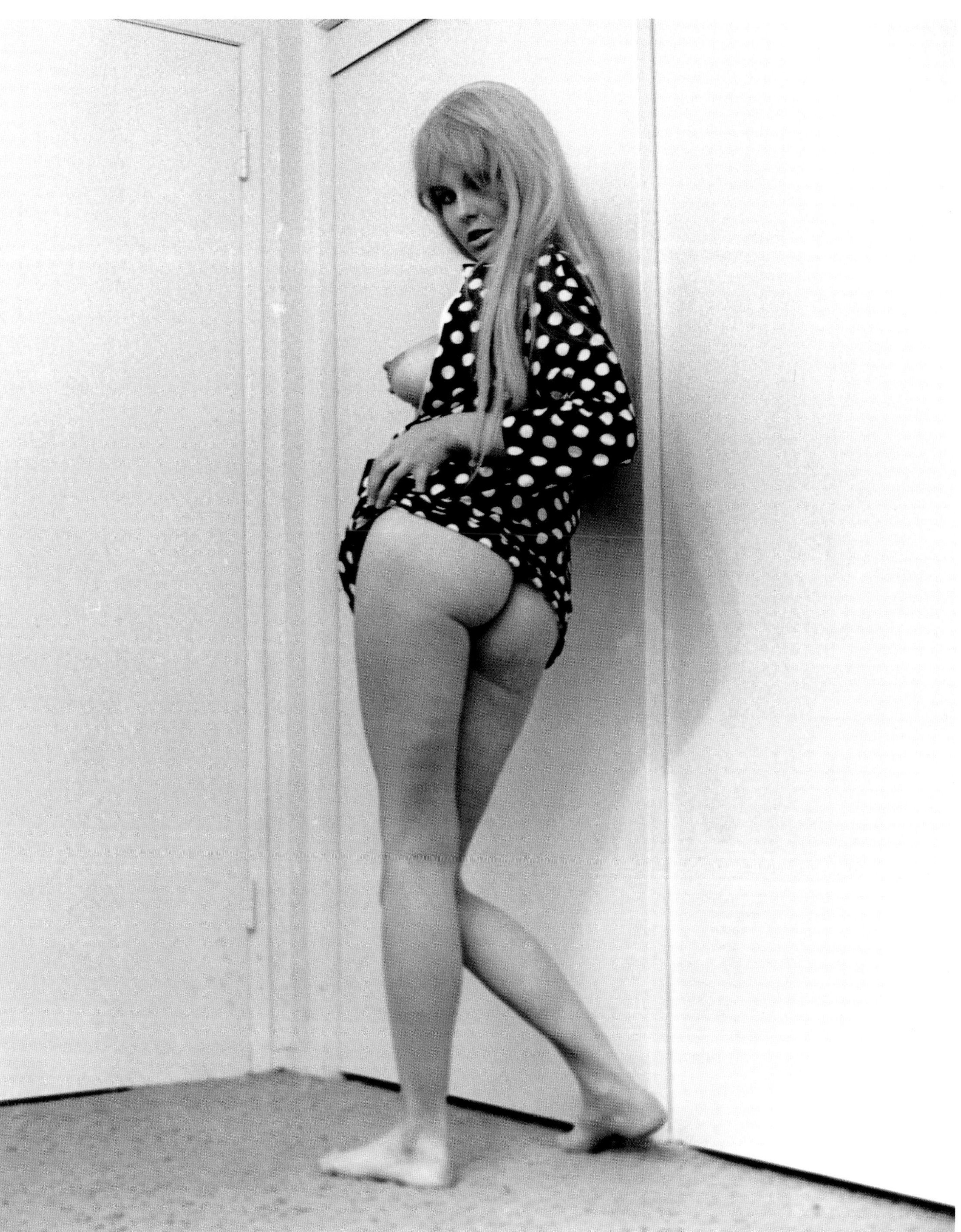

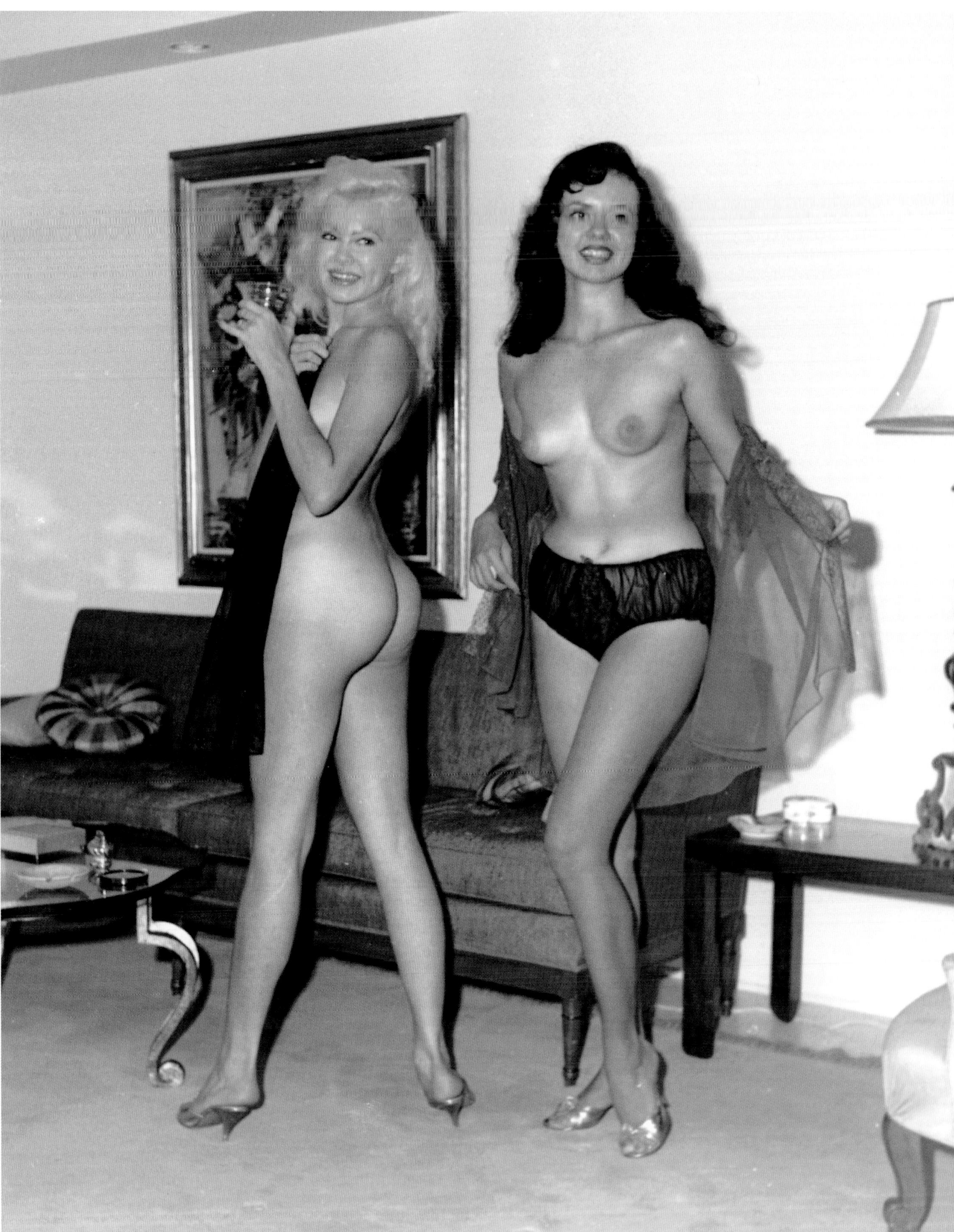

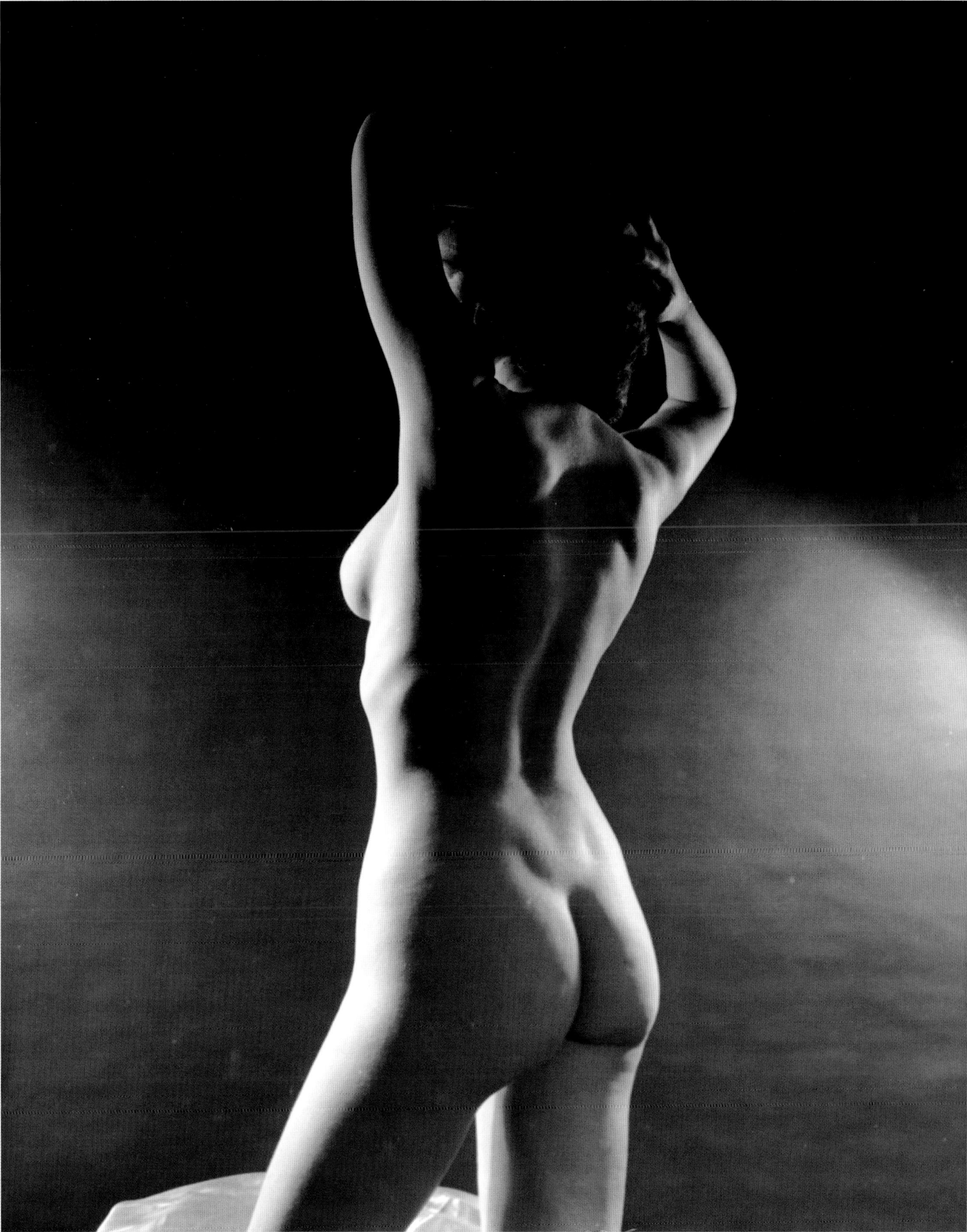

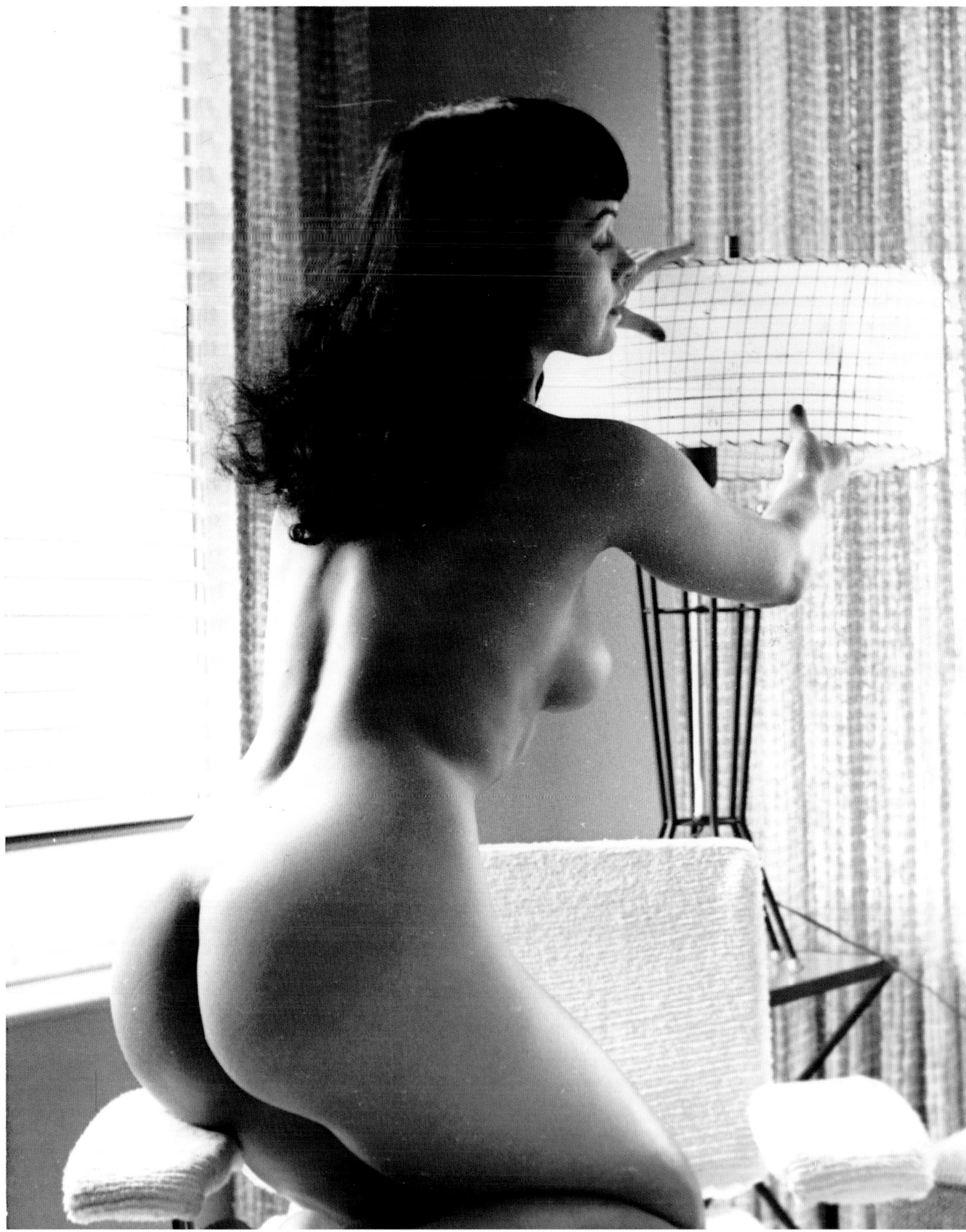

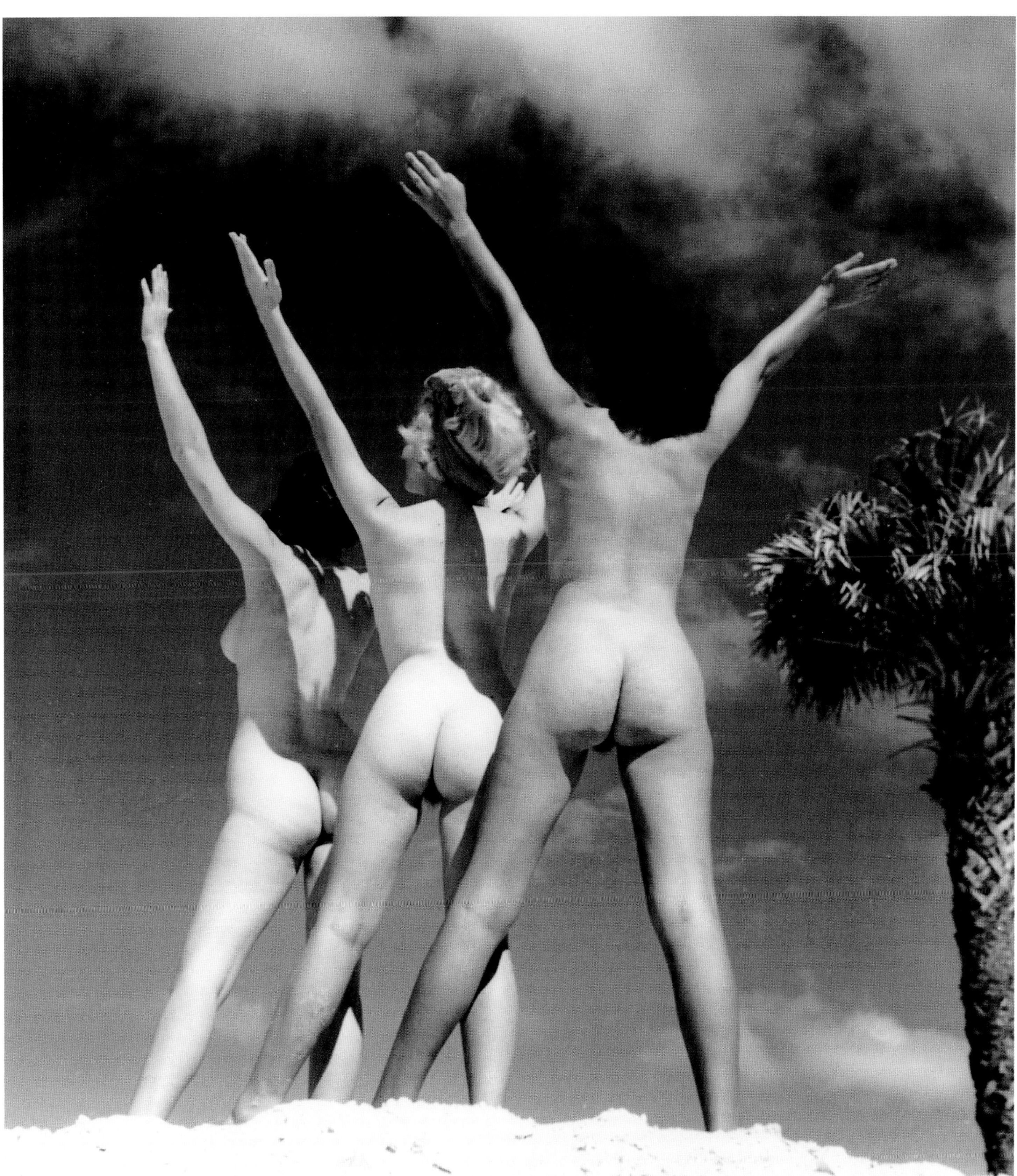

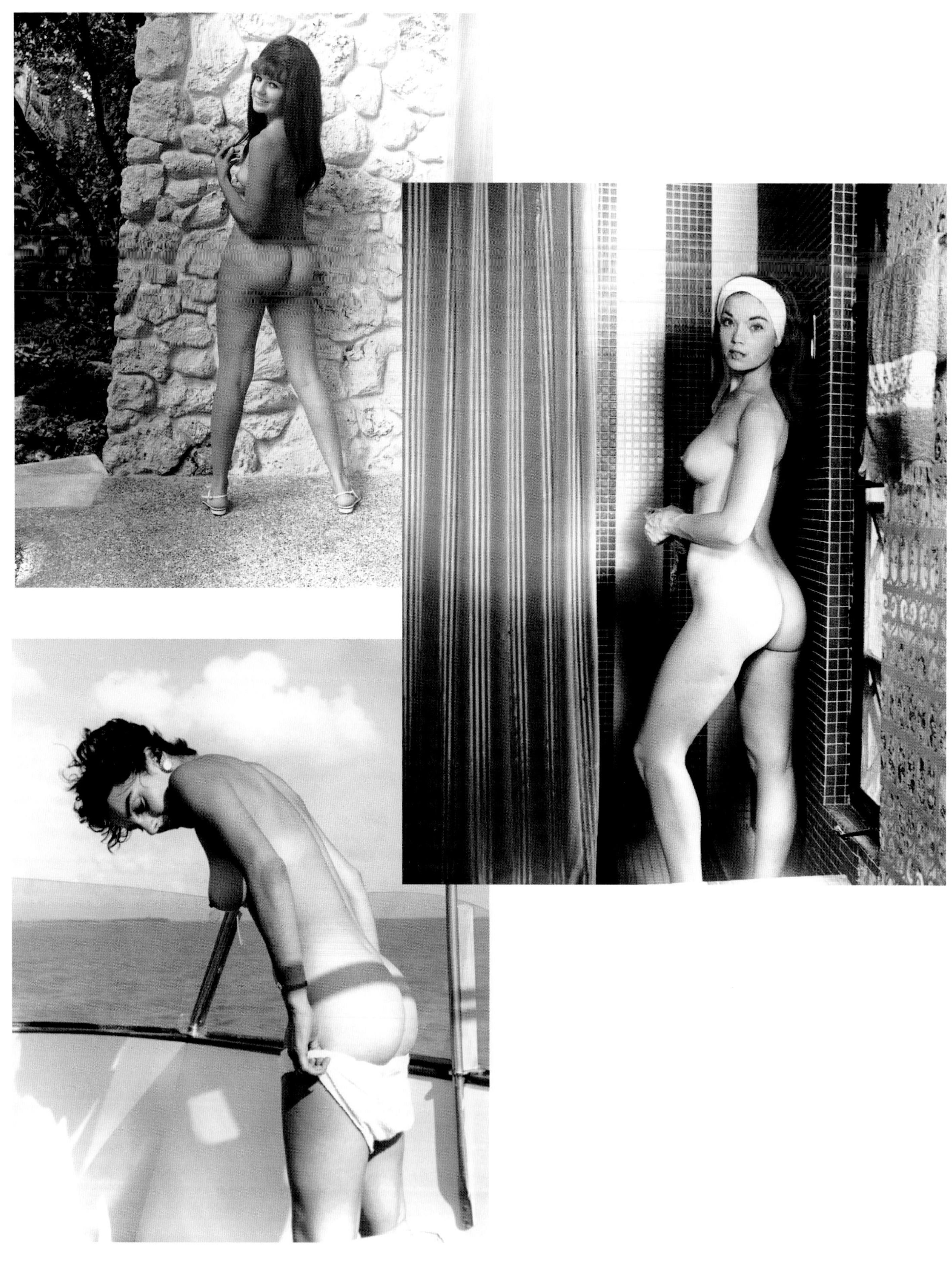

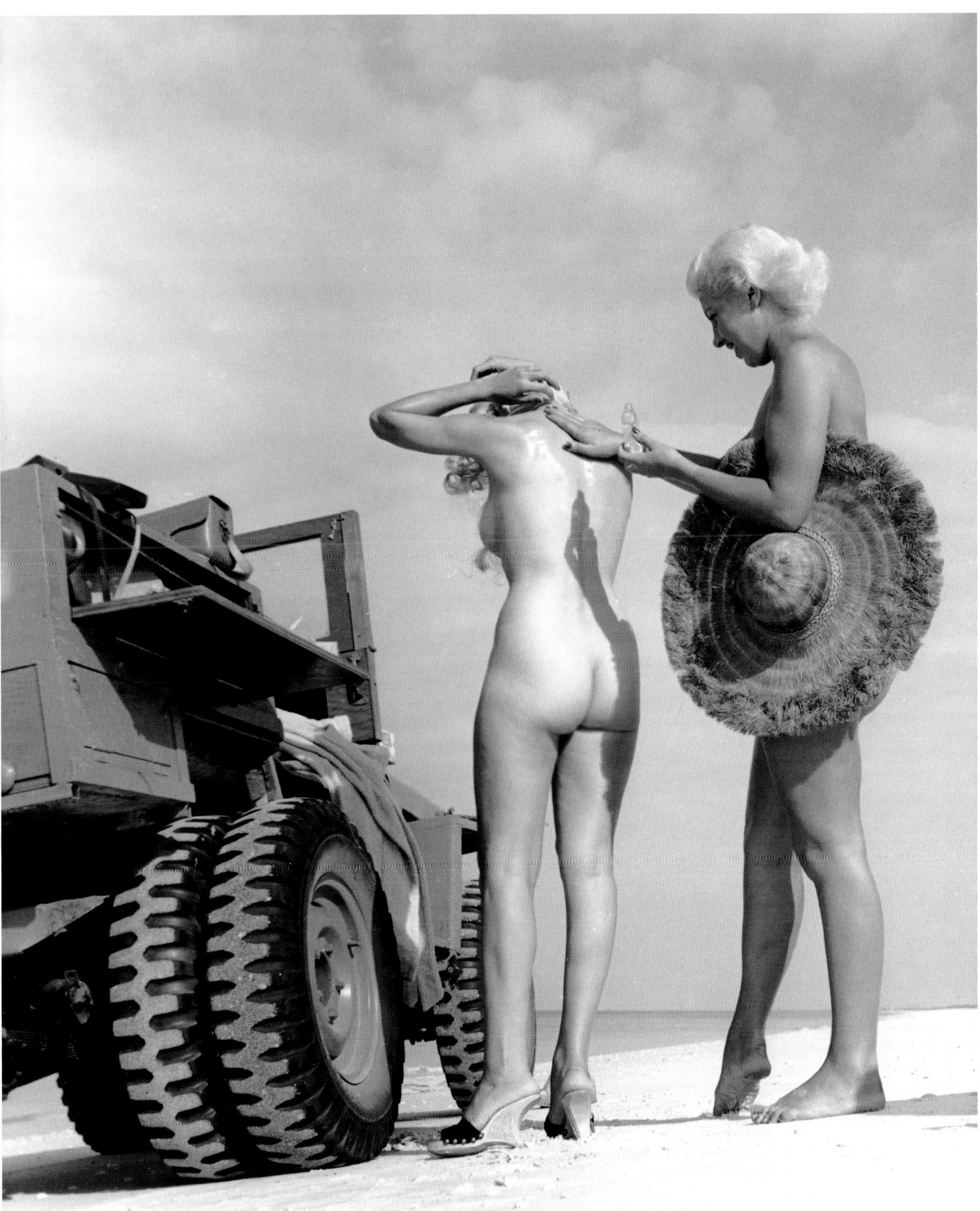

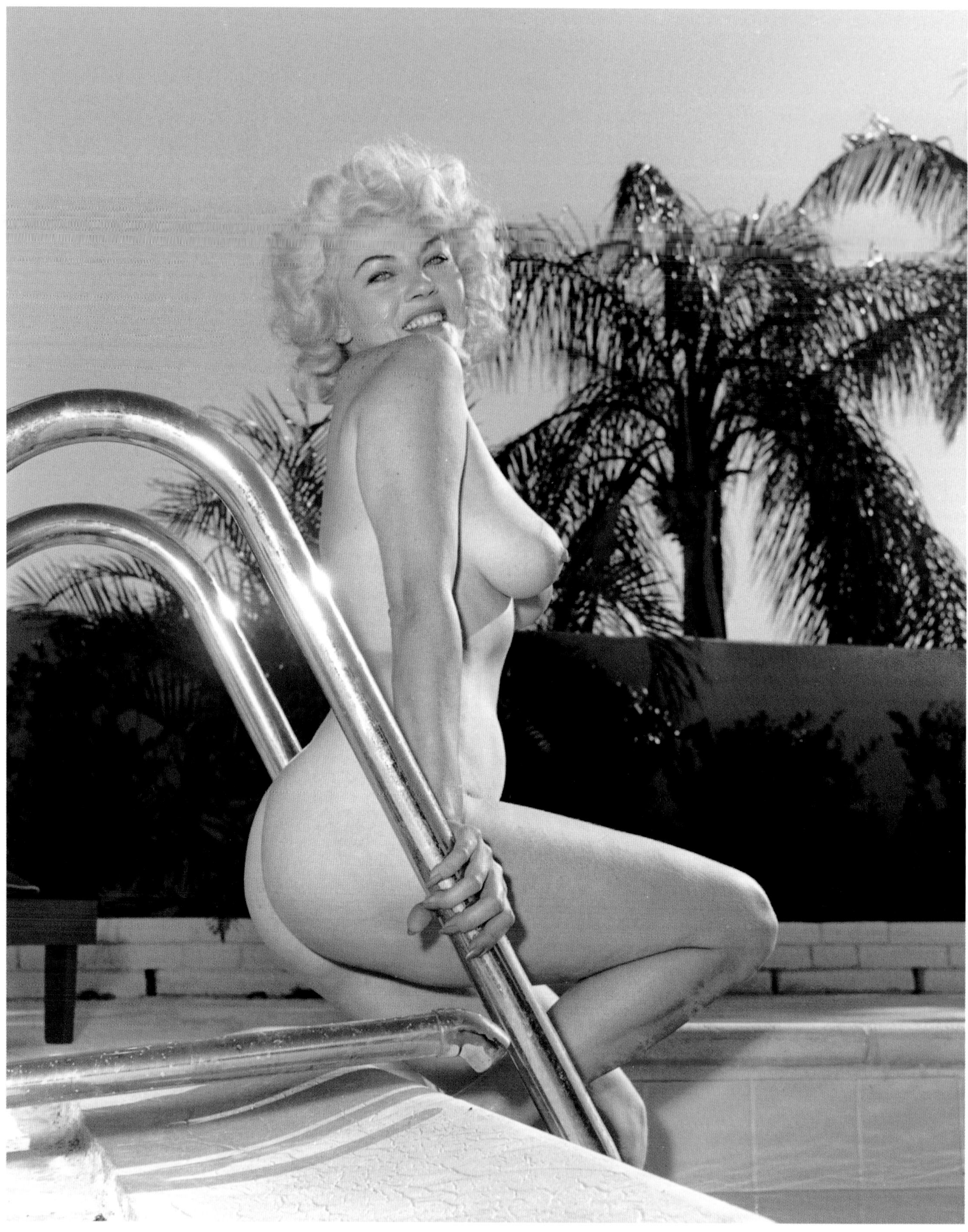

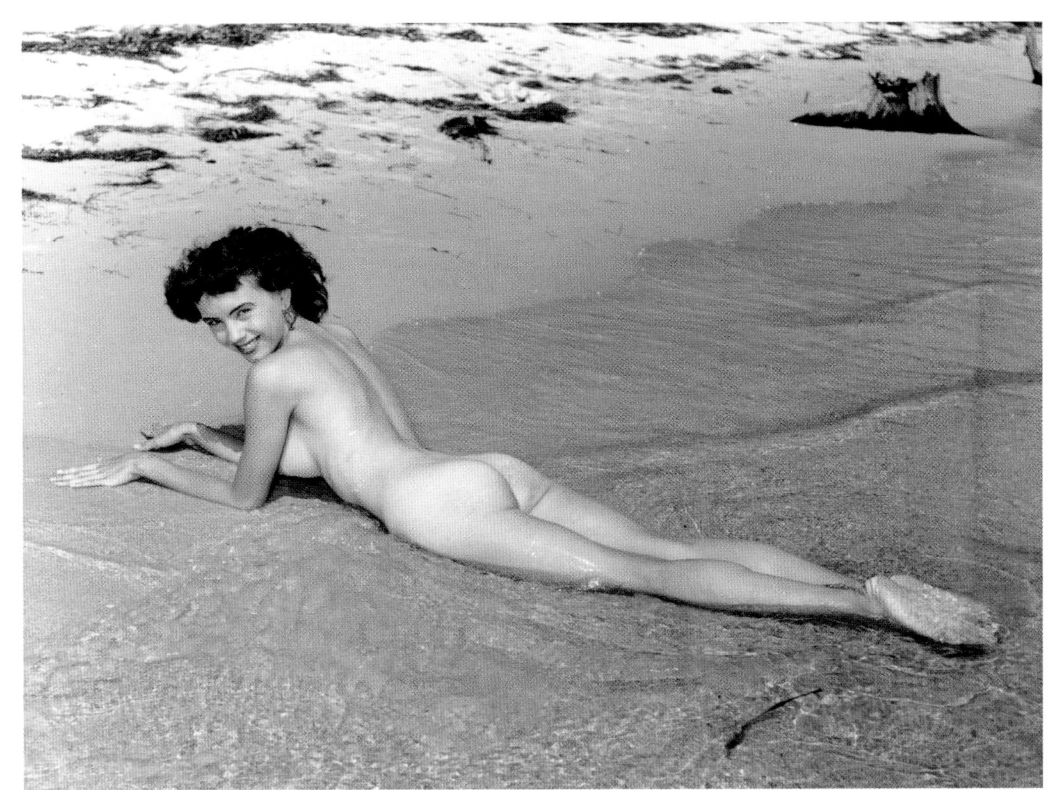

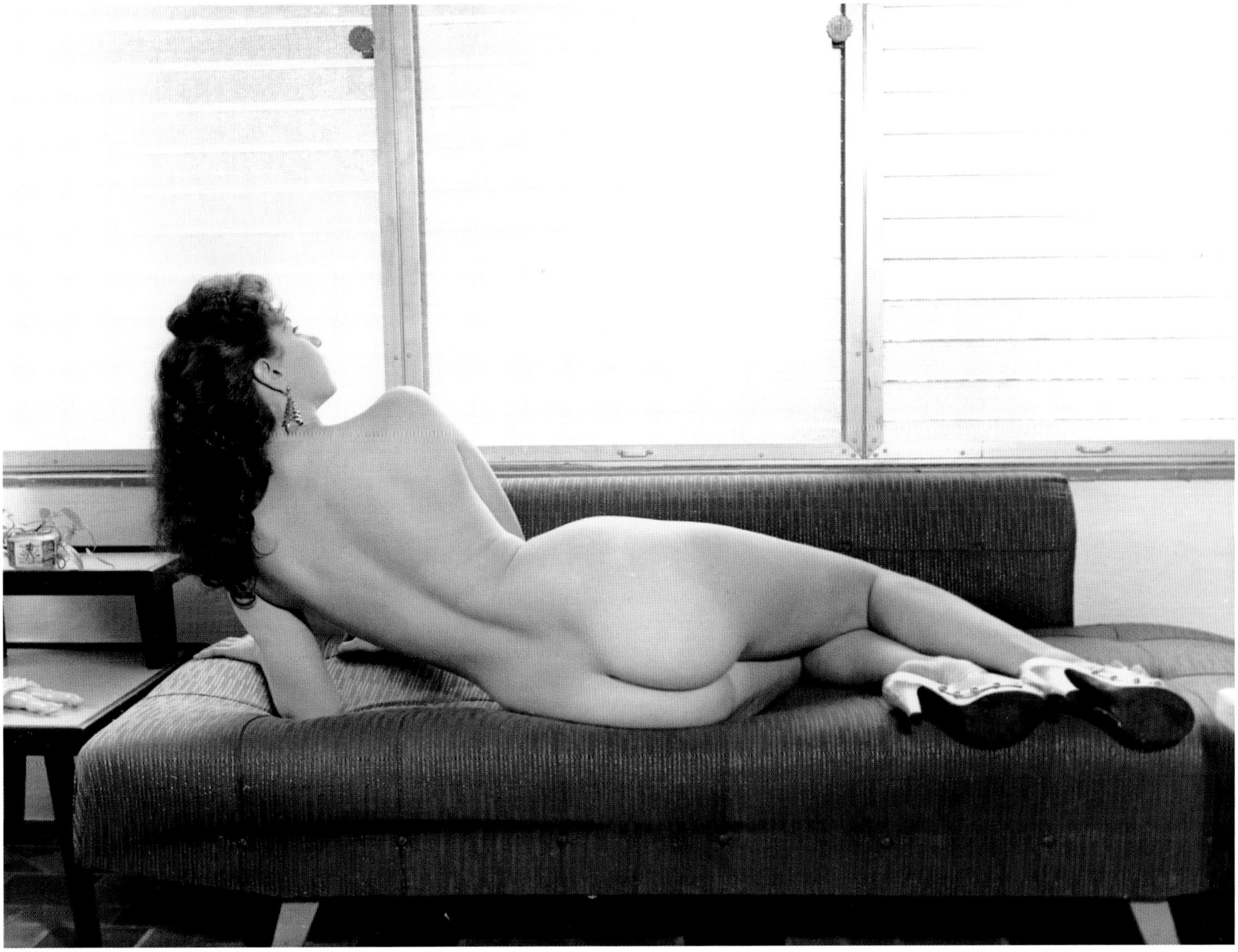

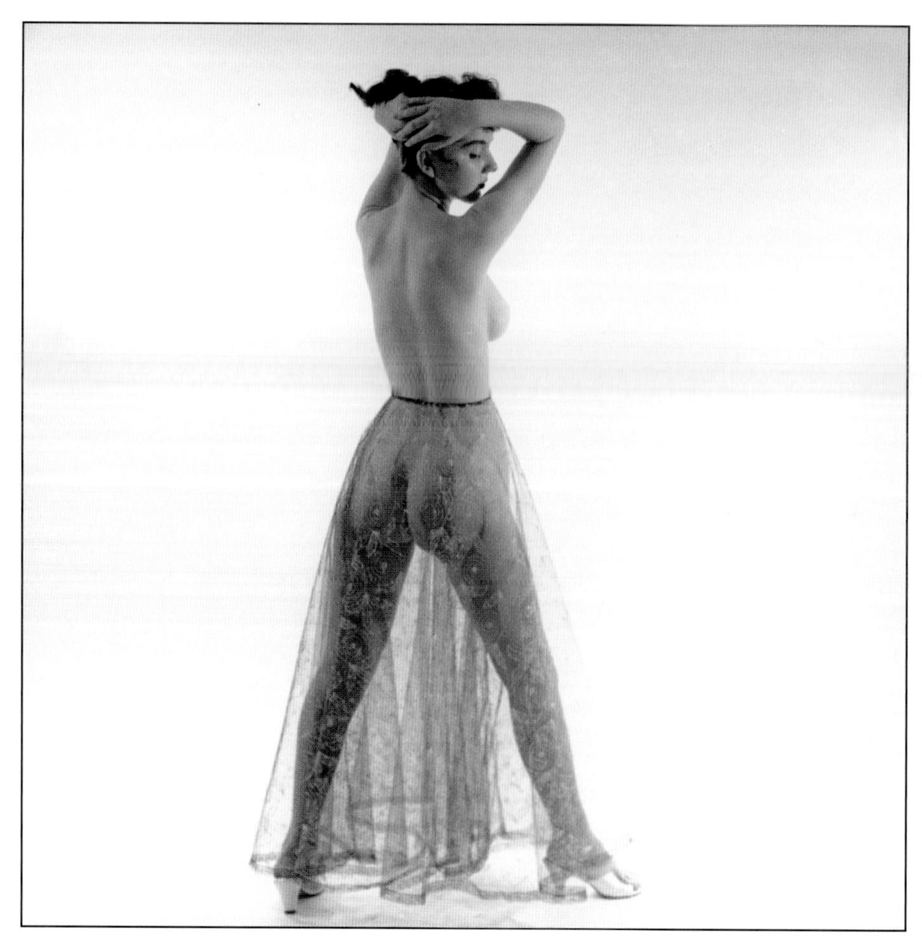

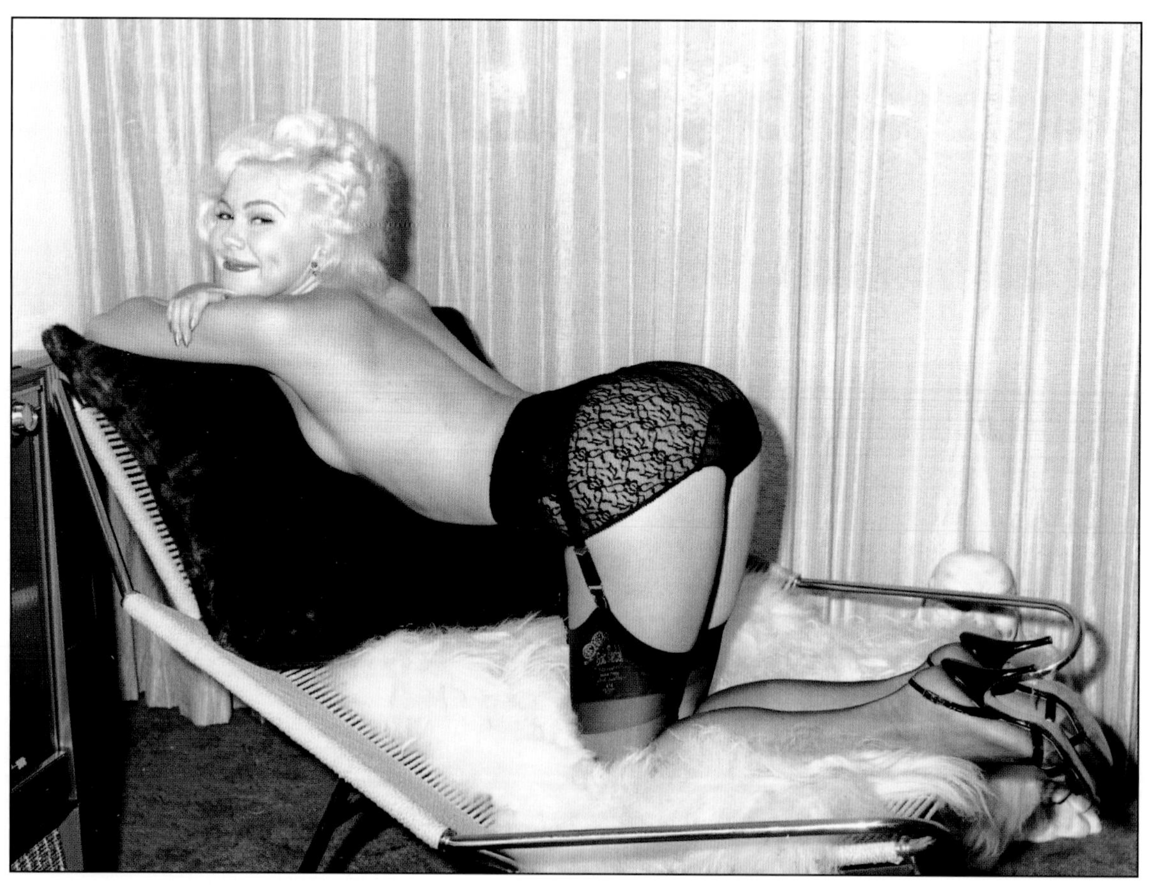

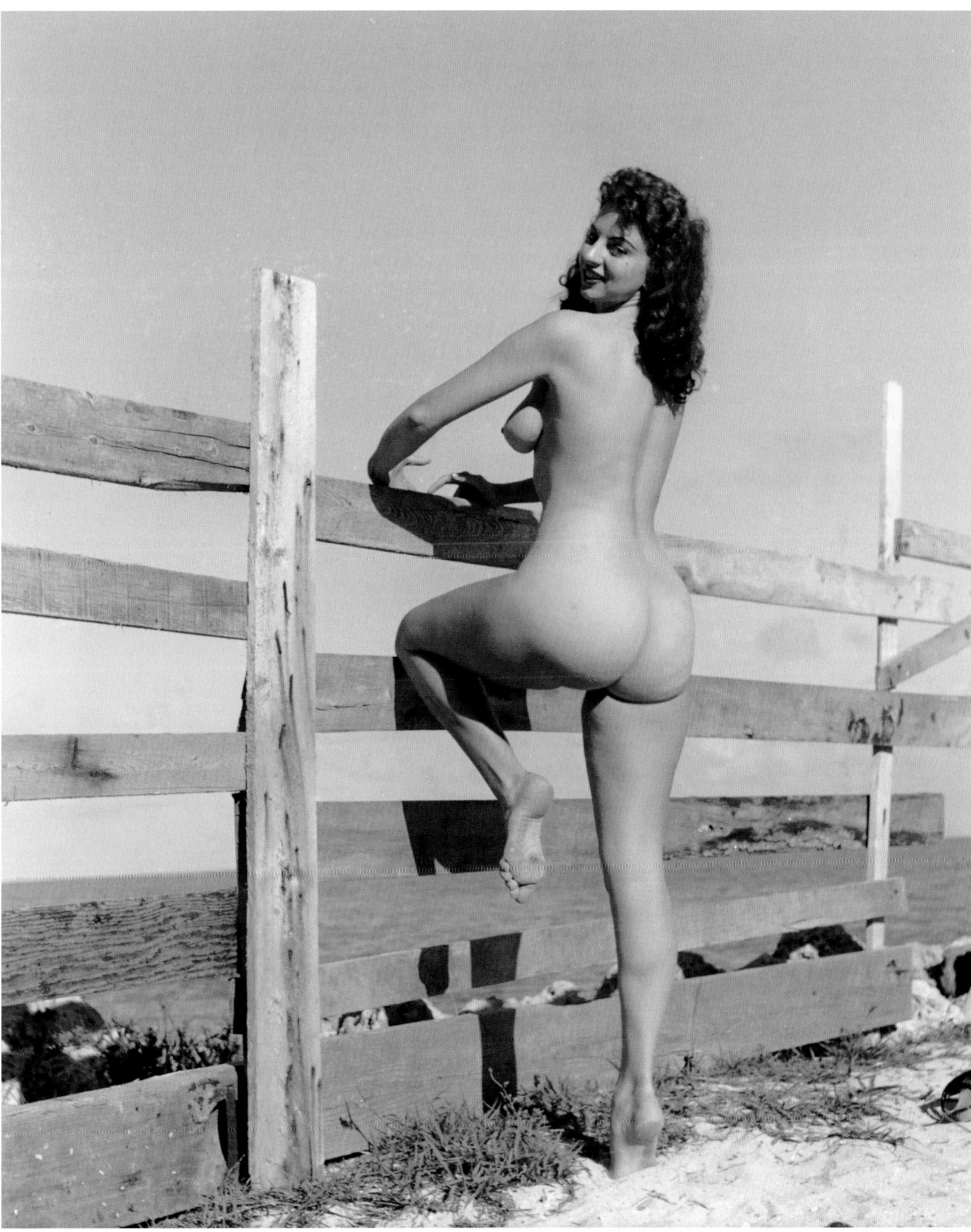

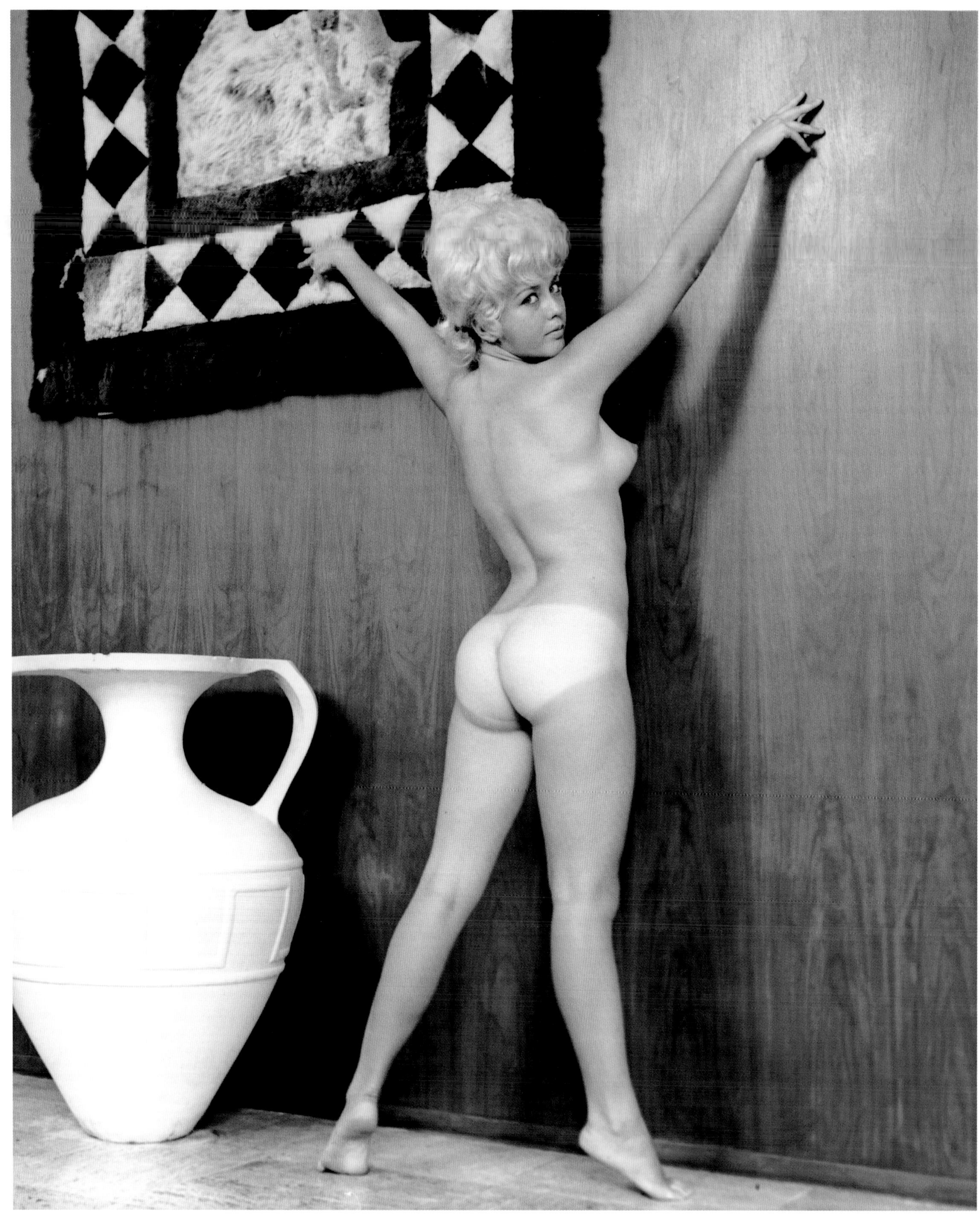

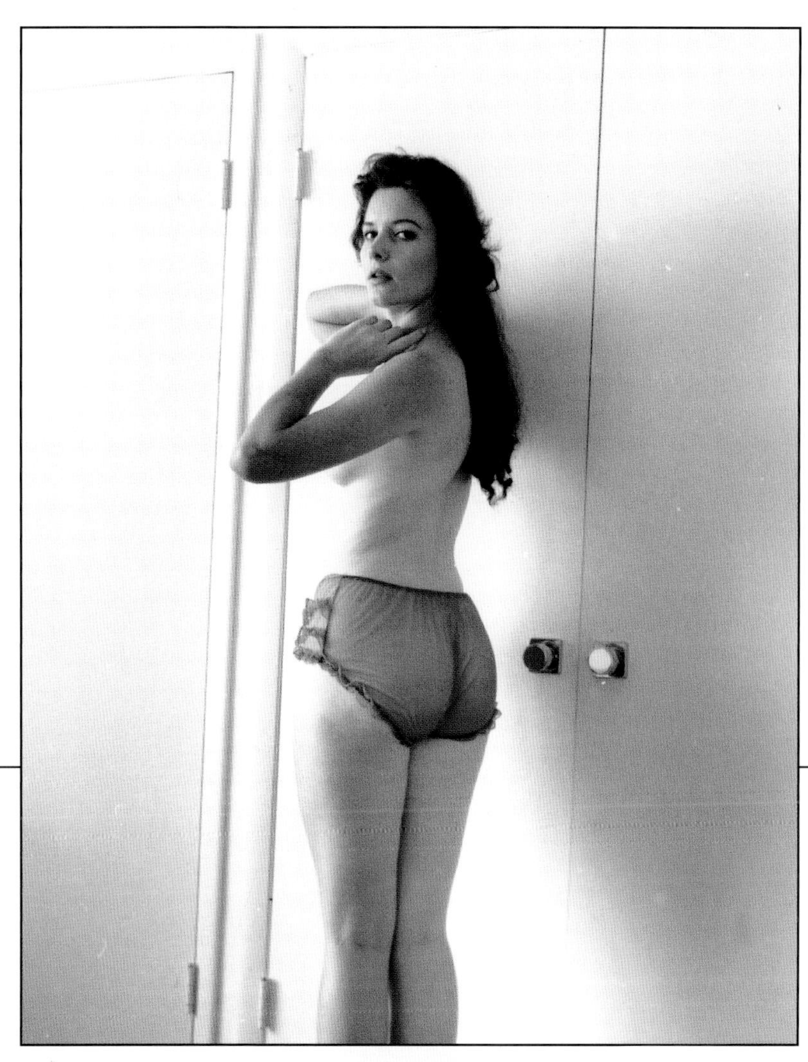

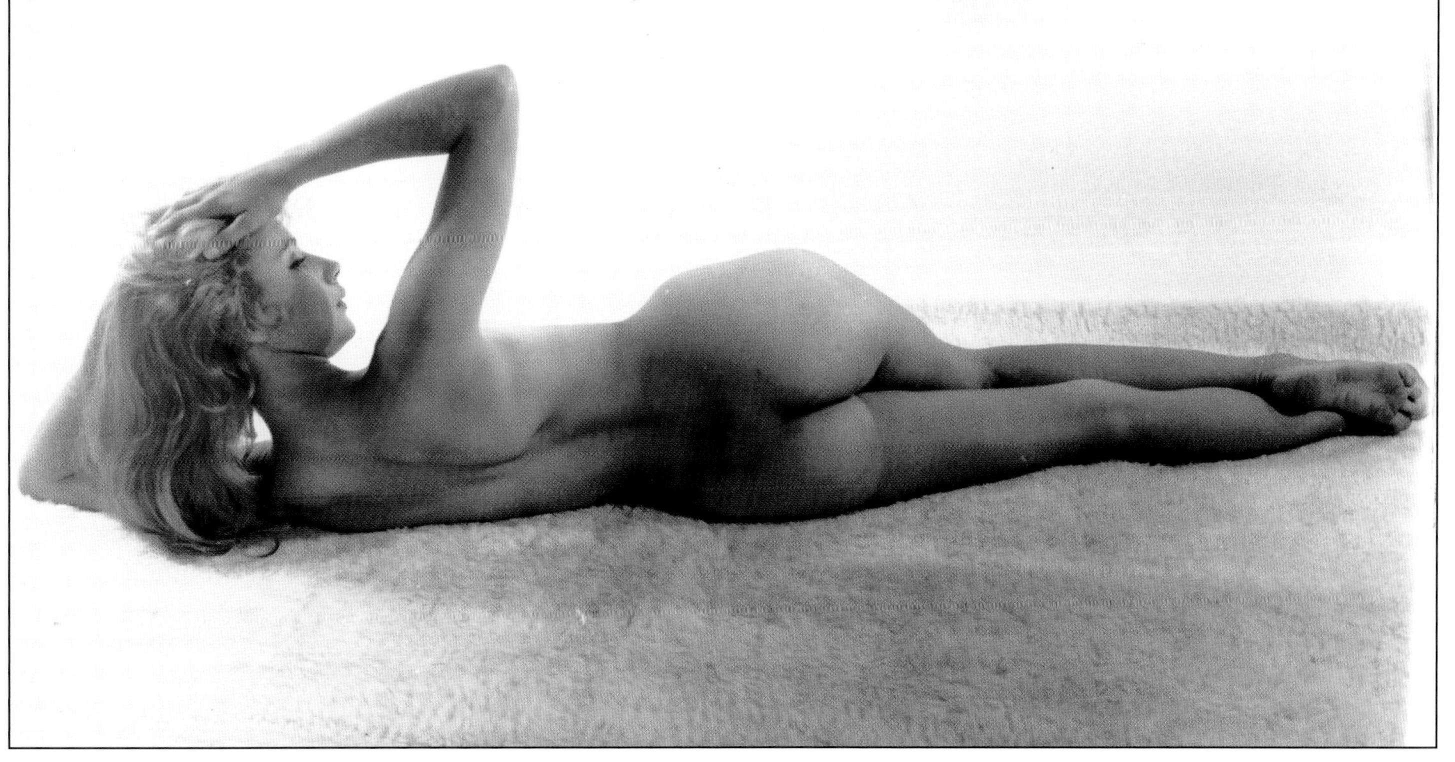

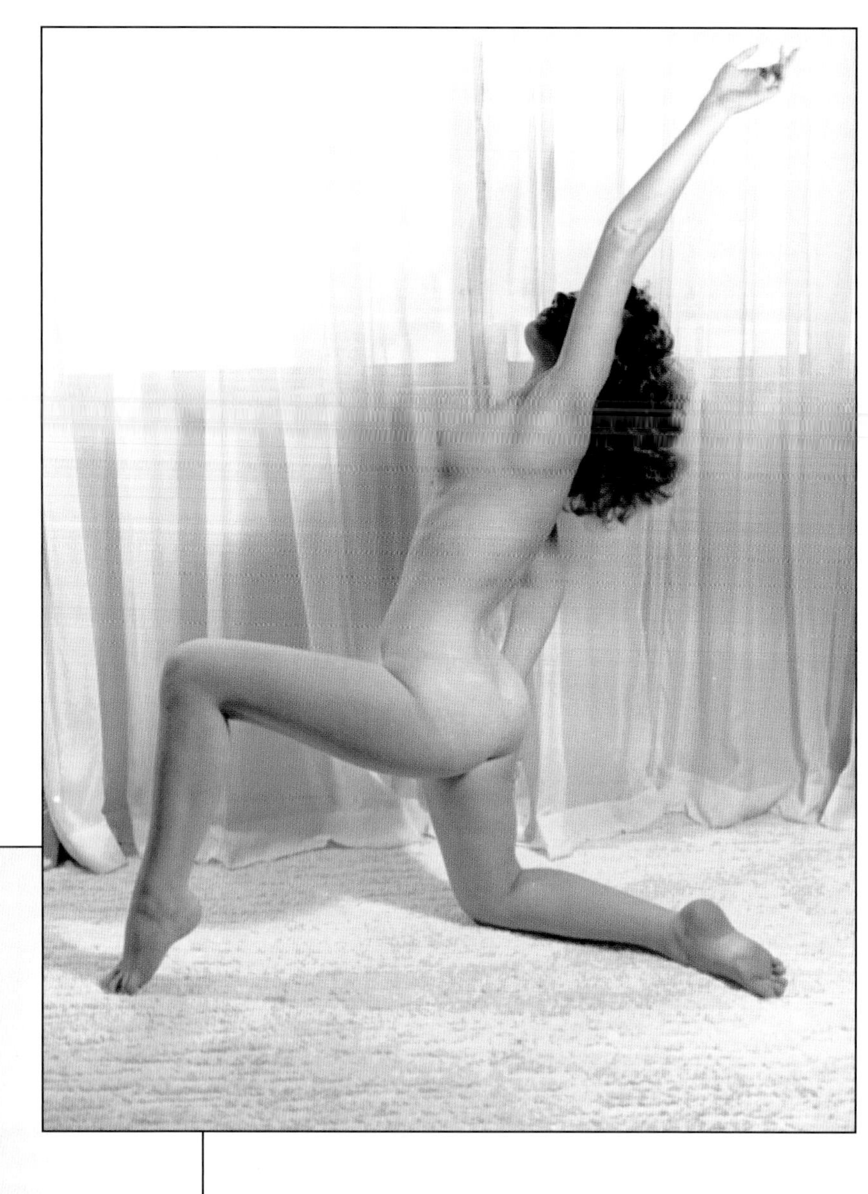

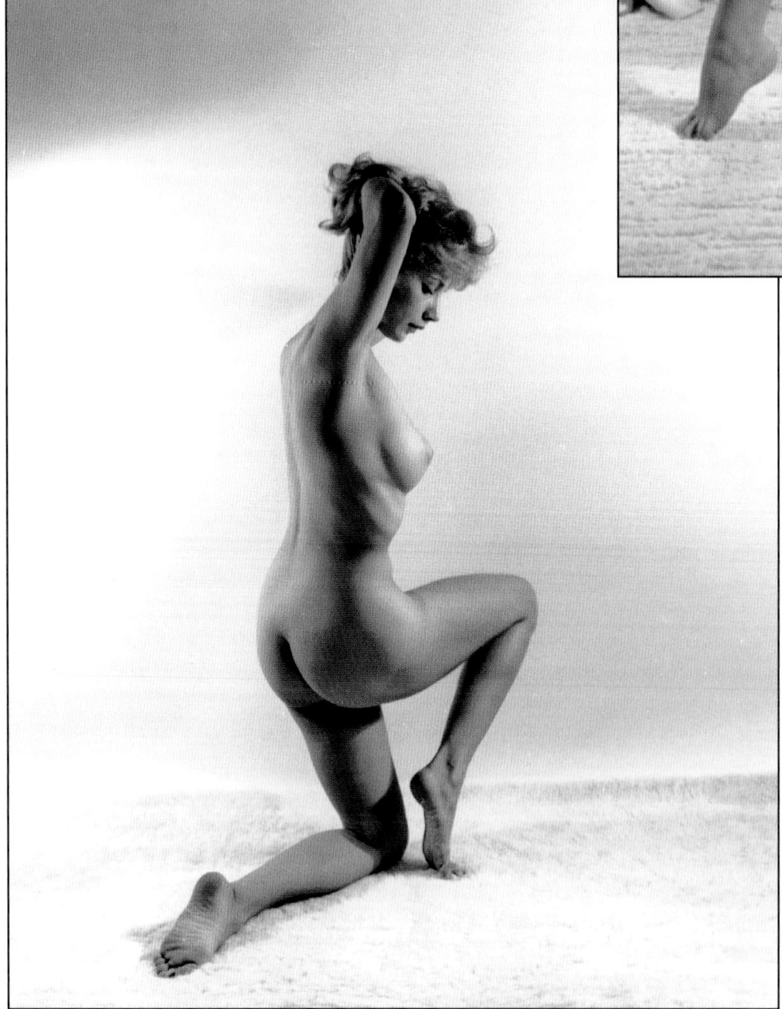

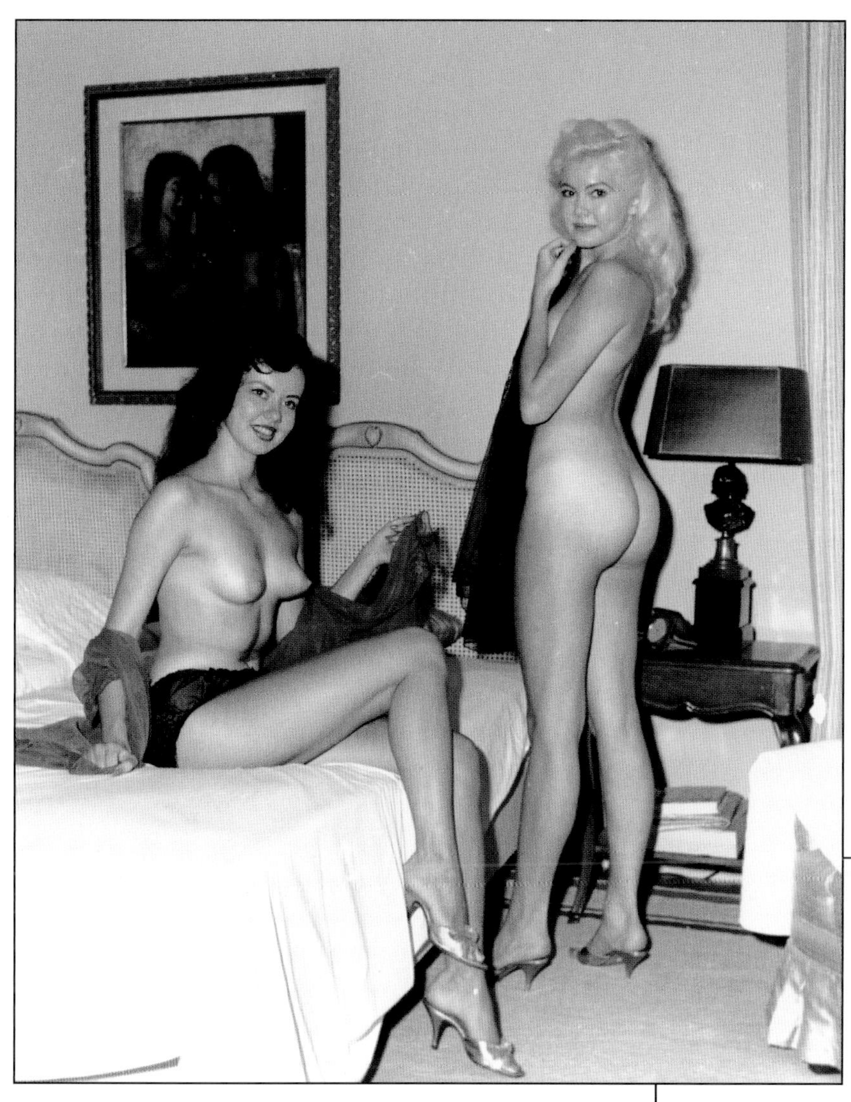

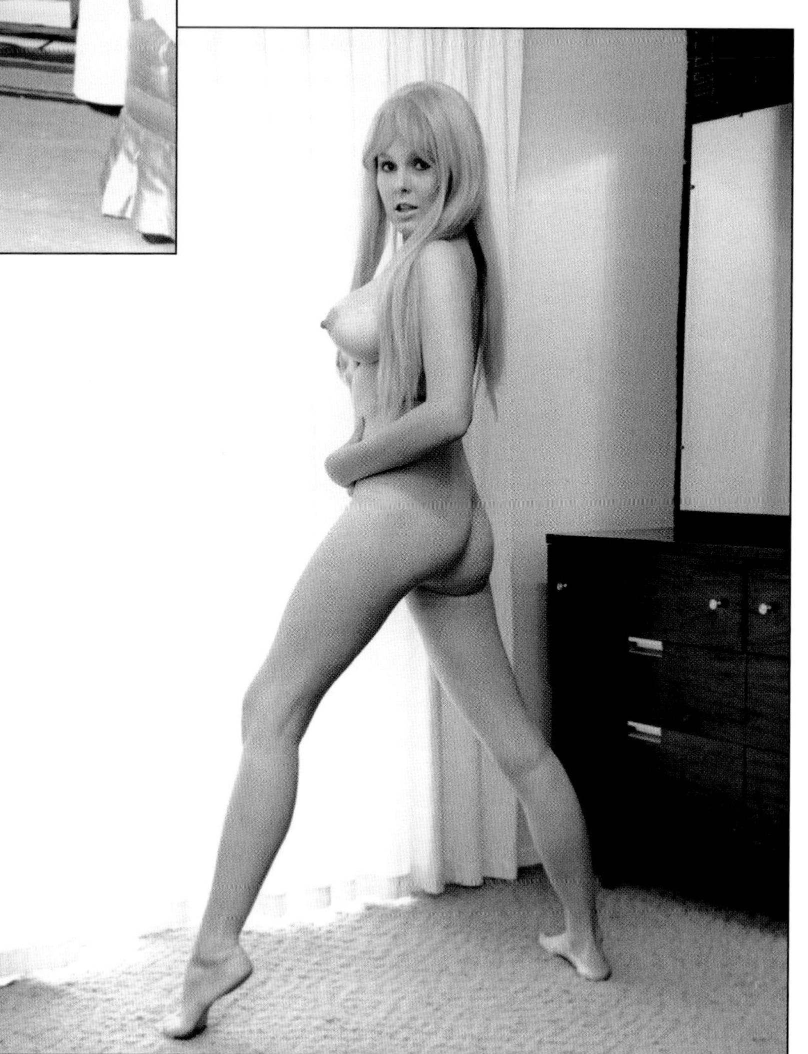

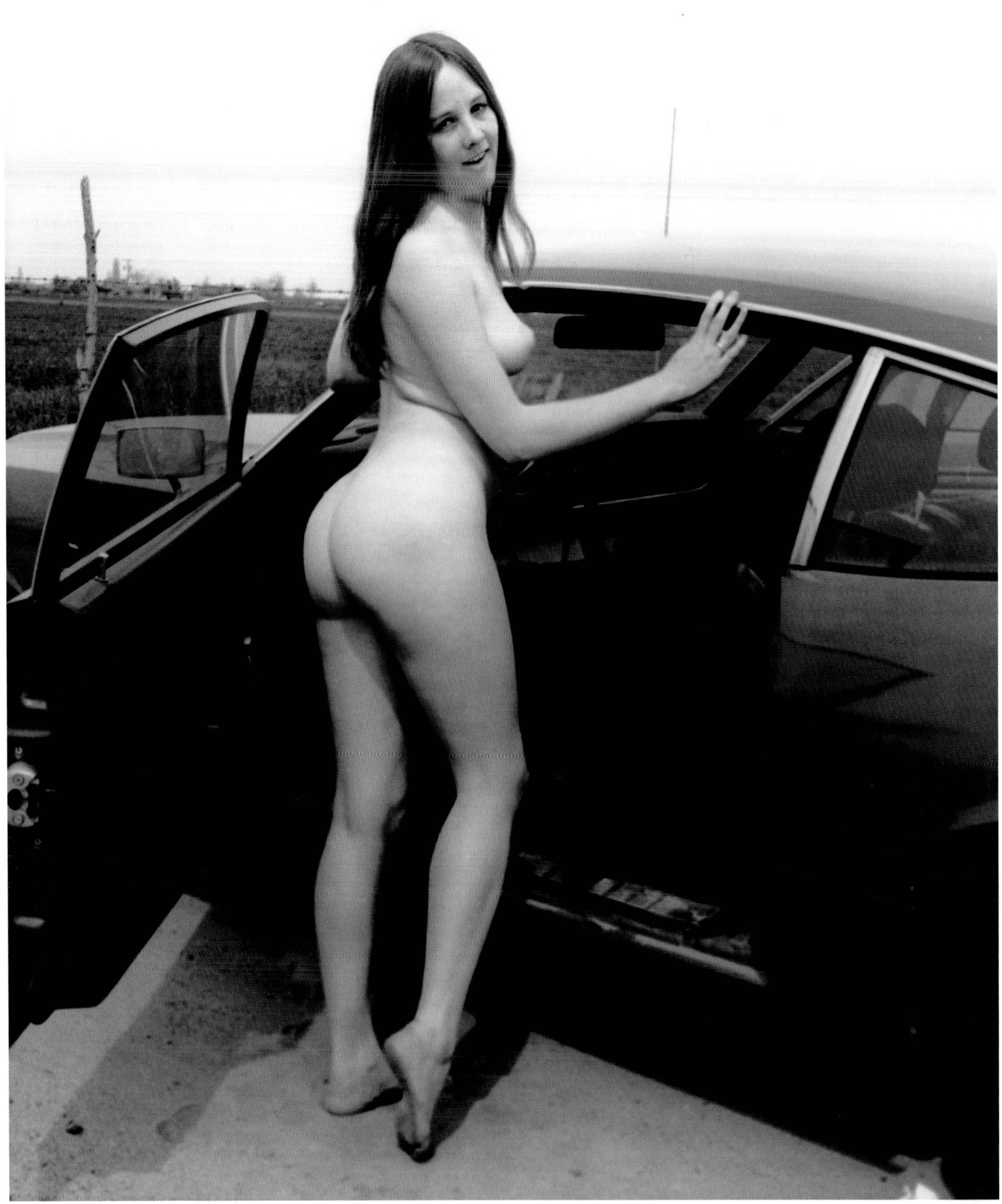

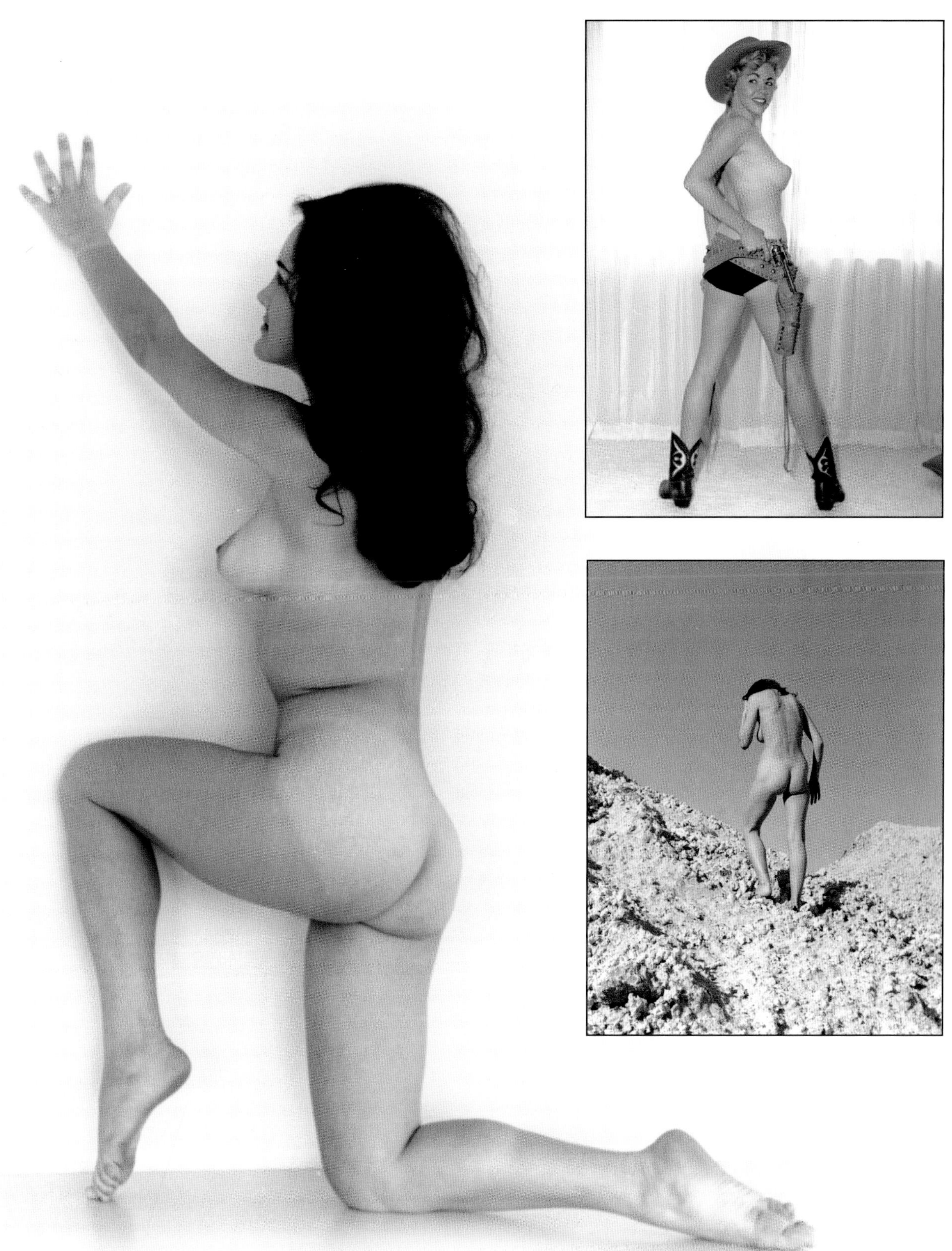

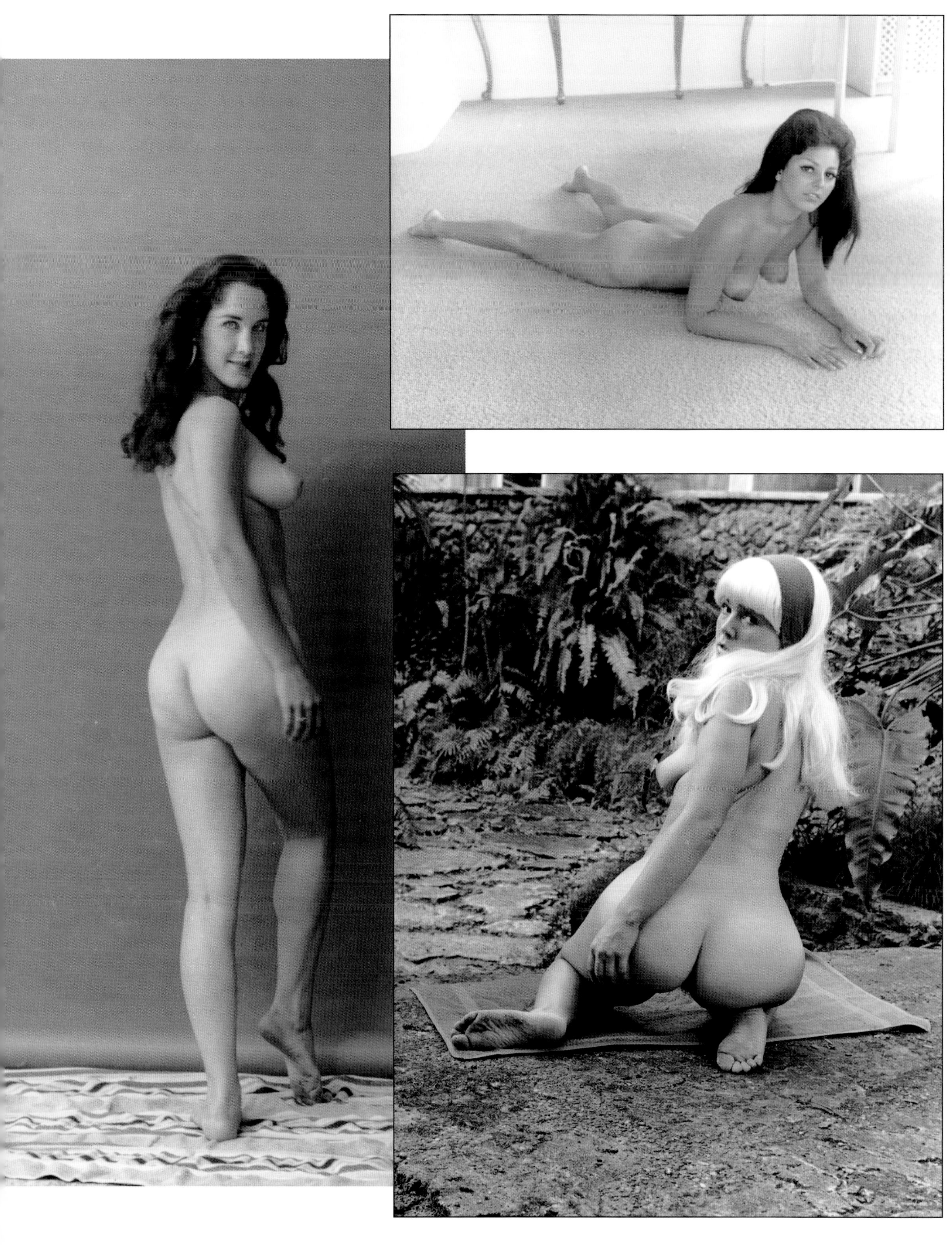

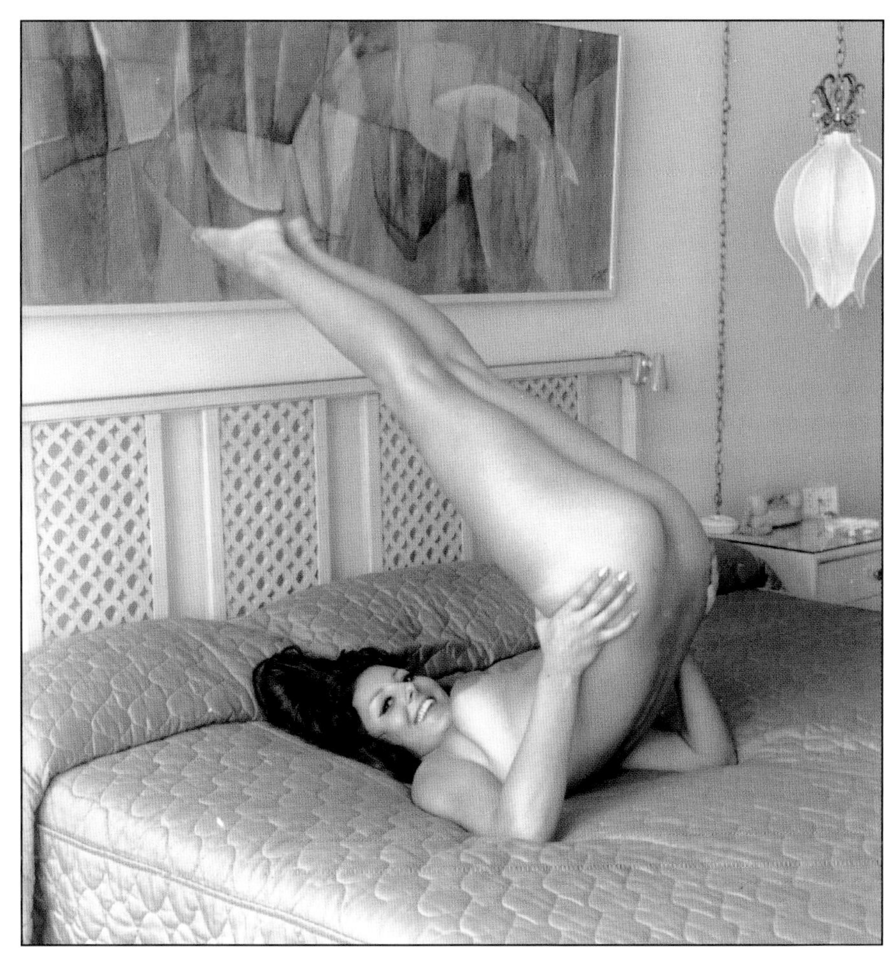

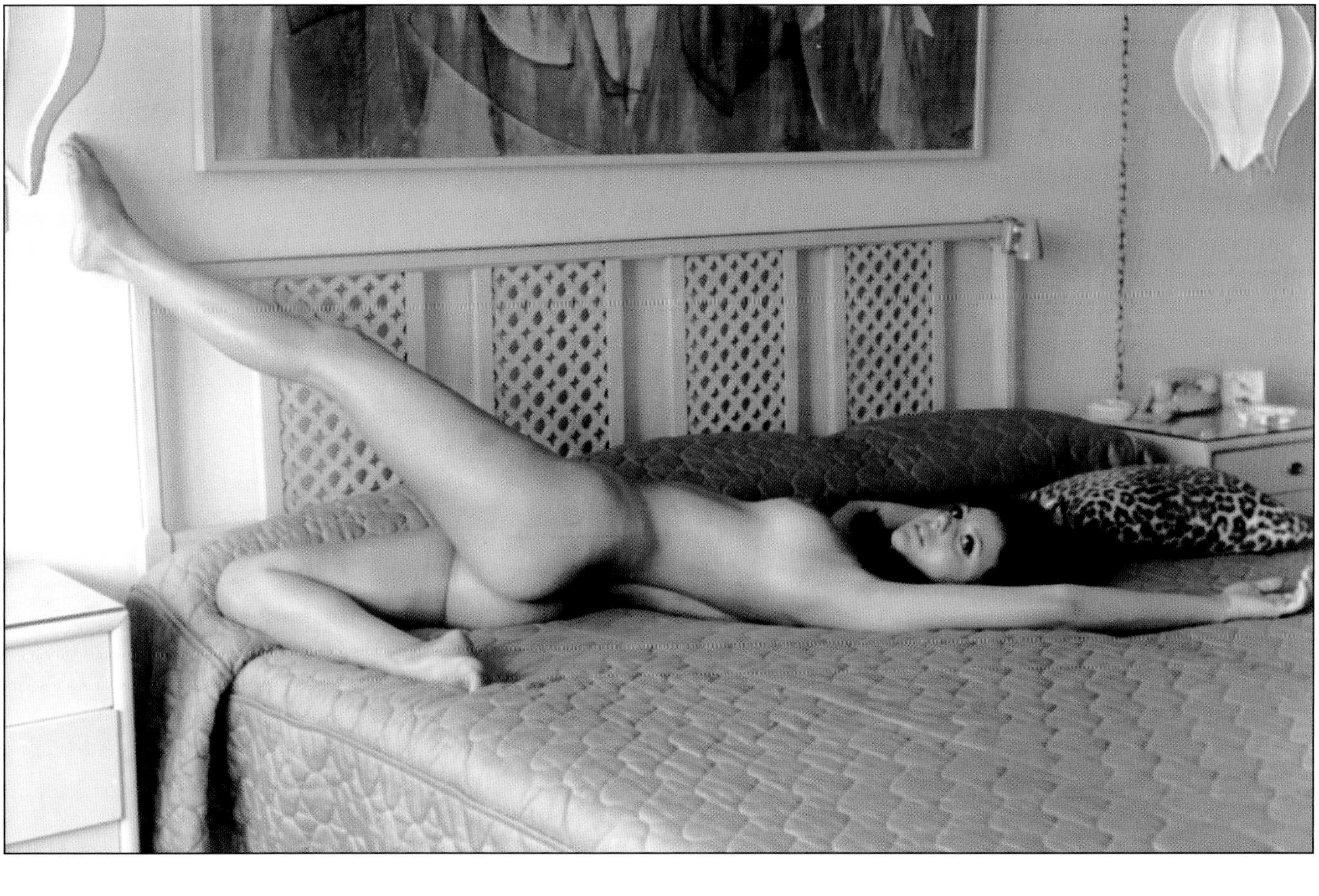

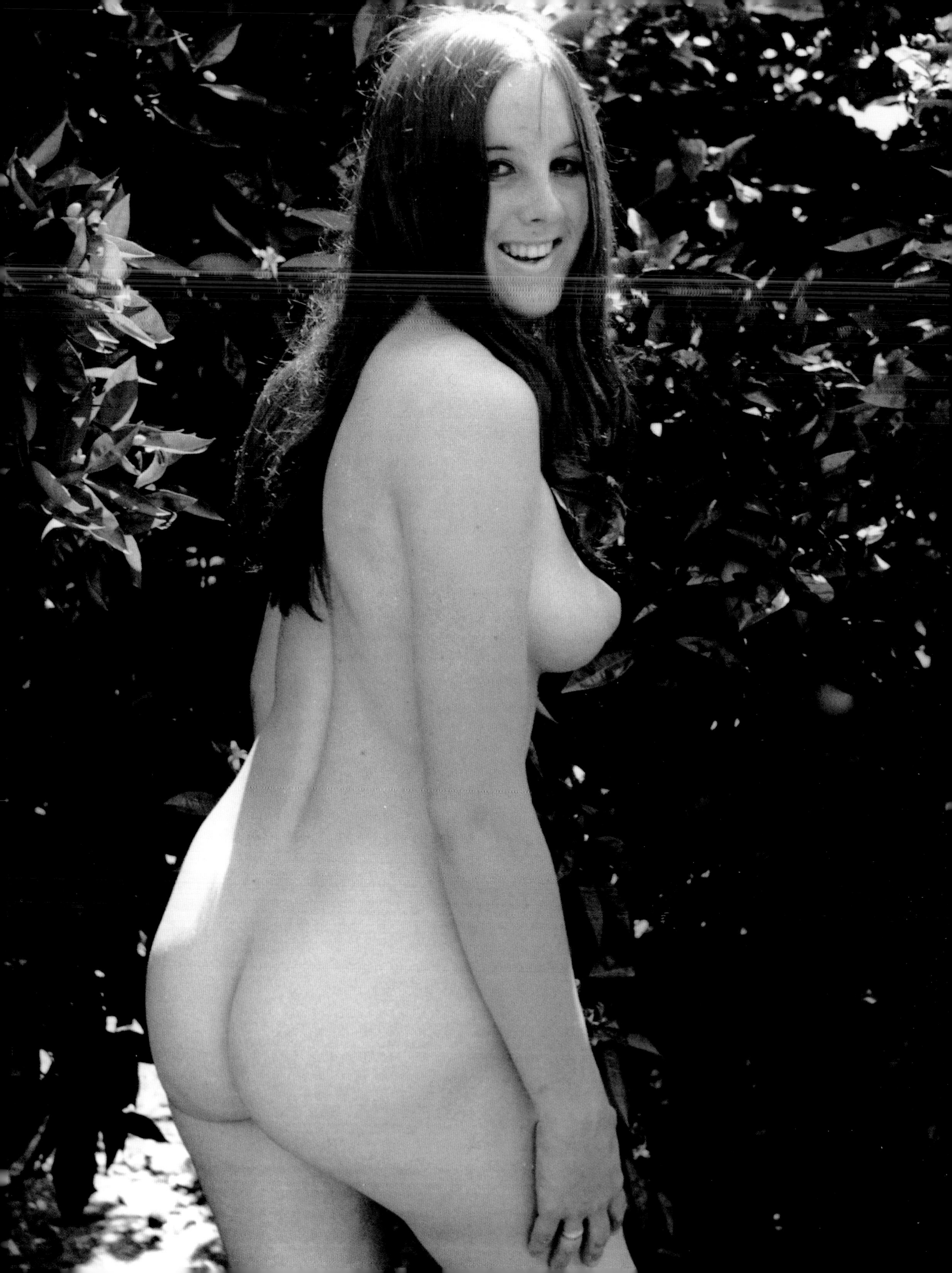

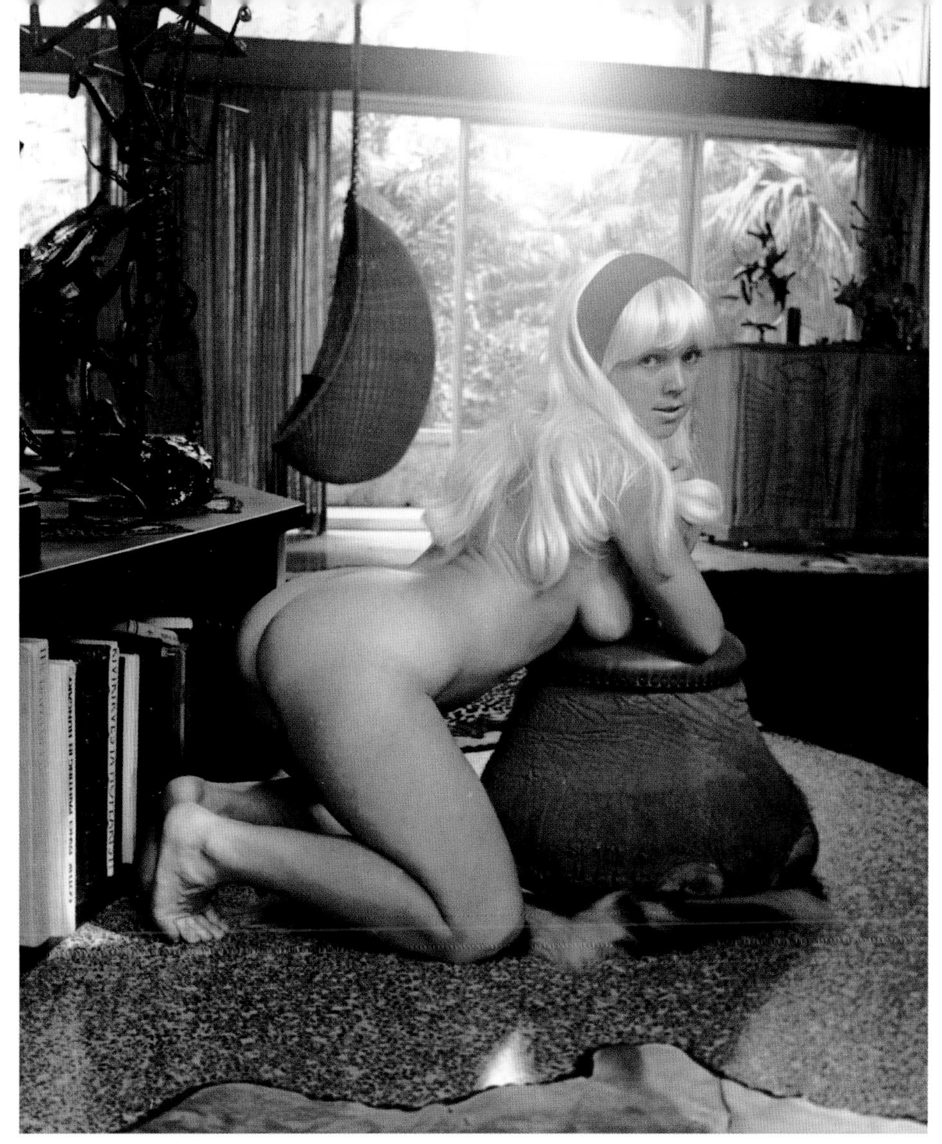

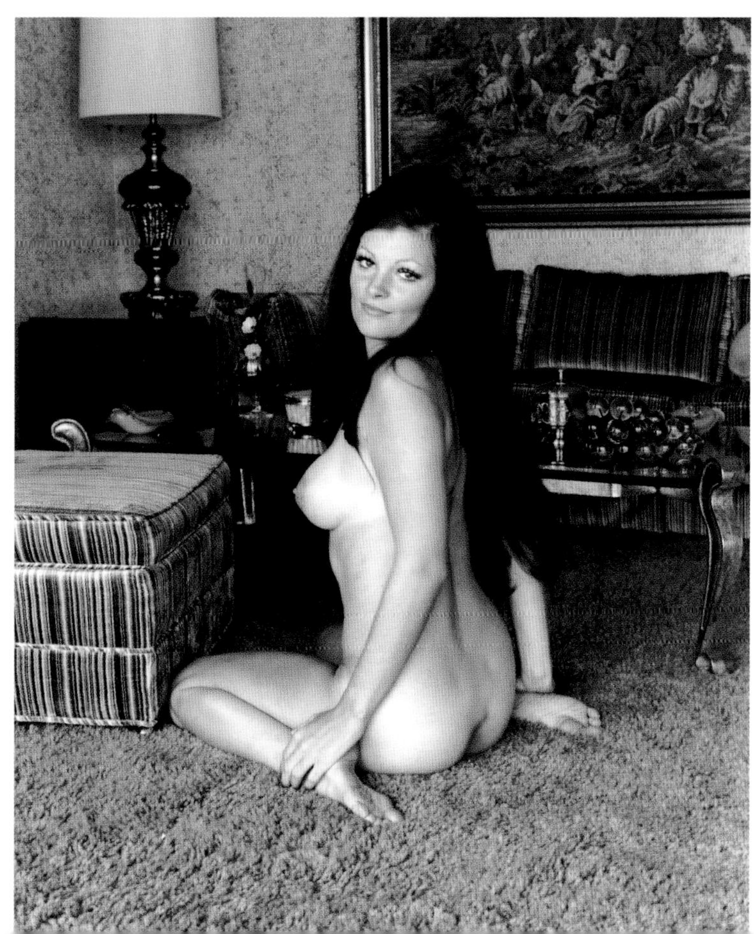

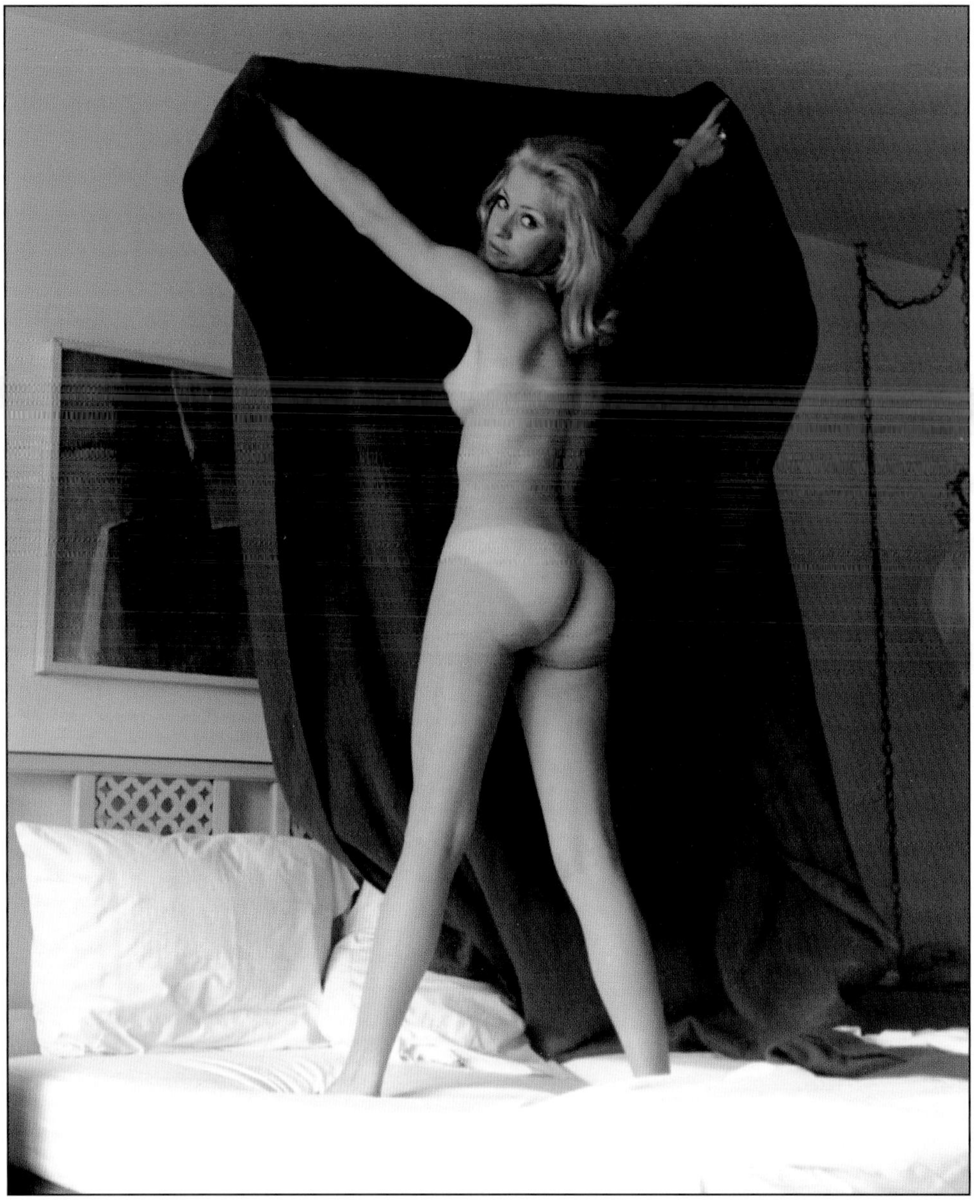

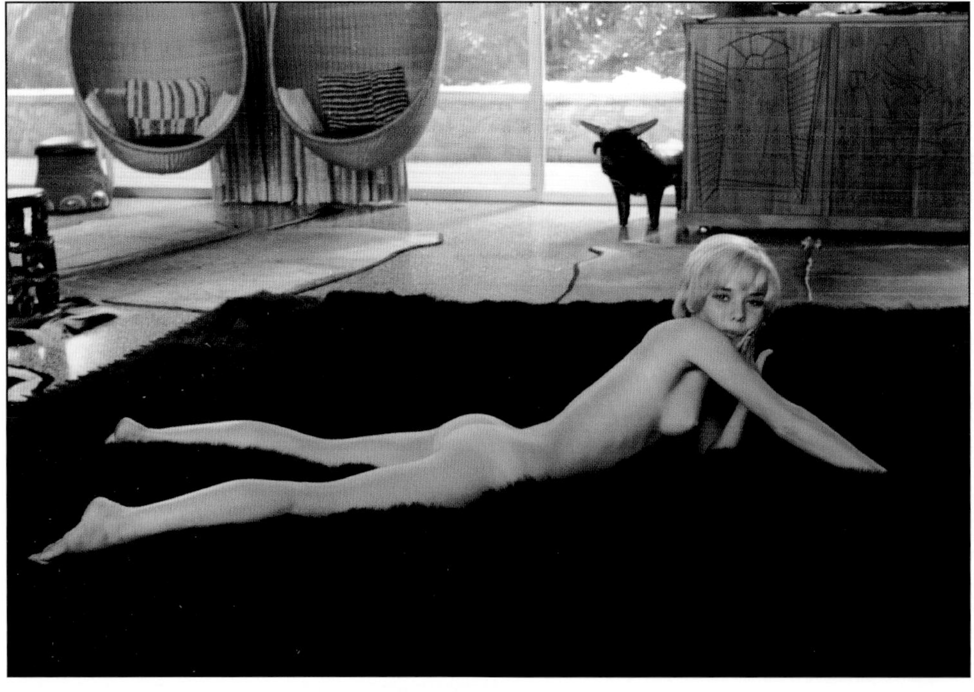

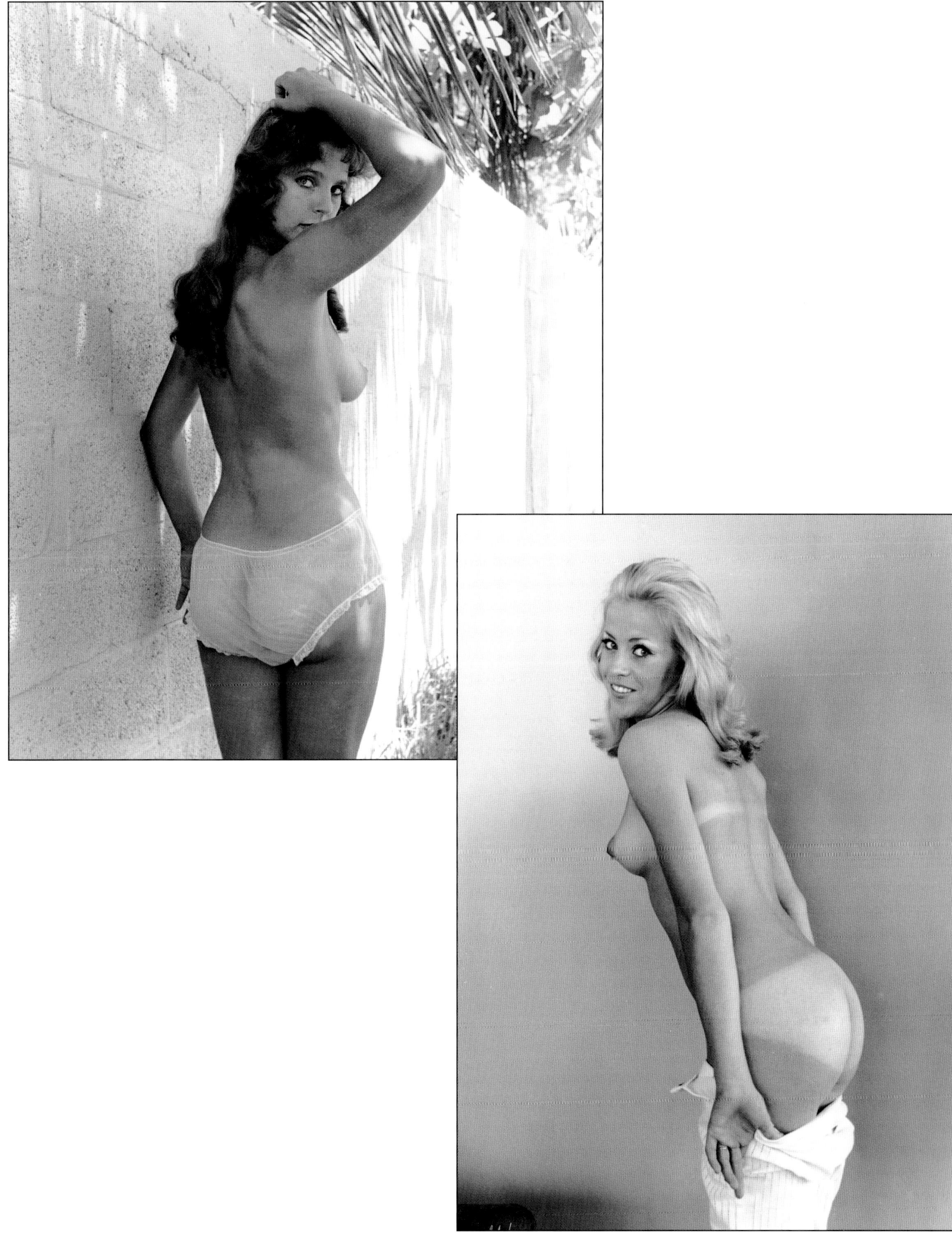

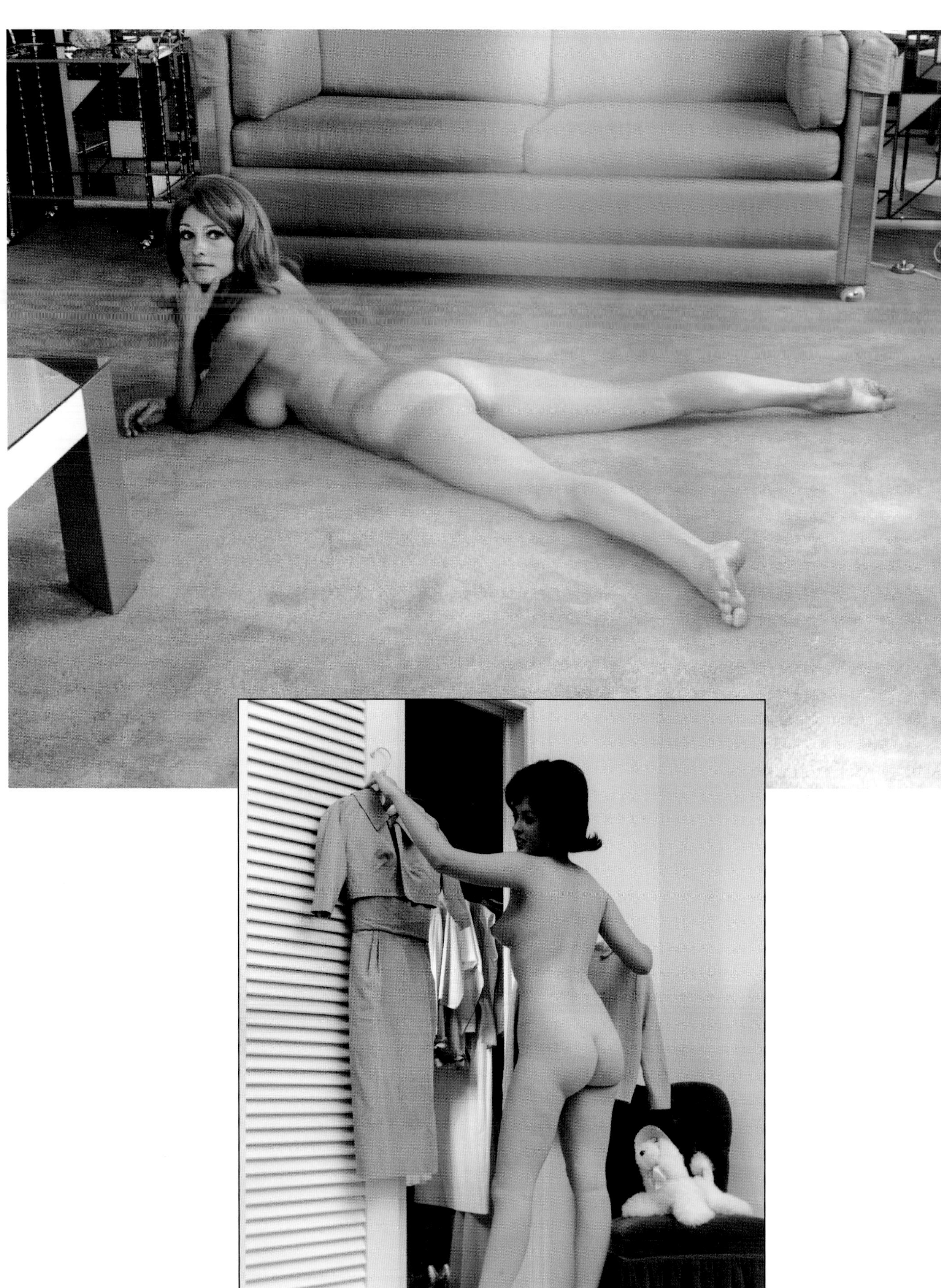

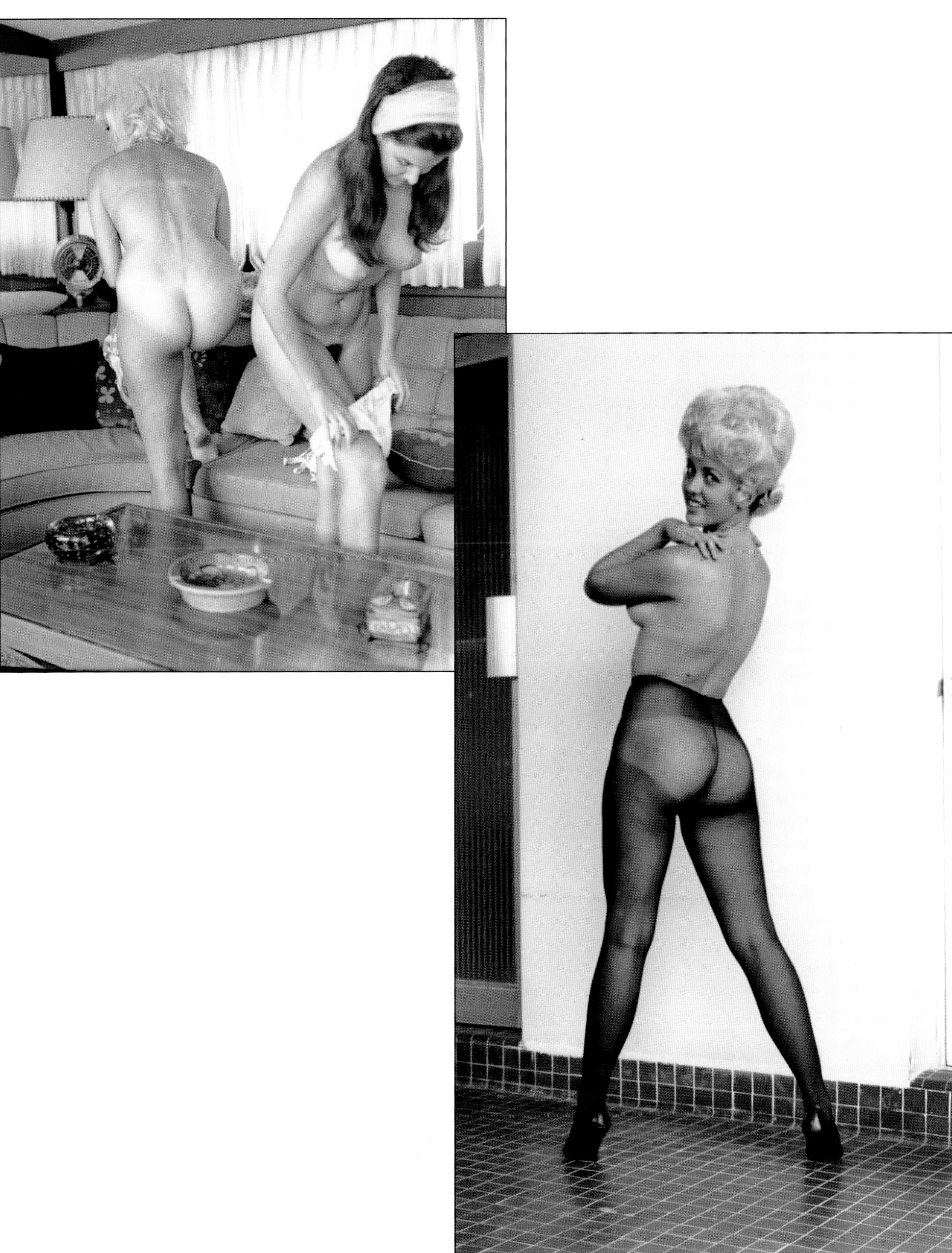

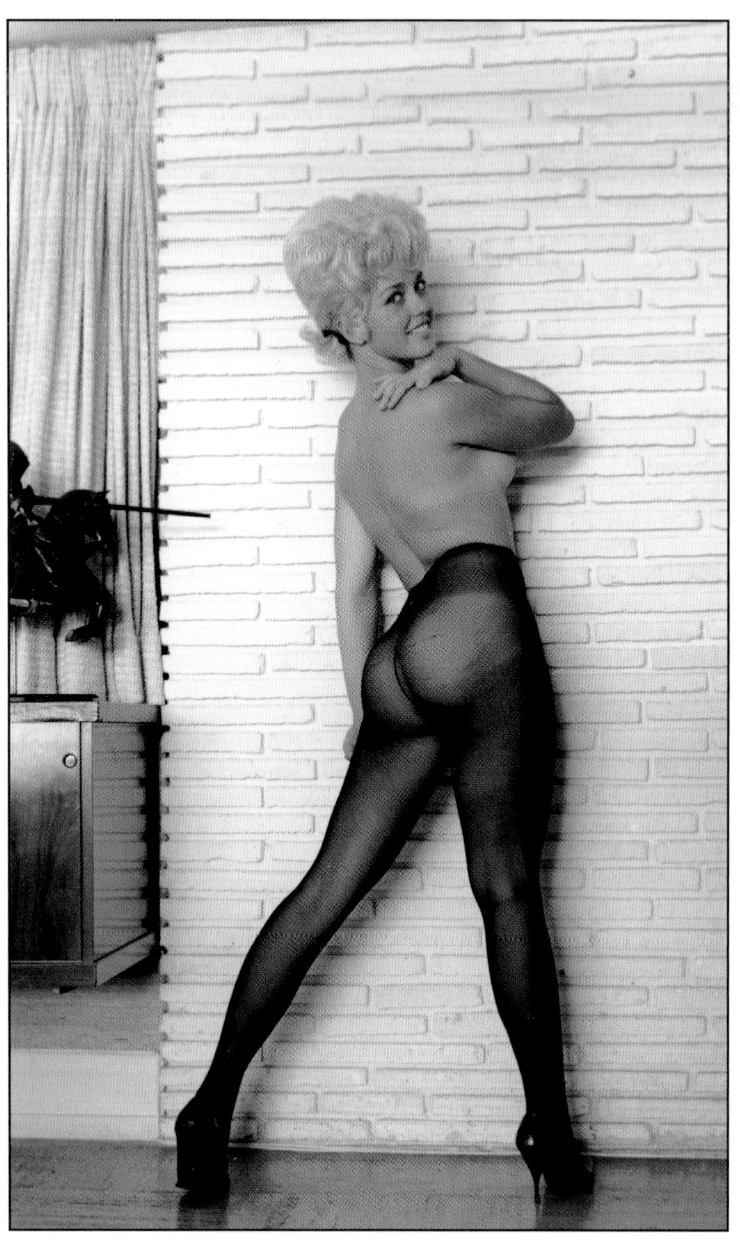

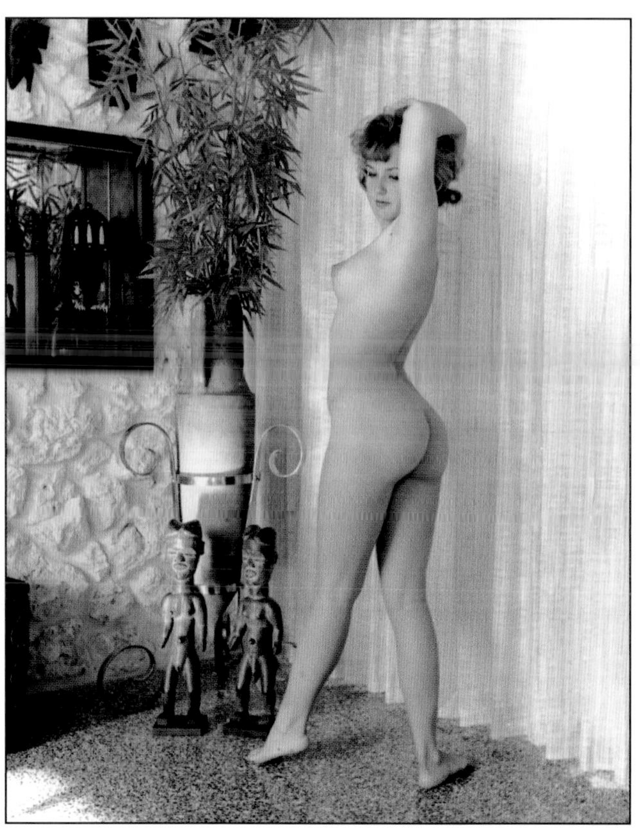

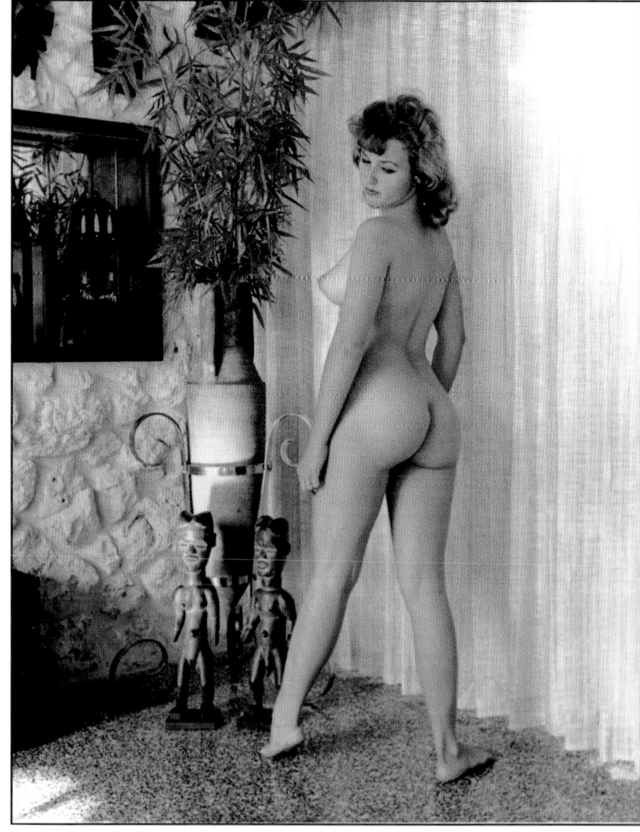

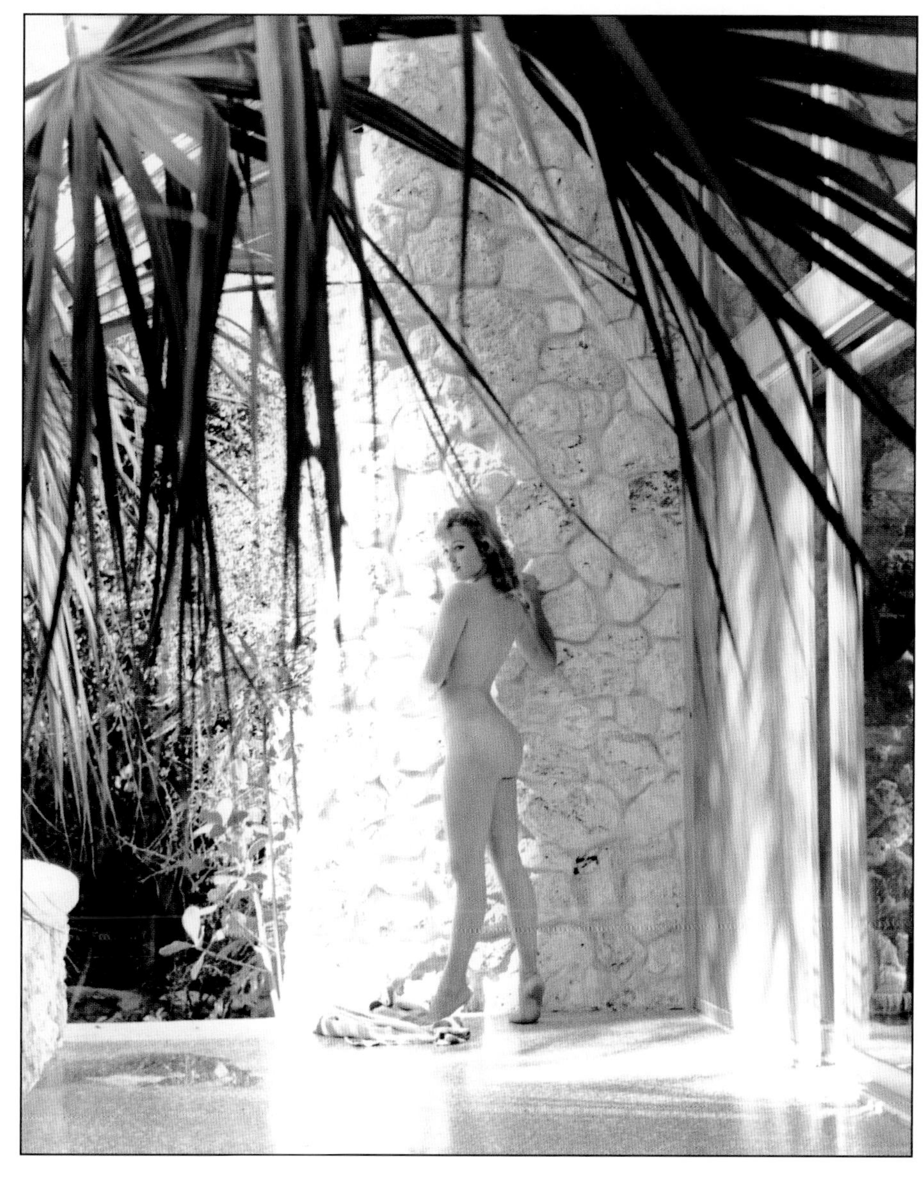

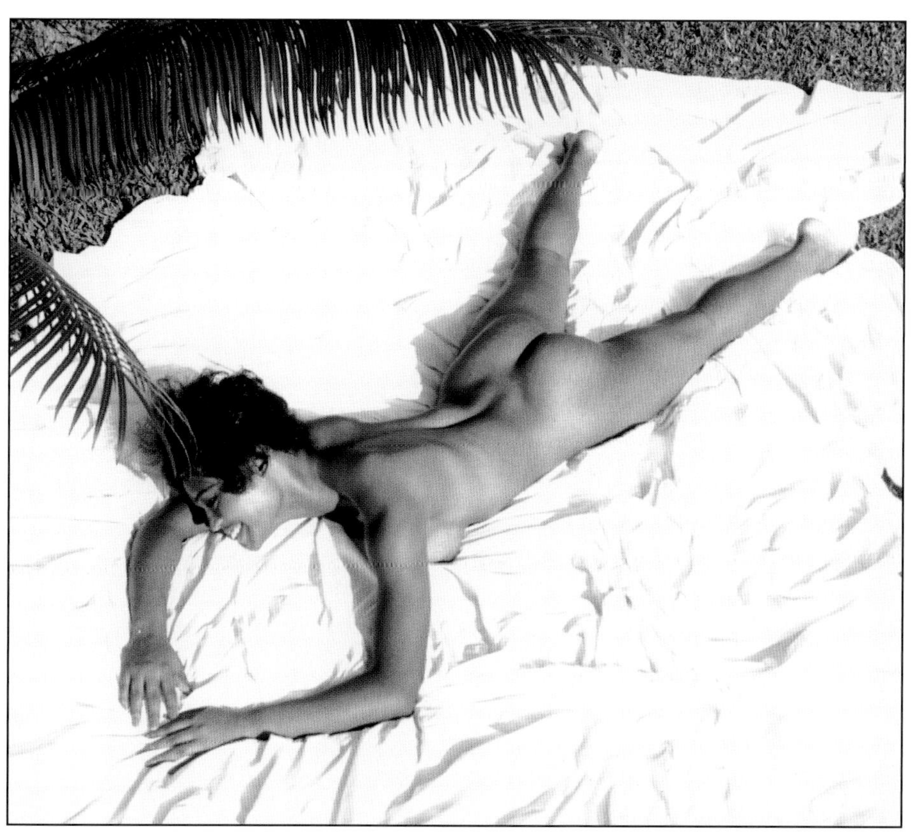

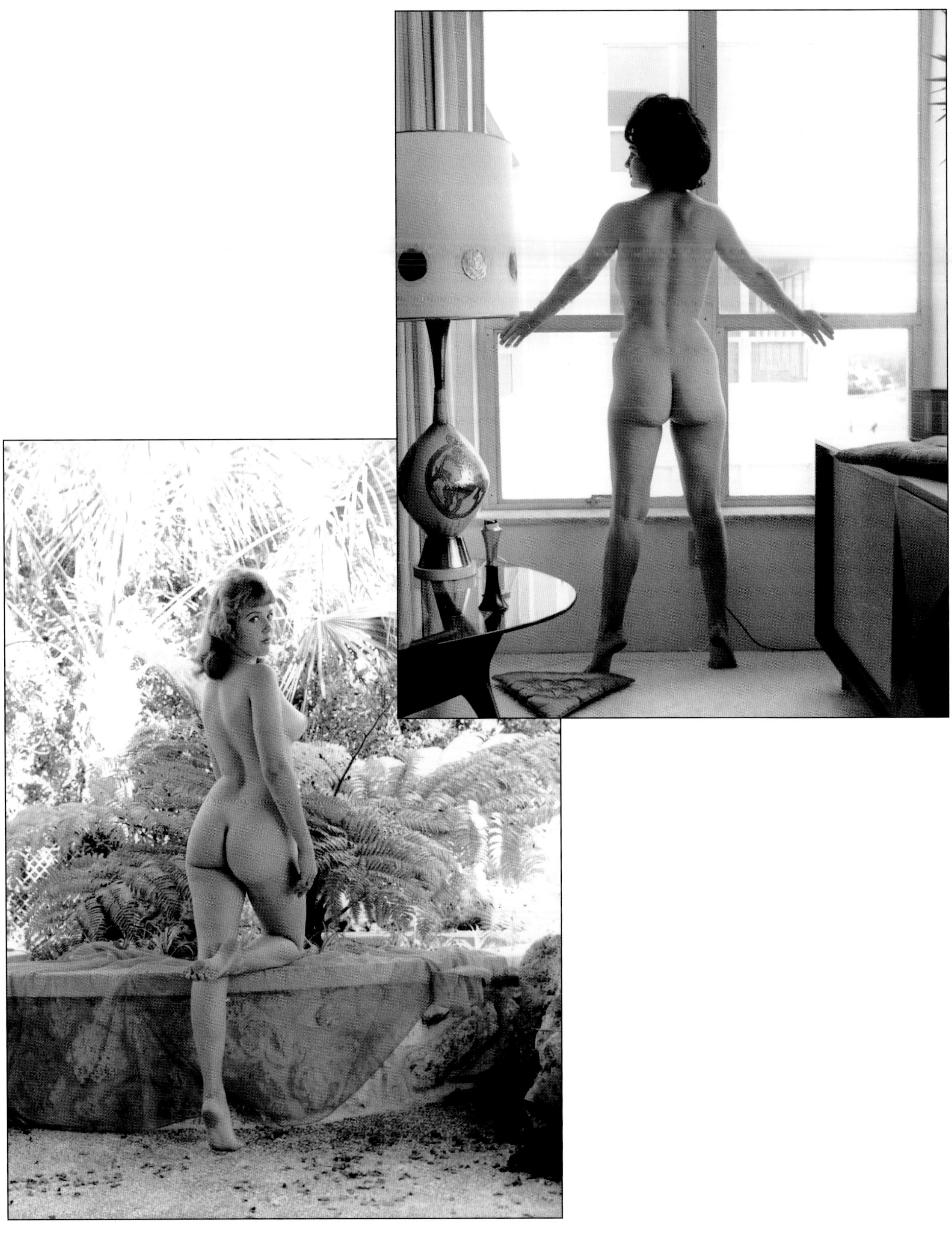

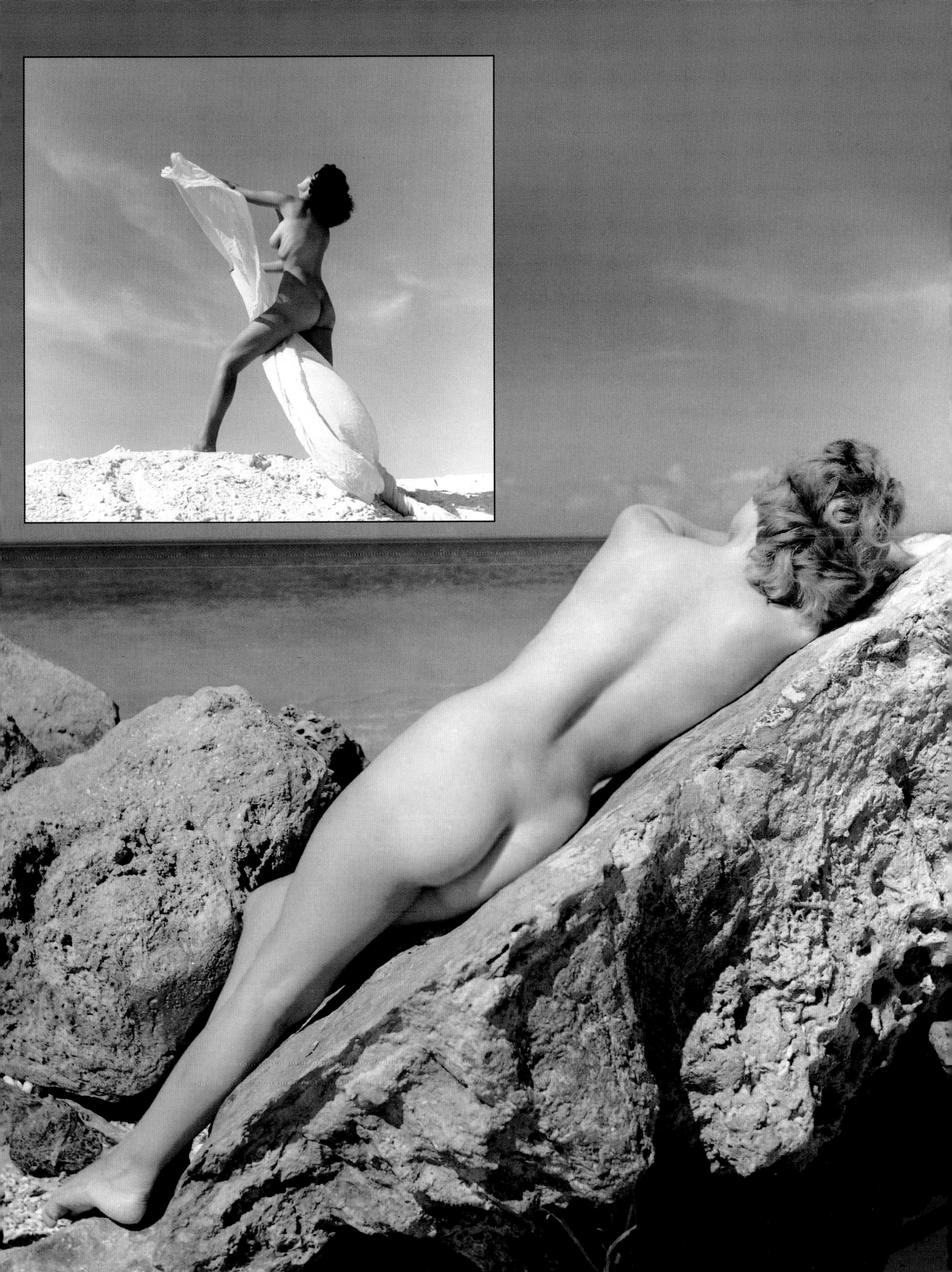

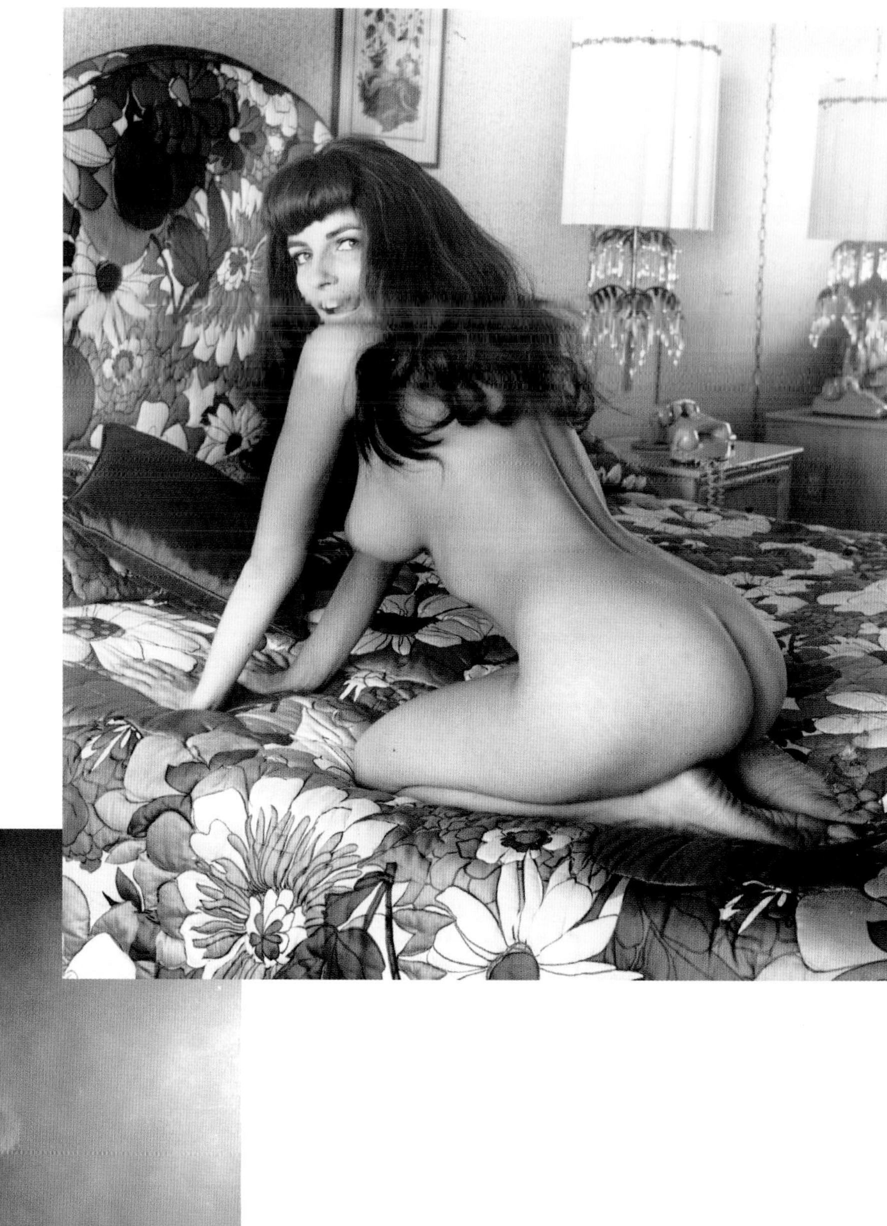

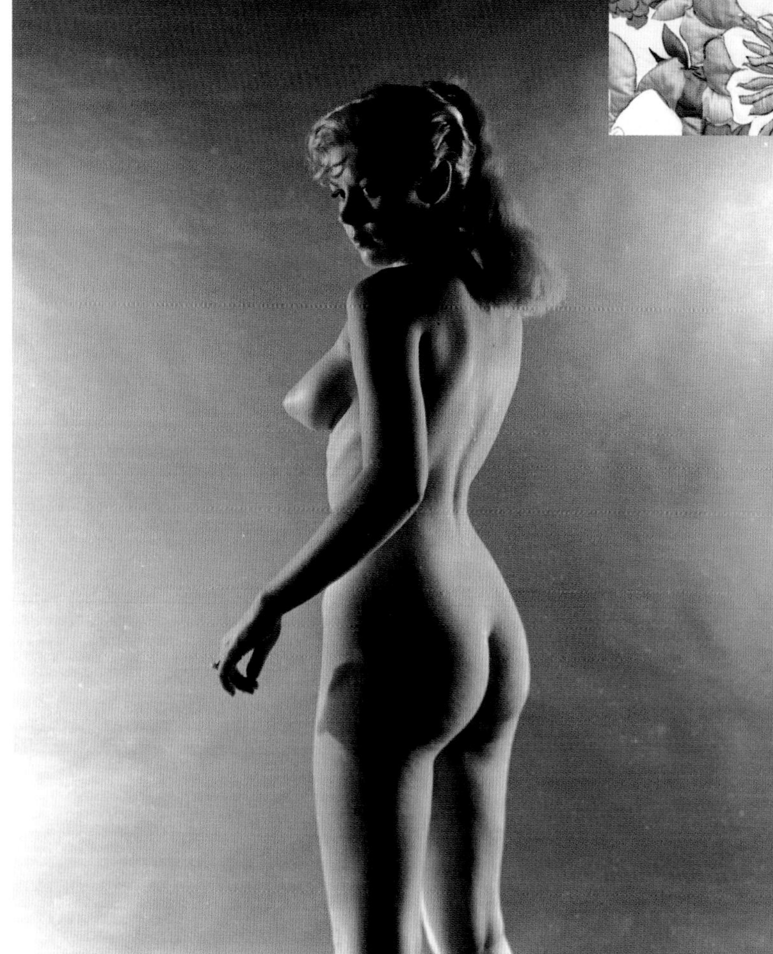

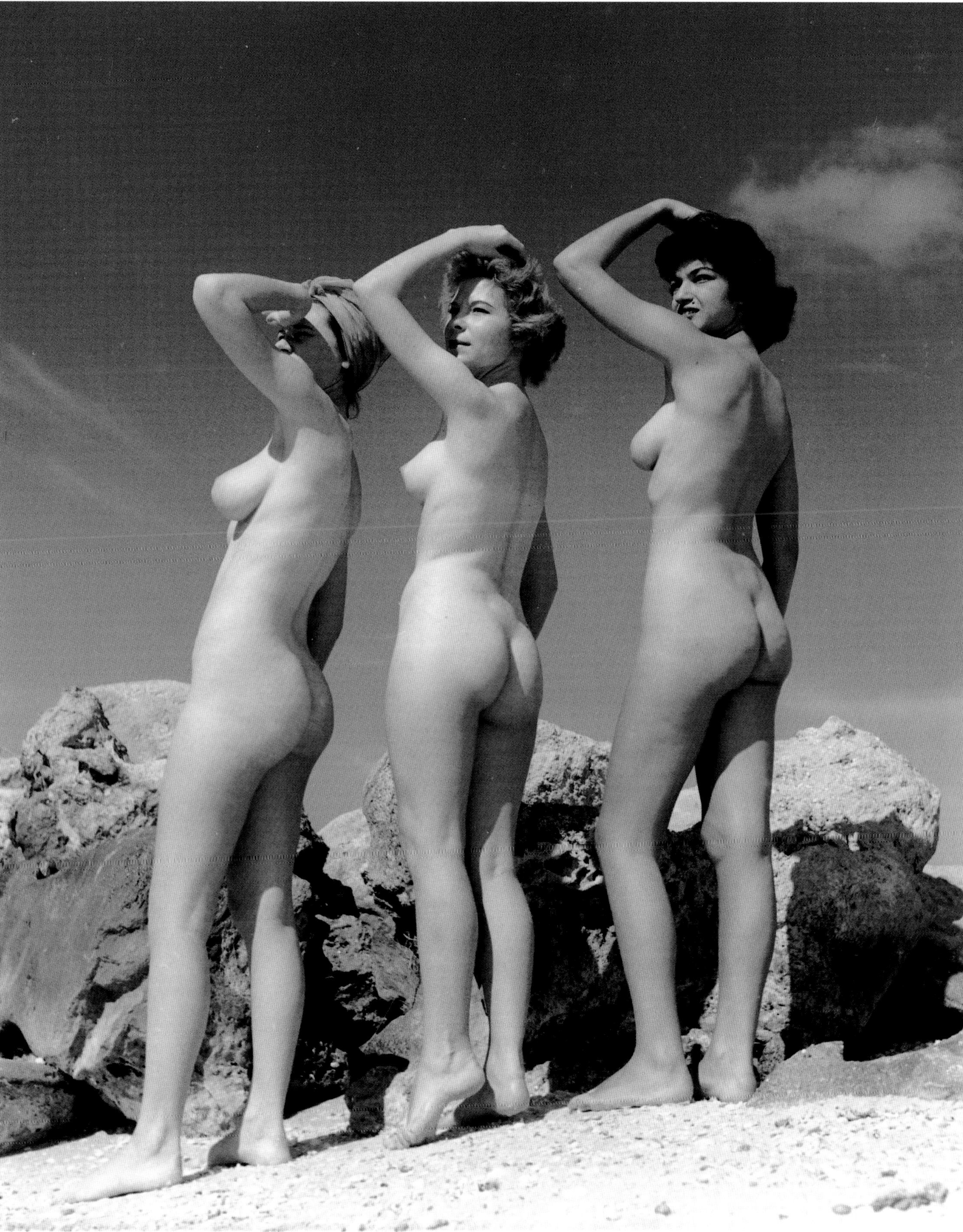

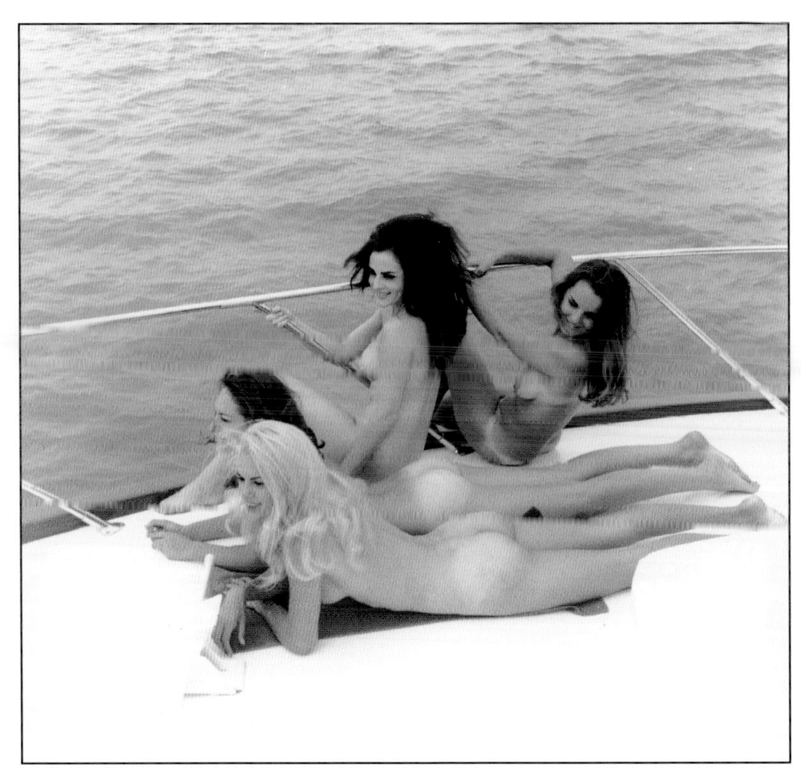

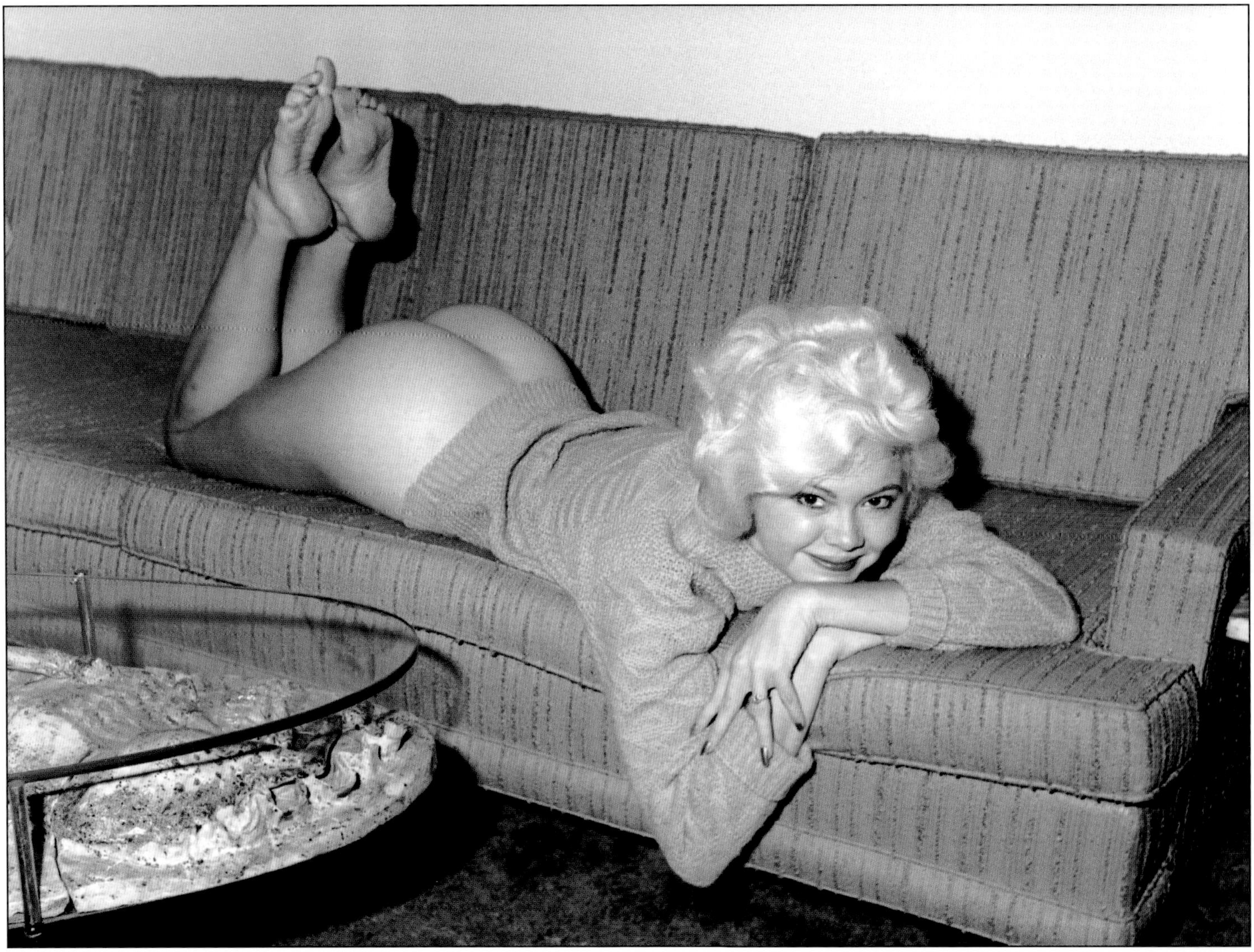

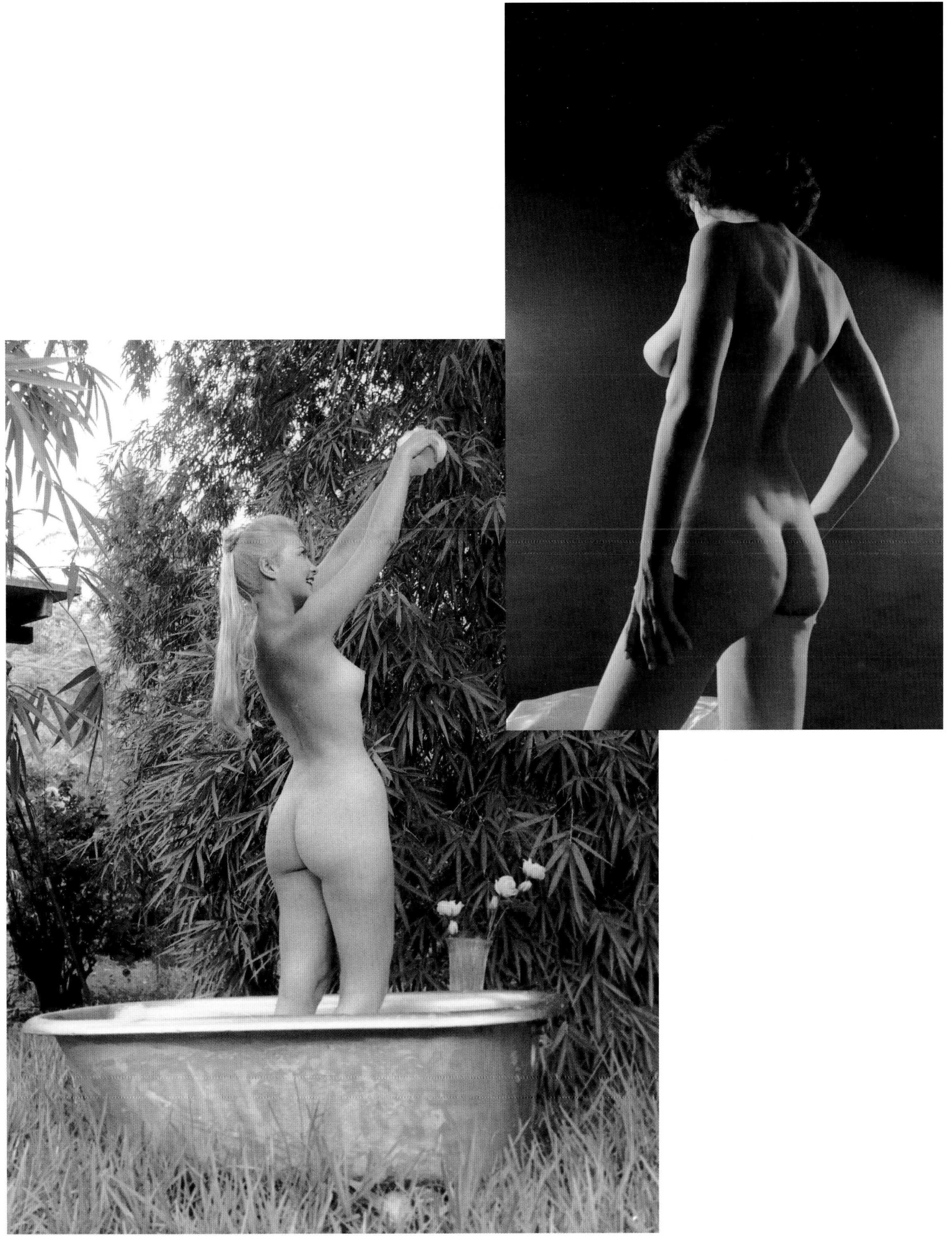

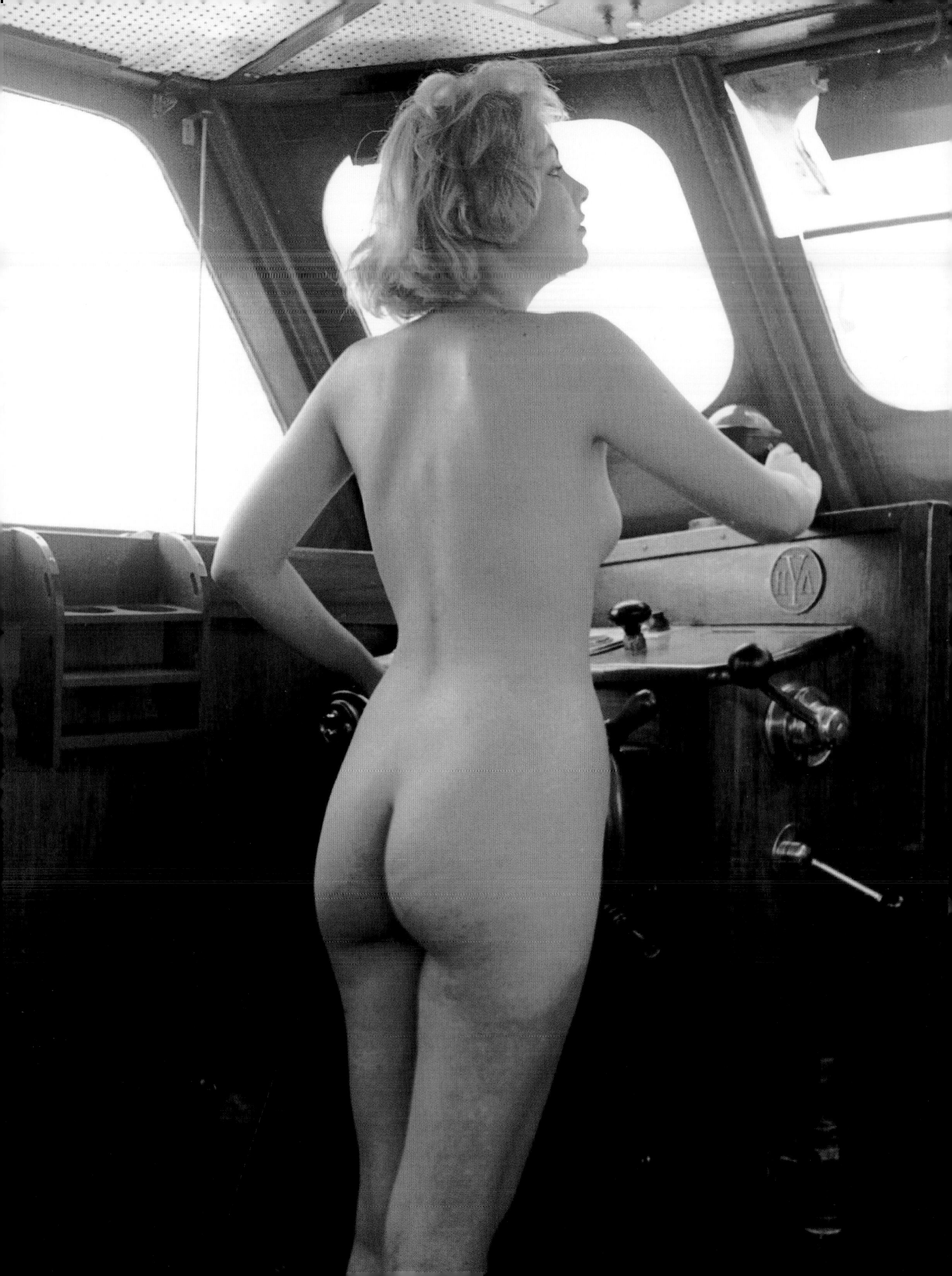

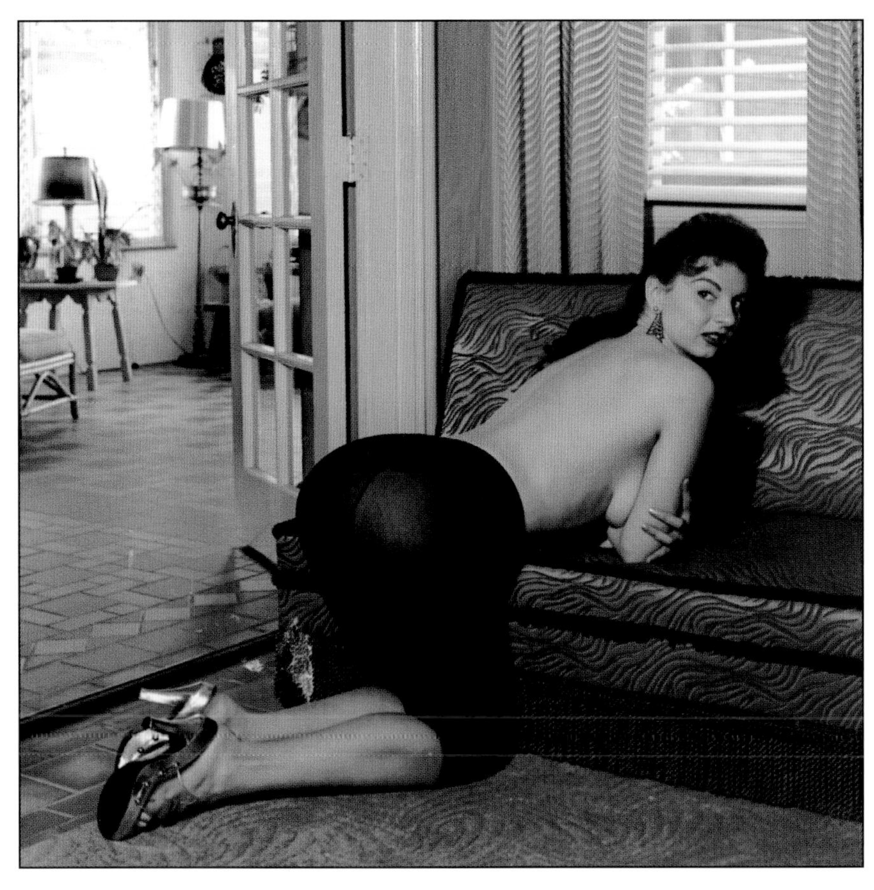

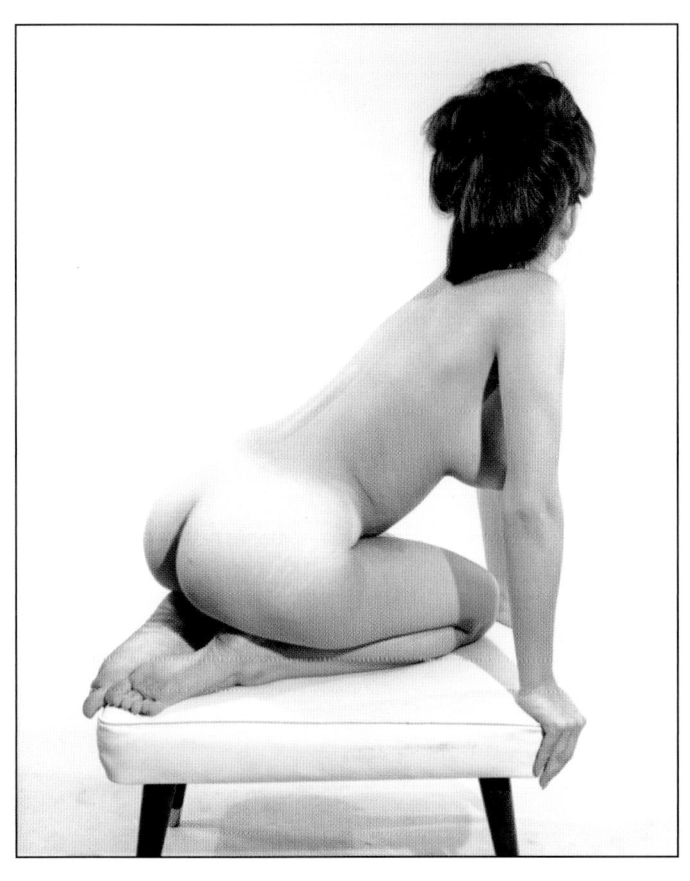

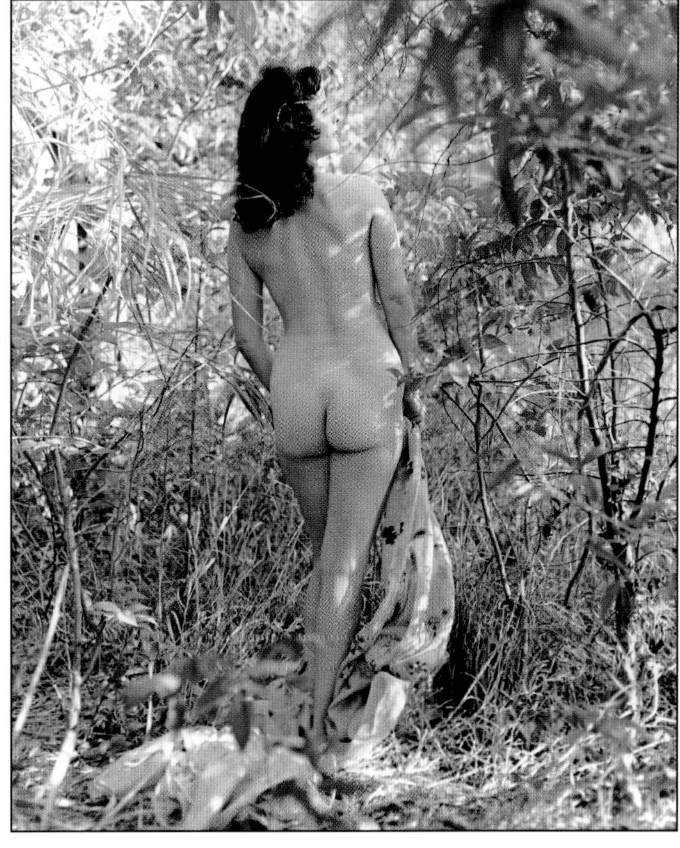

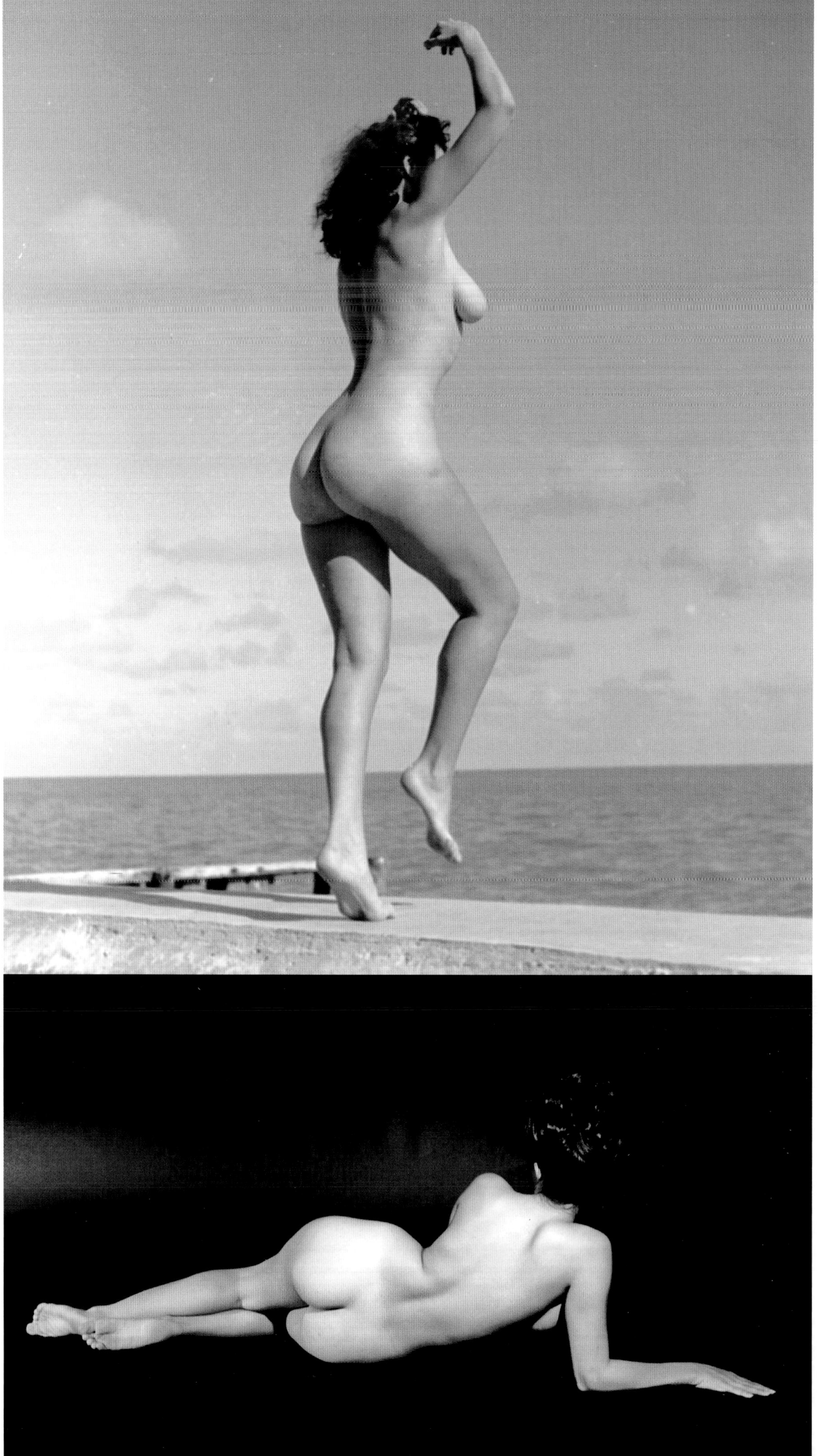

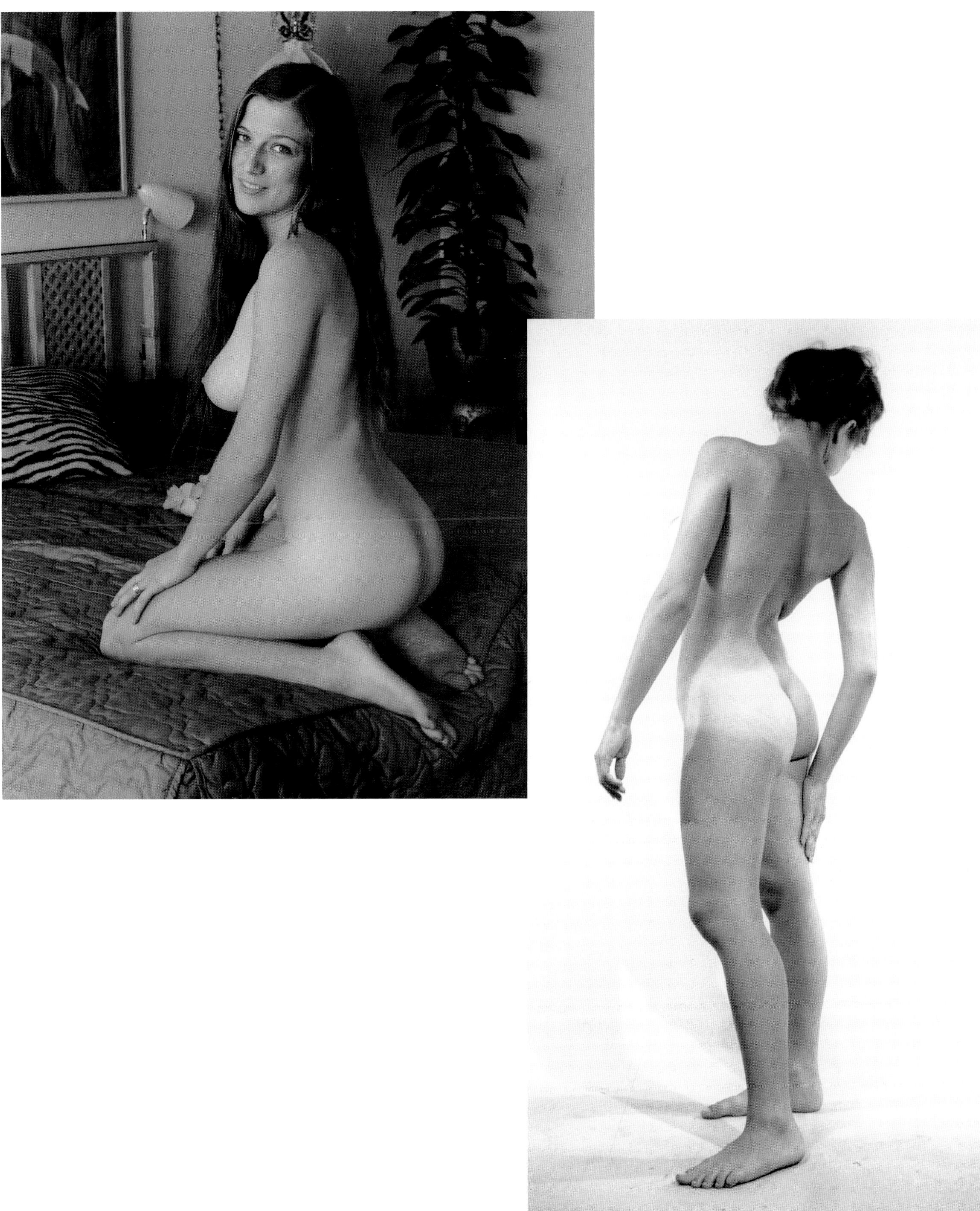

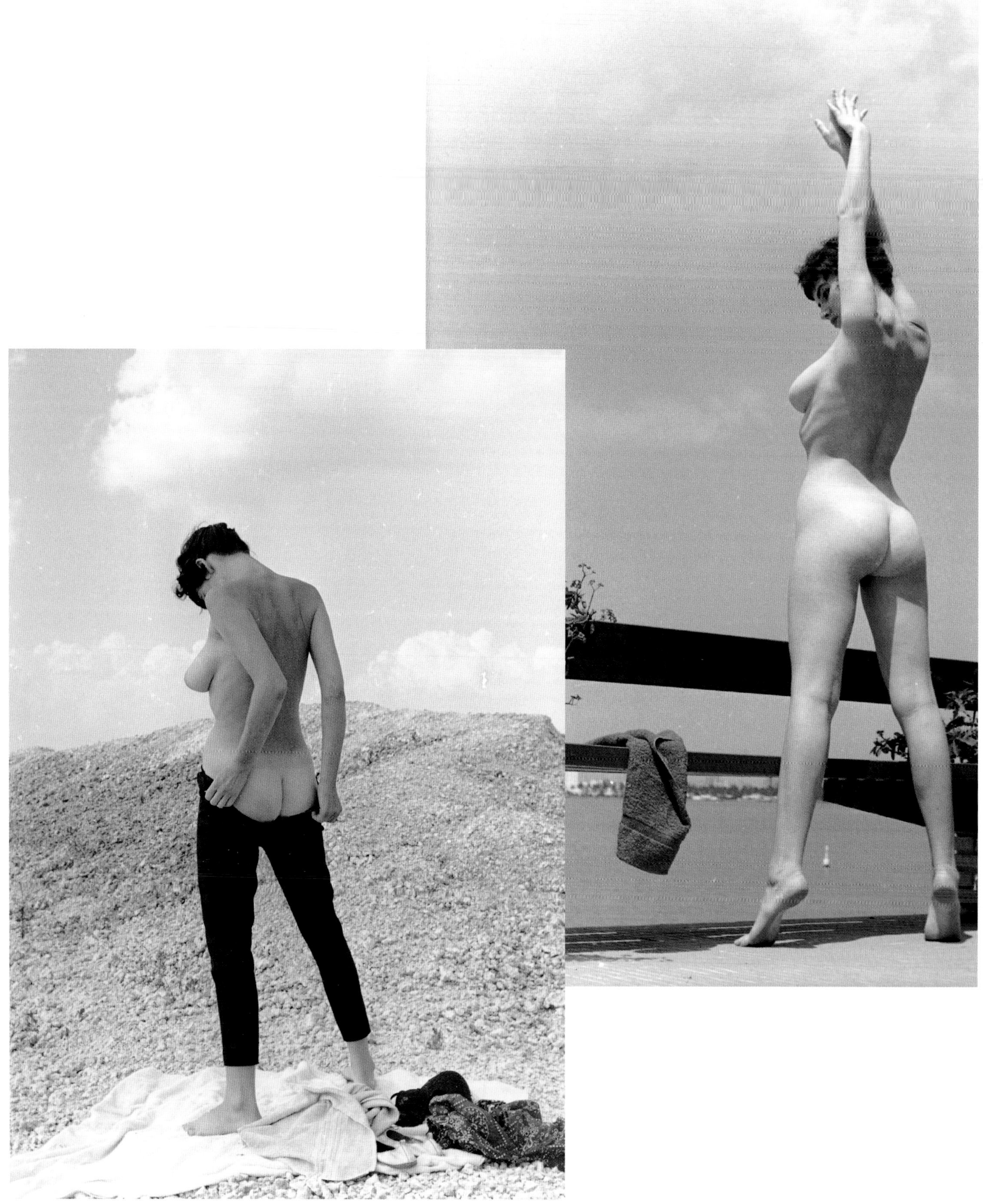

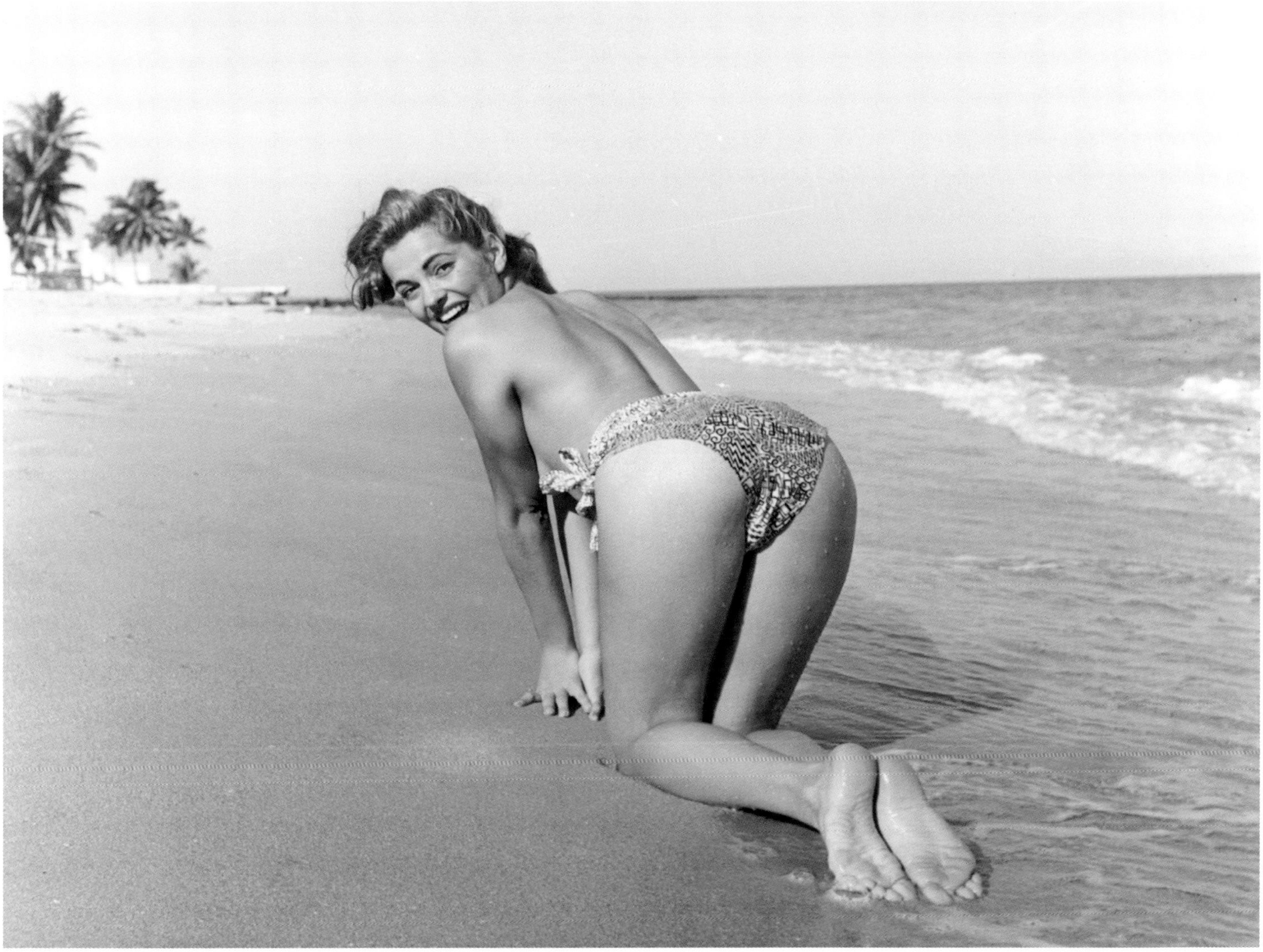

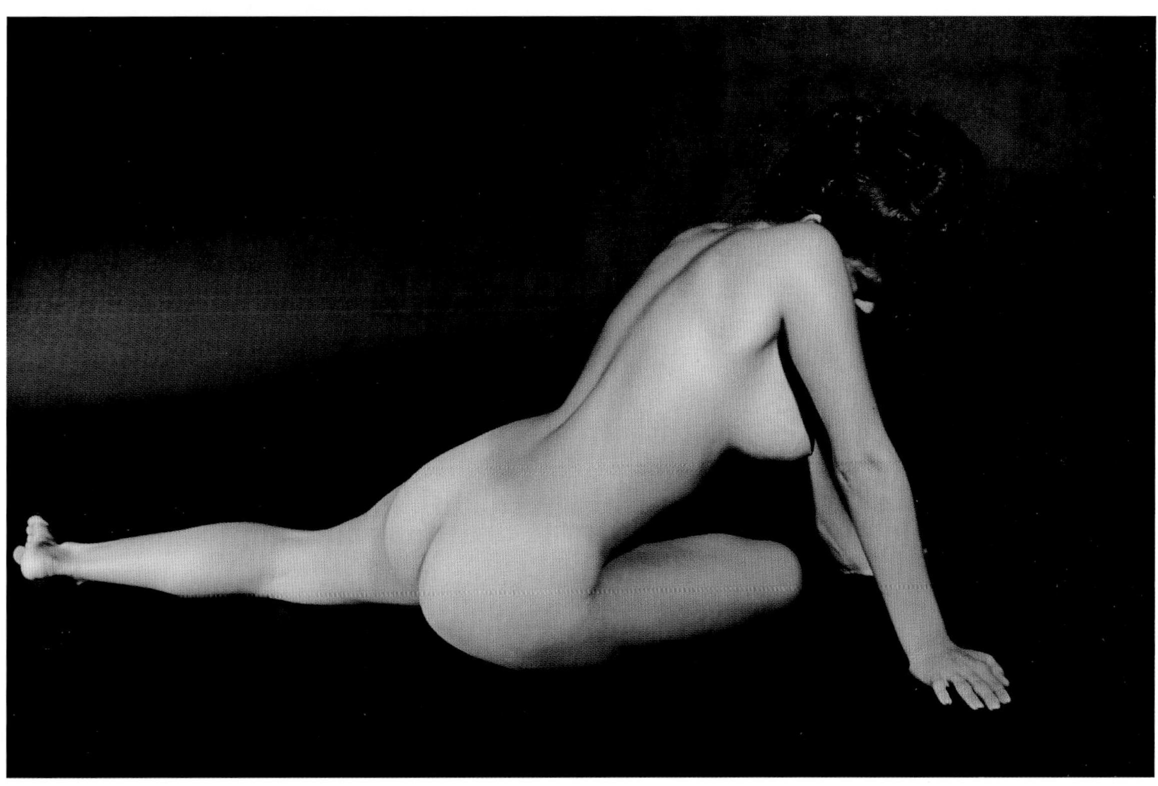

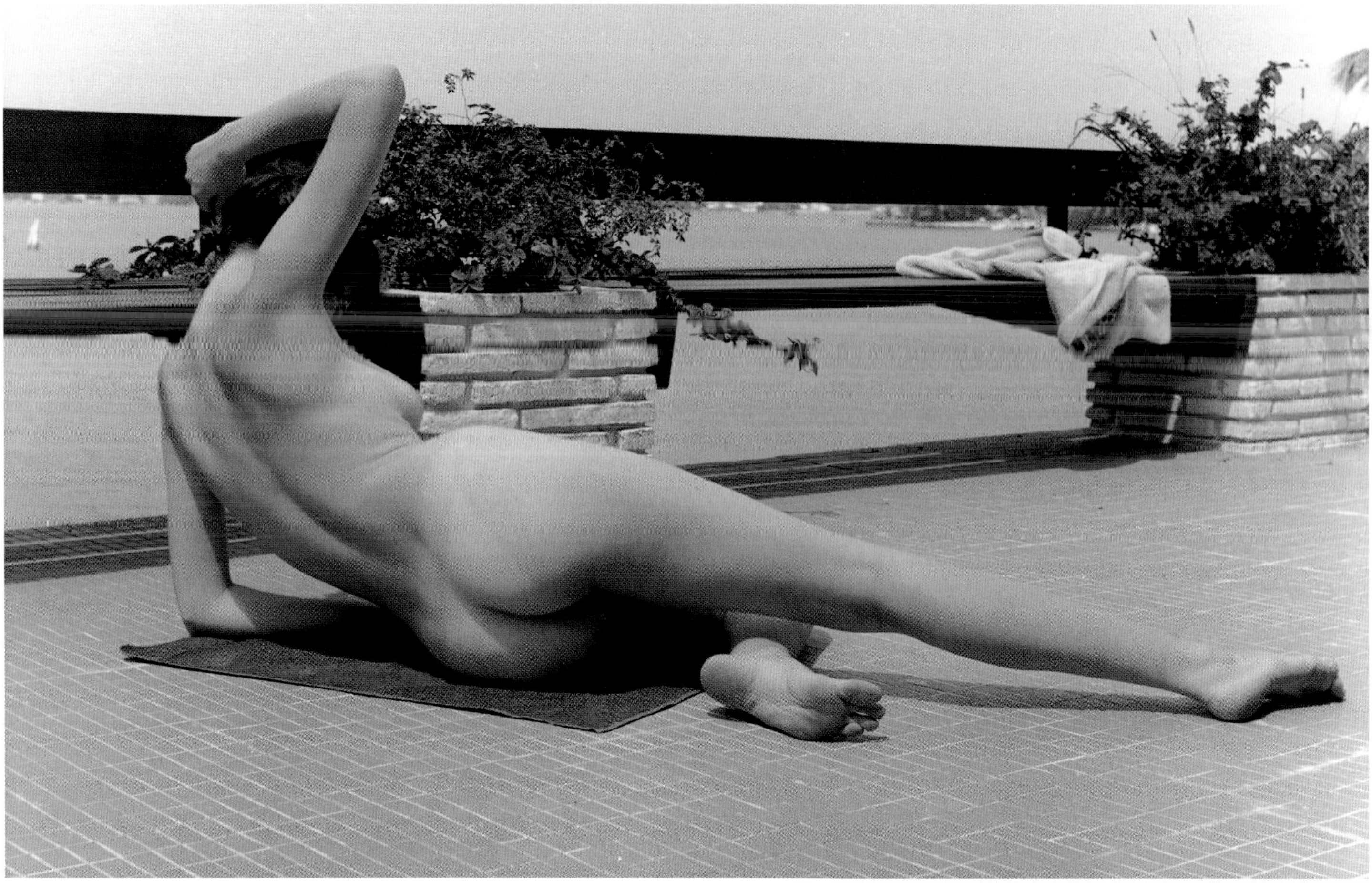

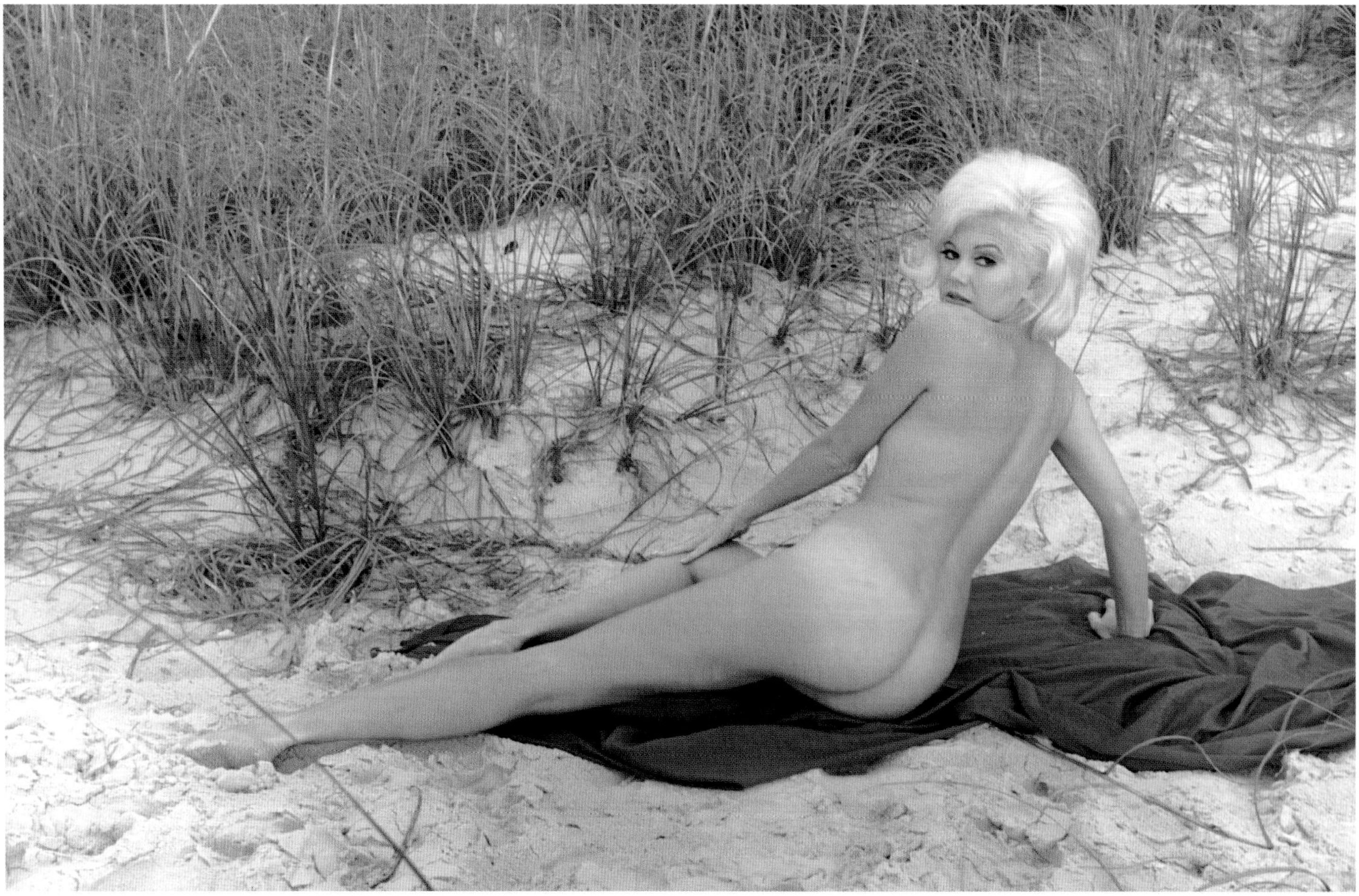

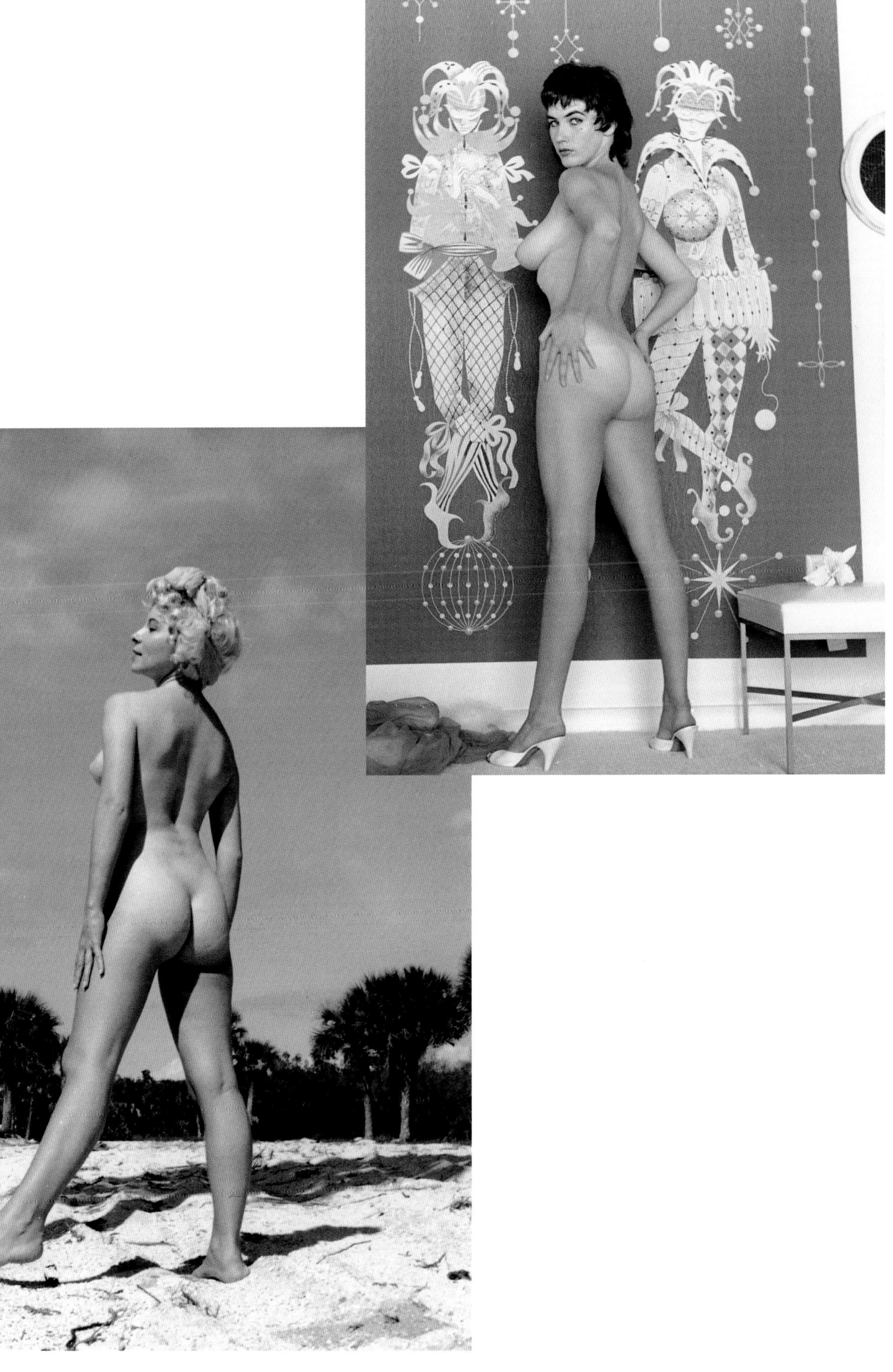

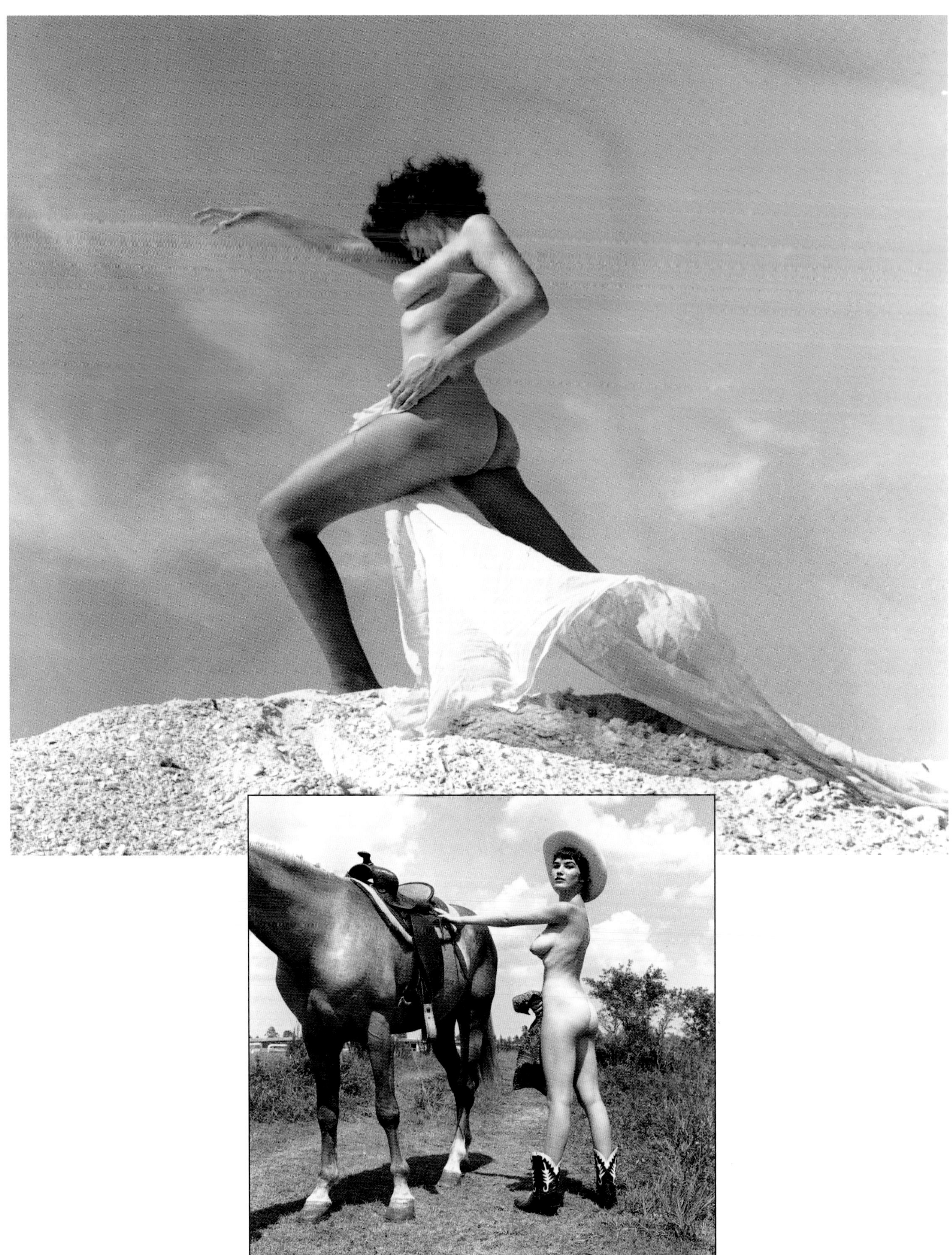

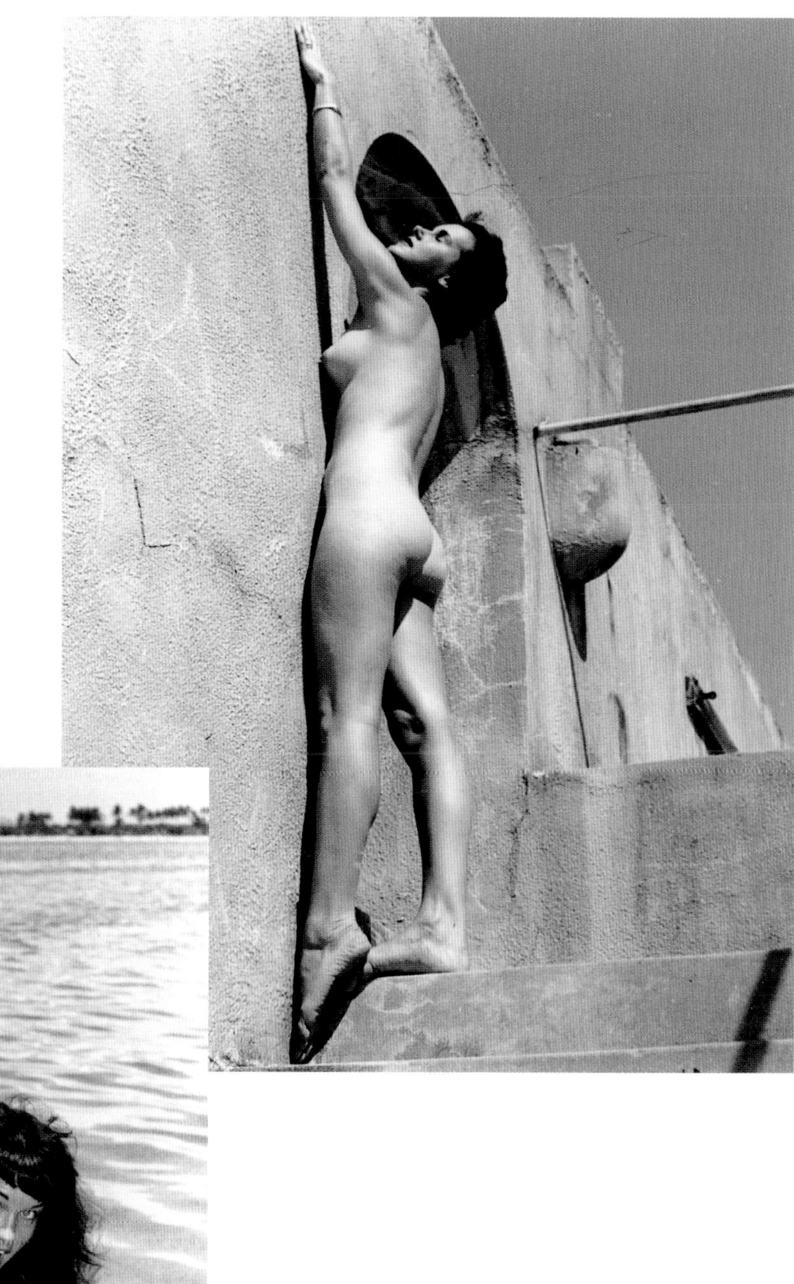

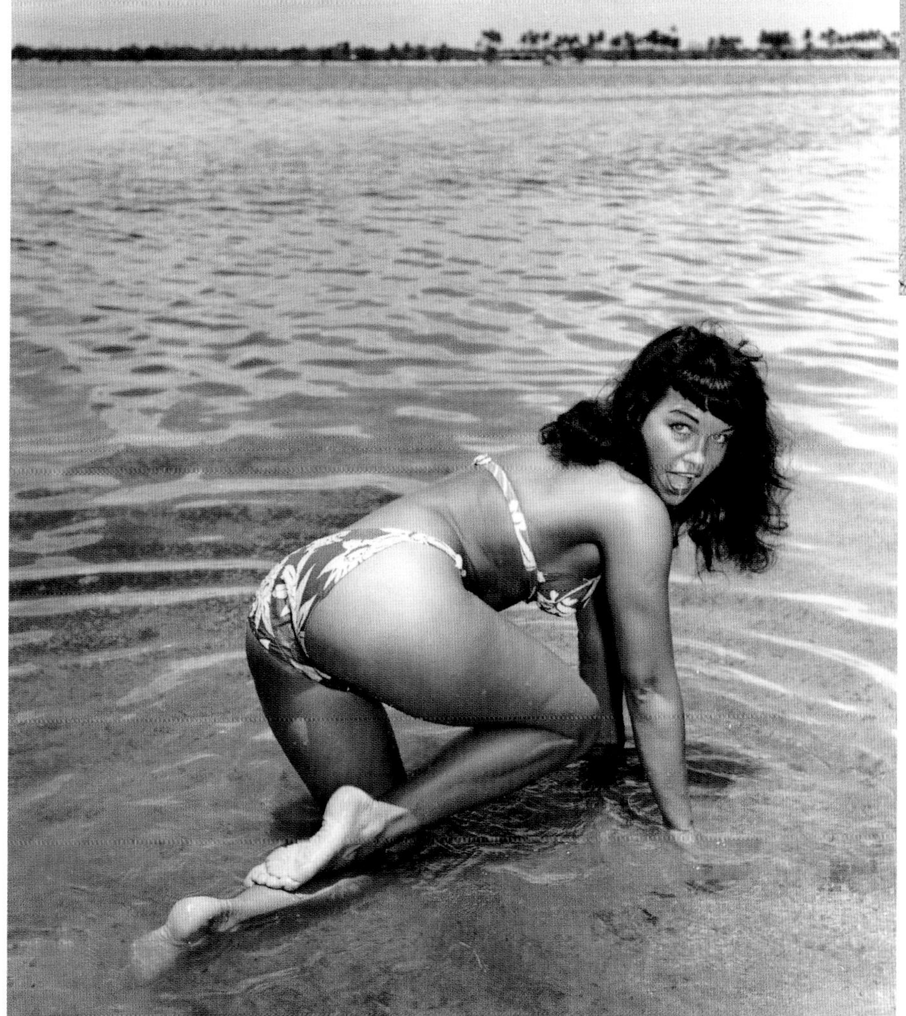

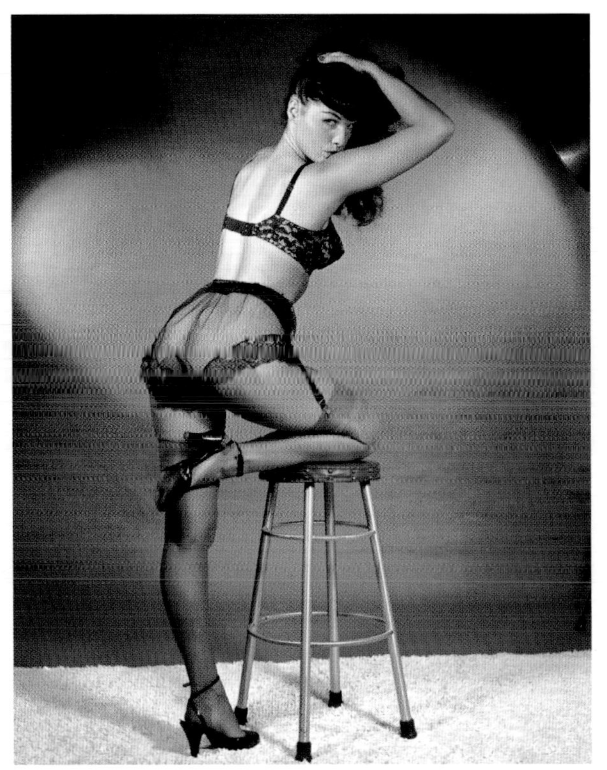

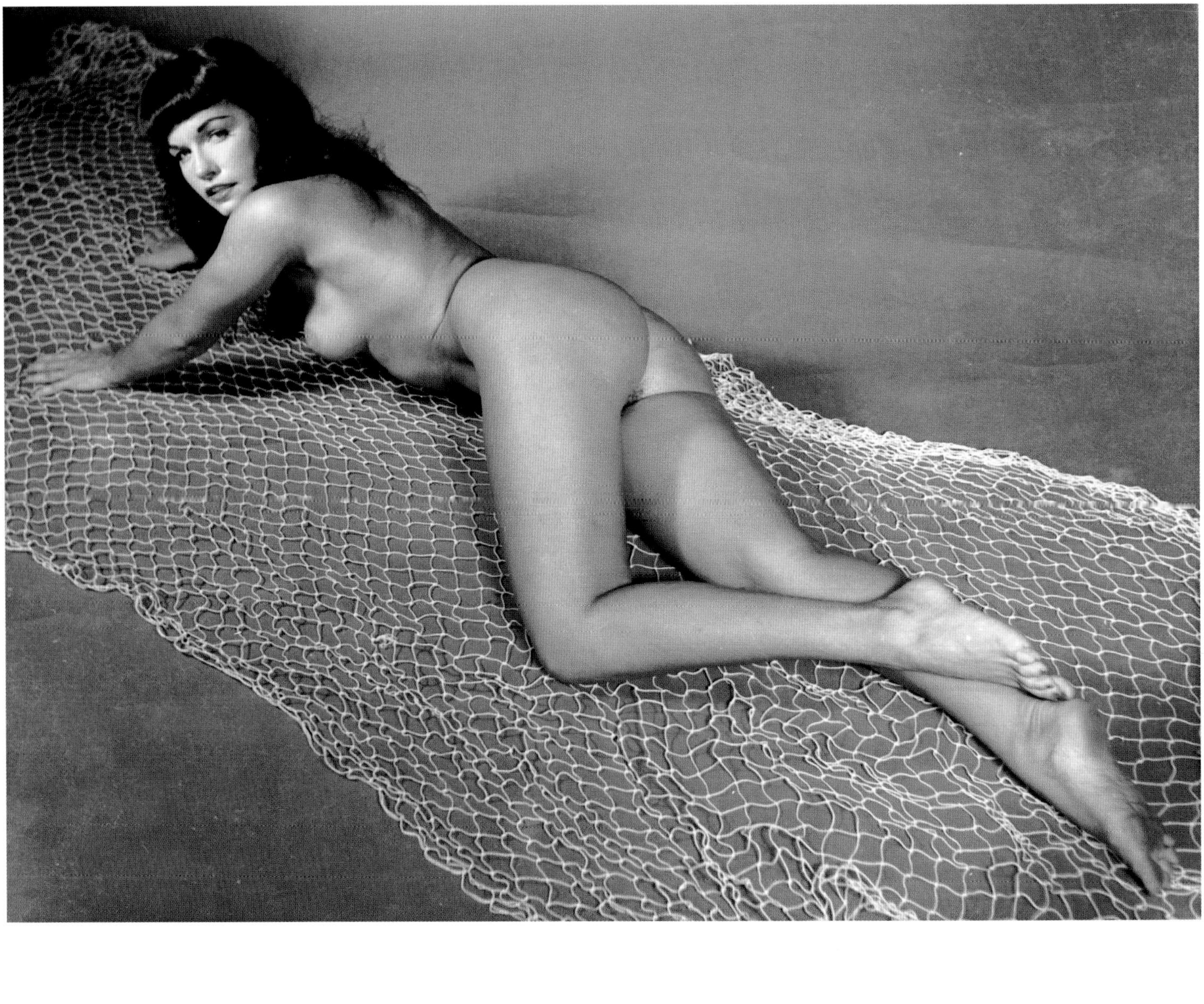